NETWORK AND SECURITY FUNDAMENTALS FOR ETHICAL HACKERS

ADVANCED NETWORK PROTOCOLS, ATTACKS, AND DEFENSES

4 BOOKS IN 1

BOOK 1
NETWORK FUNDAMENTALS FOR ETHICAL HACKERS: A BEGINNER'S GUIDE TO PROTOCOLS AND SECURITY BASICS

BOOK 2
UNDERSTANDING NETWORK ATTACKS: INTERMEDIATE TECHNIQUES AND COUNTERMEASURES

BOOK 3
ADVANCED NETWORK DEFENSE STRATEGIES: MITIGATING SOPHISTICATED ATTACKS

BOOK 4
EXPERT-LEVEL NETWORK SECURITY: MASTERING PROTOCOLS, THREATS, AND DEFENSES

ROB BOTWRIGHT

Published by Rob Botwright
Library of Congress Cataloging-in-Publication Data
ISBN 978-1-83938-525-4
Cover design by Rizzo

Disclaimer

The contents of this book are based on extensive research and the best available historical sources. However, the author and publisher make no claims, promises, or guarantees about the accuracy, completeness, or adequacy of the information contained herein. The information in this book is provided on an "as is" basis, and the author and publisher disclaim any and all liability for any errors, omissions, or inaccuracies in the information or for any actions taken in reliance on such information.

The opinions and views expressed in this book are those of the author and do not necessarily reflect the official policy or position of any organization or individual mentioned in this book. Any reference to specific people, places, or events is intended only to provide historical context and is not intended to defame or malign any group, individual, or entity.

The information in this book is intended for educational and entertainment purposes only. It is not intended to be a substitute for professional advice or judgment. Readers are encouraged to conduct their own research and to seek professional advice where appropriate.

Every effort has been made to obtain necessary permissions and acknowledgments for all images and other copyrighted material used in this book. Any errors or omissions in this regard are unintentional, and the author and publisher will correct them in future editions.

TABLE OF CONTENTS – BOOK 1 - NETWORK FUNDAMENTALS FOR ETHICAL HACKERS: A BEGINNER'S GUIDE TO PROTOCOLS AND SECURITY BASICS

TABLE OF CONTENTS – BOOK 2 - UNDERSTANDING NETWORK ATTACKS: INTERMEDIATE TECHNIQUES AND COUNTERMEASURES

TABLE OF CONTENTS – BOOK 3 - ADVANCED NETWORK DEFENSE STRATEGIES: MITIGATING SOPHISTICATED ATTACKS

TABLE OF CONTENTS – BOOK 4 - EXPERT-LEVEL NETWORK SECURITY: MASTERING PROTOCOLS, THREATS, AND DEFENSES

Introduction

In an era where information flows ceaselessly across the digital landscape, the need for safeguarding networks and systems has never been more critical. With the ever-increasing connectivity of our world, the role of ethical hackers has evolved into an indispensable force in defending against cyber threats. To become a proficient guardian of the digital realm, one must journey through the intricacies of network and security fundamentals and ascend to the zenith of advanced protocols, attacks, and defenses.

Welcome to the "Network and Security Fundamentals for Ethical Hackers" book bundle—an immersive voyage designed to equip you with the knowledge, skills, and strategies needed to thrive in the dynamic field of cybersecurity. Comprising four distinct volumes, this comprehensive collection guides you from the rudimentary principles of networking to the advanced realms of threat mitigation and expert-level security.

Book 1 - Network Fundamentals for Ethical Hackers: A Beginner's Guide to Protocols and Security Basics
Our journey commences with a solid foundation in "Book 1." Here, we delve into the very core of networking, demystifying protocols and elucidating security fundamentals. Whether you're new to the world of cybersecurity or looking to reinforce your grasp of networking essentials, this volume provides the essential building blocks. From the anatomy of data transmission to the principles of encryption, you will emerge from this book with a clear understanding of how networks function and

the paramount importance of security in the digital landscape.

Book 2 - Understanding Network Attacks: Intermediate Techniques and Countermeasures
As you progress to "Book 2," we embark on a deeper exploration of the threats that loom in the digital shadows. This volume navigates the intricate world of network attacks, offering insights into intermediate-level techniques employed by malicious actors. Here, you will become proficient in recognizing, dissecting, and mitigating a wide array of cyber threats. Armed with this knowledge, you will be ready to fortify networks against real-world intrusions, becoming a vigilant sentinel in the ever-evolving battlefield of cybersecurity.

Book 3 - Advanced Network Defense Strategies: Mitigating Sophisticated Attacks
The journey continues in "Book 3," where we ascend to the upper echelons of network defense. In this volume, we equip you with advanced strategies to thwart even the most sophisticated adversaries. From intrusion detection and prevention to threat intelligence and incident response, you will possess the tools and techniques required to proactively defend networks against relentless and cunning attacks. Your role as a guardian of digital realms will be elevated to one of strategic resilience and adaptive defense.

Book 4 - Expert-Level Network Security: Mastering Protocols, Threats, and Defenses
In the final installment, "Book 4," we culminate our exploration by delving into the intricate web of expert-level network security. Here, we dissect complex protocols, analyze cutting-edge threats, and introduce you to state-of-

the-art defense mechanisms. This book is not merely a culmination of knowledge; it is an invitation to master the art of network security. Armed with the insights and strategies from this volume, you will stand among the elite— capable of safeguarding networks against the most formidable of adversaries.

As you embark on this immersive journey through the pages of these books, remember that ethical hacking is a noble endeavor—one that demands continuous learning, adaptability, and a commitment to defending the digital realm against all odds. Whether you are a novice taking your first steps into the world of network security or an expert seeking to hone your skills further, this book bundle is your passport to becoming a proficient guardian of the digital frontier.

Prepare to delve deep into the world of network and security fundamentals, to understand the intricacies of advanced protocols, to recognize and thwart network attacks, and to emerge as a master of network security. Welcome to the "Network and Security Fundamentals for Ethical Hackers" bundle—your gateway to a world where knowledge is power, and security is paramount.

BOOK 1
NETWORK FUNDAMENTALS FOR ETHICAL HACKERS
A BEGINNER'S GUIDE TO PROTOCOLS AND SECURITY BASICS

ROB BOTWRIGHT

Chapter 1: Understanding the Basics of Computer Networks

Networking fundamentals are essential for anyone delving into the world of ethical hacking and cybersecurity. To understand how to protect networks from threats, it's crucial to comprehend how they operate and where their vulnerabilities lie. In this chapter, we will explore the basics of computer networks, providing a foundation for our journey into network security.

Computer networks are the backbone of modern communication. They enable the exchange of data, whether it's a simple email or a high-definition video stream. These networks consist of interconnected devices, such as computers, servers, routers, and switches, all working together to transmit data from one point to another.

At the core of every network is the concept of data packets. Data is broken down into smaller chunks, or packets, before being transmitted across the network. These packets contain not only the data itself but also information about its source and destination. Think of them as virtual envelopes, each with a sender's address, a recipient's address, and the message inside.

To manage the flow of data across a network, we rely on network protocols. These are a set of rules and conventions that govern how data is formatted, transmitted, and received. Some of the most common network protocols include TCP/IP, HTTP, FTP, and DNS. Each protocol serves a specific purpose, whether it's ensuring reliable data delivery (TCP), facilitating web browsing (HTTP), or resolving domain names to IP addresses (DNS).

A critical concept in networking is the OSI (Open Systems Interconnection) model. This model divides network communication into seven distinct layers, each responsible for a specific aspect of the process. These layers, from bottom to top, are the Physical, Data Link, Network, Transport, Session, Presentation, and Application layers. Understanding this model helps us analyze and troubleshoot network issues effectively.

The Physical layer deals with the actual transmission of raw binary data over physical mediums like cables and wireless connections. The Data Link layer is responsible for organizing raw data into frames and managing access to the physical medium. The Network layer handles routing, ensuring that data reaches its intended destination. The Transport layer is responsible for end-to-end communication, maintaining data integrity and reliability.

The Session, Presentation, and Application layers are collectively responsible for managing the user interface and application-level interactions. They handle tasks like session management, data encryption and decryption, and application-specific communication. This layering approach allows for modular design and troubleshooting of network systems.

Network topologies define how devices are connected in a network. Common topologies include the star, bus, ring, and mesh. The choice of topology impacts factors such as fault tolerance, scalability, and ease of maintenance. For instance, a star topology is easy to troubleshoot but may not be as fault-tolerant as a mesh topology.

Now, let's dive into network addressing. In a TCP/IP network, devices are identified by unique IP addresses. IPv4, the older version, uses a 32-bit address format, while IPv6 uses a 128-bit format to accommodate the growing number of devices on the internet. IP addresses are further divided into network and host portions, with subnet masks used to determine the boundaries.

Subnetting is a technique that allows network administrators to divide an IP address space into smaller, manageable subnetworks. This practice aids in efficient IP address allocation and routing within a larger network. Subnet masks and CIDR notation are essential tools in subnetting.

Network security starts with understanding the potential threats. In this context, threats can be anything that poses a risk to the confidentiality, integrity, or availability of data. Common threats include malware, viruses, hackers, and even insider threats from within the organization.

To counter these threats, various security measures and best practices are employed. One such measure is encryption, which converts readable data into a scrambled format that can only be deciphered with the correct decryption key. Encryption is used to protect data both in transit and at rest.

Firewalls are another crucial component of network security. These devices act as gatekeepers, monitoring incoming and outgoing traffic and enforcing a set of predetermined security rules. Firewalls can be hardware-based or software-based, and they help block malicious traffic while allowing legitimate data to pass through.

Virtual Private Networks (VPNs) are commonly used for secure remote access to corporate networks or for encrypting data traffic over untrusted networks, such as the internet. VPNs create a secure "tunnel" for data to travel through, protecting it from eavesdropping.

Network security also involves the practice of access control, which ensures that only authorized individuals or devices can access specific resources on the network. Access control mechanisms include usernames and passwords, biometric authentication, and access control lists (ACLs).

Intrusion Detection Systems (IDS) and Intrusion Prevention Systems (IPS) are used to identify and respond to potential security breaches. IDS monitors network traffic for suspicious activity, while IPS can take immediate action to block or mitigate threats.

Network security isn't just about defending against external threats. Insider threats, whether intentional or accidental, can be just as damaging. This is where user awareness training and monitoring play a significant role. Employees and users should be educated about security best practices and potential risks.

The field of network security is continually evolving. New threats emerge, and security professionals must stay up-to-date with the latest trends and technologies. Continuous monitoring, regular security audits, and vulnerability assessments are essential to maintaining a secure network environment.

In summary, network fundamentals are the building blocks of network security. Understanding how networks operate, the protocols they use, and the threats they face is crucial for anyone entering the field of ethical hacking and cybersecurity. As we delve deeper into the realm of network security, we will explore advanced techniques and strategies to protect networks from increasingly sophisticated threats.

The OSI (Open Systems Interconnection) model is a fundamental framework used to understand how network communication works. It divides the process into seven layers, each responsible for specific tasks. Starting from the bottom, the Physical layer deals with the actual hardware components and the transmission of raw binary data. Above that is the Data Link layer, which organizes raw data into frames and manages access to the physical medium. The Network layer handles routing, ensuring data reaches its intended destination. The Transport layer maintains data integrity and reliability, managing end-to-end communication. Then, we have the Session, Presentation, and Application layers, collectively responsible for the user interface and application-level interactions. This layered approach allows for modular design and effective troubleshooting of network systems. Consider this model as a blueprint for how data travels through a network. Each layer has its own specific responsibilities, but they work together to ensure data is transmitted accurately and reliably. Think of it as an assembly line where each worker has a unique role, contributing to the final product. The Physical layer is the foundation of the OSI model. It deals with the actual hardware, such as cables, switches, and network interface cards. At this level, data is in the form of electrical signals, light pulses, or radio waves. The Data Link layer comes next. It's responsible for organizing data into frames, which are packets of information. This layer also manages access to the physical medium to prevent collisions in shared network segments. Ethernet is a common example of a Data Link layer protocol. Moving up to the Network layer, we find routers and switches. This layer focuses on routing data packets from the source to the destination. It deals with logical addressing, such as IP addresses, to determine where data should go. Imagine it as a postal service that decides how to deliver a letter based on the address. The Transport layer is like the quality control of the OSI model. It ensures data arrives intact and in the correct order. Two common Transport layer protocols are TCP (Transmission Control Protocol) and UDP (User Datagram Protocol). TCP is like a phone call where you confirm that the other person hears you correctly. UDP, on the other hand, is like sending a letter; you don't know if it arrived, but it's faster. Now, let's explore the Session, Presentation, and Application layers. The Session layer manages sessions or connections between devices. It helps establish, maintain, and terminate connections. Think of it as the conversation you have with someone, including the greetings and farewells. The Presentation layer deals with data translation and encryption. It ensures that data sent by one system can be read by another. For example, it converts text into a format that can be displayed correctly on different devices. Finally, we have the Application layer, which is where users interact with the network. This layer includes applications and services like web browsers, email clients, and file transfer programs. It's what you see and use when you access the internet or send emails. Together, these seven layers form the OSI model, providing a structured way to understand network communication. Remember that the OSI model is a conceptual framework. It helps us visualize and discuss how networks function, but it's not a strict set of rules that all networks must follow. In reality, networks often use a combination of protocols and technologies from multiple OSI layers. For instance, the internet primarily relies on the TCP/IP suite of protocols, which doesn't neatly align with the OSI model. Nonetheless, understanding the OSI model is valuable for troubleshooting network issues and designing effective network solutions. Imagine it as a map that helps you navigate the complex world of networking. As you encounter different network technologies and protocols, you can map them to the appropriate OSI layers. This mapping makes it easier to identify the source of problems and implement solutions. So, whether you're a network administrator, a developer, or simply someone curious about how the internet works, the OSI model is a fundamental concept that will serve you well. It provides a common language and framework for discussing and understanding network communication. With this knowledge, you can better grasp the intricacies of networking and make informed decisions when working with or troubleshooting networks. In our journey through the world of networking, the OSI model is just the beginning. We'll explore various network protocols, security measures, and advanced concepts that will deepen your understanding and empower you to navigate the ever-evolving landscape of modern technology. So, let's embark on this adventure together and delve deeper into the fascinating realm of networks and communication.

Chapter 2: Introduction to Internet Protocols

TCP/IP, short for Transmission Control Protocol/Internet Protocol, is the backbone of the modern internet. It's the set of rules and conventions that govern how data is transmitted, received, and routed across the vast global network we know as the internet. TCP/IP defines how devices on the internet communicate with each other, ensuring that data packets sent from one device reach their intended destination accurately and reliably. Imagine TCP/IP as the language spoken by all devices connected to the internet; it allows them to understand each other and work together seamlessly. At the heart of TCP/IP lies the concept of packets. When data is transmitted over the internet, it's divided into small, manageable units known as packets. Each packet contains a portion of the data, along with information about its source, destination, and position within the overall data stream. Think of these packets as individual letters within a long book, each with its sender, recipient, and a page number. One of the key components of TCP/IP is the IP address. An IP address is a unique numerical label assigned to each device on a network, including the internet. It serves as the device's "address" in the digital world, allowing data to be directed to the right place. Much like a postal address for physical mail, an IP address ensures data packets reach their intended destination. IPv4 and IPv6 are two versions of IP addresses. IPv4, the older version, uses a 32-bit format and is represented as four sets of numbers, like "192.168.1.1." However, the increasing number of devices connected to the internet has led to the adoption of IPv6, which uses a 128-bit format and allows for a virtually limitless number of unique addresses. Imagine IPv6 as an address book with enough pages to list every building in every city on Earth. When you enter a web address, like "www.example.com," your device uses a domain name system (DNS) server to translate that human-readable name into an IP address. DNS acts like a digital phonebook, ensuring your device can find the correct IP address to reach the website you want. So, when you type "www.example.com" in your web browser, it's the DNS server that translates it into something like "192.0.2.1." Now, let's talk about some of the core protocols within the TCP/IP suite. HTTP, or Hypertext Transfer Protocol, is one you've likely encountered frequently. It's the protocol used for transferring web pages and other resources on the World Wide Web. When you open your web browser and visit a website, your device uses HTTP to request and receive the web pages and associated content. Think of HTTP as the language spoken between your device and a web server, enabling the exchange of web pages and data. FTP, or File Transfer Protocol, is another important protocol within the TCP/IP suite. It's used for transferring files between computers over a network. If you've ever downloaded a file from the internet or uploaded a document to a server, you've likely used FTP or a related protocol. SMTP, or Simple Mail Transfer Protocol, is the backbone of email communication. When you send an email, SMTP is responsible for routing it to the recipient's email server. SMTP ensures that your email reaches its intended destination, much like a postal service for digital messages. POP3 (Post Office Protocol version 3) and IMAP (Internet Message Access Protocol) are protocols used to retrieve email from a server. They allow you to access your email messages, whether you're using a desktop email client or a mobile app. Think of POP3 and IMAP as the keys to your digital mailbox, allowing you to retrieve and manage your messages. TCP and UDP are two fundamental transport layer protocols within the TCP/IP suite. TCP, or Transmission Control Protocol, provides reliable, connection-oriented communication. It ensures that data is delivered accurately and in the correct order, making it suitable for applications like web browsing and file downloads. Imagine TCP as a diligent courier who verifies that every page of a book arrives in order and without errors. UDP, or User Datagram Protocol, is a simpler, connectionless protocol. It's well-suited for applications that prioritize speed over reliability, such as real-time video streaming and online gaming. Think of UDP as a courier who delivers messages quickly but doesn't check if every page of the book arrived. These protocols work in harmony to provide the foundation for internet communication. When you browse a website, your web browser may use both TCP and UDP to retrieve web pages and load multimedia content. For instance, TCP ensures that the text and images on a webpage load accurately, while UDP handles the real-time streaming of videos or online gaming data. In this way, TCP/IP adapts to the specific needs of different types of internet communication. Now, let's delve into the concept of ports. In the world of TCP/IP, a port is like a numbered gateway that allows data to flow in and out of a device. Ports help devices distinguish between different types of data and direct it to the appropriate application or service. Think of ports as different entrances to a large building, with each entrance leading to a different floor or department. Common ports include Port 80 for HTTP, Port 25 for SMTP, and Port 21 for FTP. When you access a website, your web browser sends a request to the web server on Port 80, indicating that it wants to retrieve a web page. The server receives the request on Port 80, processes it, and sends back the requested web page through the same port. It's like sending a letter to a specific department in a building by using the correct entrance. The internet is a vast interconnected network of devices, and TCP/IP is the universal language that enables them to communicate. It's the foundation of everything you do online, from sending emails and browsing websites to streaming videos and playing online games. Whether you're aware of it or not, TCP/IP is working behind the scenes to ensure that data flows seamlessly across the internet, connecting people, devices, and services around the world. Understanding the basics of TCP/IP and how it underpins the internet is essential for anyone who wants to navigate the digital landscape effectively. In the next chapters, we'll dive deeper into the world of networking, exploring topics such as network security, protocols, and advanced networking concepts. So, let's continue our journey through the exciting realm of computer networks and discover the wonders of the digital age together.

The Internet Protocol Suite, commonly known as TCP/IP, is the foundation of modern internet communication. It's the set of protocols and conventions that govern how data is transmitted, received, and routed across the global network that we all know as the internet. TCP/IP is like the language that all devices on the internet speak; it enables them to understand each other and work together seamlessly. At its core, TCP/IP revolves around the concept of data packets. When information is sent over the internet, it's broken down into smaller, manageable units called packets. Each packet contains a portion of the data, along with essential information like its source, destination, and position within the overall data stream. Think of these packets as individual puzzle pieces, each contributing to the complete picture of the data being transmitted. One of the key components of TCP/IP is the IP address. An IP address is a unique numerical label assigned to every device on a network, including the internet. It serves as the digital address of a device, ensuring that data packets are directed to the correct destination. Much like a postal address ensures a letter reaches the right mailbox, an IP address ensures data packets reach their intended recipient. IPv4 and IPv6 are two versions of IP addresses. IPv4, the older version, uses a 32-bit format and is represented as four sets of numbers, such as "192.168.1.1." However, as the number of connected devices continues to grow, IPv6 has been introduced, utilizing a 128-bit format that allows for a virtually unlimited number of unique addresses. Imagine IPv6 as an address book with pages enough to list every building in every city worldwide. When you enter a web address, like "www.example.com," your device uses a Domain Name System (DNS) server to translate that human-readable name into an IP address. DNS acts like a digital phonebook, ensuring your device can find the correct IP address to reach the website you want. So, when you type "www.example.com" in your web browser, it's the DNS server that translates it into something like "192.0.2.1." Now, let's explore some of the core protocols within the TCP/IP suite. HTTP, or Hypertext Transfer Protocol, is one you encounter frequently. It's the protocol used for transferring web pages and other resources on the World Wide Web. When you open your web browser and visit a website, your device uses HTTP to request and receive the web pages and associated content. Think of HTTP as the language of the web, allowing your device to communicate with web servers and retrieve the information you seek. FTP, or File Transfer Protocol, is another crucial protocol within TCP/IP. It's employed for transferring files between computers over a network. If you've ever downloaded a file from the internet or uploaded a document to a server, you've likely used FTP or a related protocol. SMTP, or Simple

Mail Transfer Protocol, forms the backbone of email communication. When you send an email, SMTP is responsible for routing it to the recipient's email server. SMTP ensures that your email reaches its intended destination, much like a postal service for digital messages. POP3 (Post Office Protocol version 3) and IMAP (Internet Message Access Protocol) are protocols used to retrieve email from a server. They enable you to access your email messages, whether you're using a desktop email client or a mobile app. Think of POP3 and IMAP as the keys to your digital mailbox, allowing you to retrieve and manage your messages. TCP and UDP are two fundamental transport layer protocols within TCP/IP. TCP, or Transmission Control Protocol, provides reliable, connection-oriented communication. It ensures that data is delivered accurately and in the correct order, making it suitable for applications like web browsing and file downloads. Imagine TCP as a diligent courier who checks each page of a book to ensure it arrives in order and without errors. UDP, or User Datagram Protocol, is a simpler, connectionless protocol. It's well-suited for applications that prioritize speed over reliability, such as real-time video streaming and online gaming. Think of UDP as a courier who delivers messages quickly but doesn't check if every page of the book arrived. These protocols work harmoniously to provide the foundation for internet communication. When you browse a website, your web browser may use both TCP and UDP to retrieve web pages and load multimedia content. For example, TCP ensures that the text and images on a webpage load accurately, while UDP handles the real-time streaming of videos or online gaming data. In this way, TCP/IP adapts to the specific needs of different types of internet communication. Now, let's delve into the concept of ports. In the TCP/IP world, a port is like a numbered gateway that allows data to flow in and out of a device. Ports help devices distinguish between different types of data and direct it to the appropriate application or service. Think of ports as different entrances to a large building, with each entrance leading to a different floor or department. Common ports include Port 80 for HTTP, Port 25 for SMTP, and Port 21 for FTP. When you access a website, your web browser sends a request to the web server on Port 80, indicating that it wants to retrieve a web page. The server receives the request on Port 80, processes it, and sends back the requested web page through the same port. It's like sending a letter to a specific department in a building by using the correct entrance. The internet is a vast interconnected network of devices, and TCP/IP is the universal language that enables them to communicate effectively. It's the foundation of everything you do online, from sending emails and browsing websites to streaming videos and playing online games. Whether you're aware of it or not, TCP/IP is working behind the scenes to ensure that data flows seamlessly across the internet, connecting people, devices, and services around the world. Understanding the basics of TCP/IP and how it underpins the internet is essential for anyone who wants to navigate the digital landscape effectively. In the next chapters, we'll delve deeper into the world of networking, exploring topics such as network security, protocols, and advanced networking concepts. So, let's continue our journey through the exciting realm of computer networks and discover the wonders of the digital age together.

Chapter 3: Essential Network Devices and Topologies

Let's delve into the fascinating world of networking devices, starting with routers, switches, and hubs. These devices play a crucial role in the functioning of computer networks, connecting devices and enabling the flow of data. First, let's explore routers. A router is like the traffic cop of a network, directing data packets between different networks. It serves as the gateway between your local network and the larger network, usually the internet. Imagine it as the bridge between your home network and the vast digital world beyond. Routers use a routing table to determine the best path for data to travel from source to destination. They examine the IP address of incoming packets and decide where to send them next. It's like the router reading the address on a letter and deciding which postal route it should take. Routers are also responsible for Network Address Translation (NAT), which allows multiple devices on a local network to share a single public IP address.

This feature helps conserve IPv4 addresses and adds an extra layer of security by hiding internal IP addresses from the internet. Now, let's talk about switches. A switch is like the dispatcher in a busy train station, efficiently directing data packets to their intended destinations within a local network. Unlike hubs, which blindly broadcast data to all connected devices, switches are smarter and more selective. When a device on a switch-based network sends data, the switch learns the device's MAC (Media Access Control) address and creates a MAC address table. This table keeps track of which devices are connected to which ports on the switch. When data arrives at the switch, it checks the MAC address table to determine which specific port to send the data to, ensuring that it reaches the correct device. Think of it as a switchboard operator connecting phone calls to the right recipients. Switches enhance network efficiency by reducing unnecessary data traffic and collisions. They're essential for modern networks, where multiple devices share the same network segment. Now, let's turn our attention to hubs. A hub, in contrast to routers and switches, is a simpler device that operates at the Physical layer of the OSI model. It's like a megaphone that amplifies and broadcasts data to all connected devices on a network segment. Hubs don't have the intelligence to make decisions about where data should go; instead, they mindlessly repeat data to all connected devices. This broadcasting approach can lead to network congestion and inefficiency, as all devices on the network segment receive every packet, regardless of whether it's meant for them. Think of it as everyone in a room hearing a message even if it's intended for just one person. Hubs are considered outdated for most modern networking scenarios due to their limitations. However, they can still find use in specific situations, such as network troubleshooting or simple network setups. In summary, routers, switches, and hubs are integral components of computer networks. Routers act as gateways, directing data between different networks and providing functions like NAT.

Switches efficiently manage data traffic within local networks, directing data to specific devices using MAC addresses. Hubs, on the other hand, broadcast data to all connected devices on a network segment and are less common in contemporary networks. Understanding the roles and functions of these devices is essential for anyone involved in network management or troubleshooting. In the next chapters, we'll continue our journey through the world of networking, exploring topics like network topologies, addressing, and security measures. So, let's keep our curiosity alive and continue to unravel the mysteries of computer networks together. Let's embark on a journey through the world of network topologies, exploring the various ways in which devices can be interconnected to form computer networks. Network topology refers to the physical or logical layout of devices in a network and how they communicate with one another. Think of it as the blueprint that outlines the structure and design of a network. One of the simplest and most common network topologies is the bus topology. In a bus topology, all devices are connected to a single central cable or "bus." Data travels along this cable, and each device listens for data addressed to it.

It's like passengers on a single bus route, where everyone can hear announcements, but only the one with the matching destination gets off. Bus topologies are straightforward to set up, but they have limitations, such as being susceptible to cable failures that can disrupt the entire network. Another common topology is the star topology. In a star topology, devices are connected to a central hub or switch. All data traffic flows through this central point, which manages the communication between devices. Think of it as a central post office where letters from different senders are sorted and then delivered to their respective recipients. Star topologies offer better reliability and ease of management compared to bus topologies. If one device or cable fails, it doesn't affect the entire network. However, the central hub or switch becomes a single point of failure, and if it goes down, the entire network may be disrupted. Next, let's explore the ring topology. In a ring topology, devices are connected in a closed-loop or ring configuration. Data travels in one direction along the ring, passing through each device until it reaches its destination. Imagine it as a circular conveyor belt in a factory where products move from one station to the next until they're assembled. Ring topologies provide redundancy, as data can travel in either direction in case of a cable or device failure. However, if a single device or cable breaks, it can disrupt the entire network. Mesh topologies take redundancy to the next level. In a full mesh topology, every device is connected to every other device in the network. Data can take multiple paths to reach its destination, providing high fault tolerance. Think of it as a web of interconnected roads where you can reach any destination via multiple routes.

Mesh topologies are extremely reliable but can be costly and complex to implement, especially as the number of devices increases. A hybrid topology combines two or more of the previously mentioned topologies. For example, a network might have a star topology within each department of an organization and then connect these departmental networks using a bus topology. Hybrid topologies offer flexibility and can balance the strengths and weaknesses of different topologies. However, they can also become complex to manage as the network grows. Topology doesn't just refer to physical connections; it can also be logical. A logical topology defines how data flows in a network, regardless of its physical layout. A common logical topology is the client-server model. In this model, some devices, known as servers, provide services or resources to other devices, called clients. Think of it as a restaurant where servers (waitstaff) provide services to customers (clients) who request food and drinks. The client-server model is prevalent in modern networks, especially in businesses where servers host email, files, and web services. Another logical topology is the peer-to-peer

(P2P) model. In a P2P network, all devices have equal status and can act as both clients and servers. Each device can share resources directly with others without relying on a central server. Imagine a potluck dinner where everyone brings a dish to share, and everyone can access each other's offerings. P2P networks are common for sharing files and resources among personal devices. Now, let's explore a special type of topology known as the tree or hierarchical topology. In a tree topology, devices are organized hierarchically, forming a tree-like structure. Data flows from top-level nodes down to lower-level nodes. Think of it as an organizational chart, with a CEO at the top, followed by department heads, and then individual employees. Tree topologies are often used in wide area networks (WANs) to connect regional or branch offices to a central headquarters.

This hierarchical structure simplifies management and allows for efficient communication between the central office and branch locations. Finally, let's touch on wireless networks. Wireless networks, or Wi-Fi networks, have their own unique topology. Devices connect to a wireless access point (AP), which acts as a central hub for wireless communication. Data travels through the airwaves, enabling devices to connect without physical cables. Imagine a radio station broadcasting music to listeners with their radios. Wireless networks are incredibly convenient, allowing devices to connect from anywhere within the coverage area of an access point. However, they can be susceptible to interference and have limitations in terms of range. In summary, network topologies define how devices are connected and communicate within a network. Common physical topologies include bus, star, ring, and mesh, each with its strengths and weaknesses. Logical topologies, such as client-server and P2P, dictate how data flows within a network, while hybrid and hierarchical topologies offer flexibility and organization. Understanding these topologies is essential for designing and managing efficient and reliable networks. In our journey through the world of networking, we'll continue to explore various network concepts, protocols, and technologies that make the digital world function seamlessly. So, let's keep unraveling the mysteries of computer networks together, one topic at a time.

Chapter 4: Network Addressing and Subnetting

Let's delve into the world of IP addressing, a fundamental aspect of computer networking that plays a crucial role in ensuring data gets to where it needs to go. At its core, an IP (Internet Protocol) address is like a digital mailing address, uniquely identifying each device connected to a network. It's what enables devices to locate and communicate with each other in the vast interconnected network we call the internet. Imagine it as the postal code that ensures a letter reaches the right mailbox. IP addresses come in two main versions: IPv4 and IPv6. IPv4, the older and more widely used version, is represented as a series of four sets of numbers, like "192.168.1.1." These sets, called octets, contain numbers ranging from 0 to 255 and are separated by periods. IPv4 addresses are becoming scarce due to the exponential growth of internet-connected devices. Enter IPv6, a newer version that uses a 128-bit format, allowing for an almost limitless number of unique addresses. IPv6 addresses look like this: "2001:0db8:85a3:0000:0000:8a2e:0370:7334." Think of IPv6 as an address book with enough pages to list every building in every city on Earth. Now, let's talk about the structure of IP addresses. An IP address is typically divided into two parts: the network portion and the host portion. The network portion identifies the specific network to which a device belongs, while the host portion distinguishes individual devices within that network. It's like a zip code within a city; the zip code identifies the general area (network), while the street address pinpoints the exact location (host). To further break down IP addresses, we use subnet masks. A subnet mask is like a filter that separates the network and host portions of an IP address. It consists of a series of ones followed by a series of zeros. The ones in the subnet mask indicate the network portion, while the zeros indicate the host portion. For example, a subnet mask of "255.255.255.0" means that the first three octets are the network portion, and the last octet is the host portion. Now, let's delve into IP address classes. IP addresses are categorized into five classes: A, B, C, D, and E. Each class has a different range of possible network and host combinations. Class A addresses have a range from 1.0.0.0 to 126.0.0.0, with a subnet mask of "255.0.0.0." They provide a large number of networks, each with a massive number of host addresses. Class B addresses, from 128.0.0.0 to 191.0.0.0, have a subnet mask of "255.255.0.0" and offer a moderate number of networks and hosts. Class C addresses, ranging from 192.0.0.0 to 223.0.0.0, have a subnet mask of "255.255.255.0" and provide a smaller number of networks but a larger number of hosts per network. Class D addresses, from 224.0.0.0 to 239.0.0.0, are reserved for multicast groups and not used for regular host addressing. Class E addresses, from 240.0.0.0 to 255.0.0.0, are also reserved for special purposes and not typically used for standard host addressing. Now, let's discuss private and public IP addresses. Private IP addresses are used within private networks, such as home or corporate networks. They are not routable on the public internet and serve as internal addresses. Examples of private IP address ranges include 192.168.0.0 to 192.168.255.255 and 10.0.0.0 to 10.255.255.255. Public IP addresses, on the other hand, are assigned to devices directly connected to the internet. They are globally unique and routable across the internet. Public IP addresses are what enable devices to communicate with each other on a global scale. Think of private IP addresses as the numbers on your house door, known only to your neighbors, while public IP addresses are like your postal address, allowing mail carriers to find you from anywhere. To manage the distribution of IP addresses, there are organizations called Regional Internet Registries (RIRs) responsible for allocating IP address blocks to internet service providers (ISPs) and organizations. These RIRs ensure that IP addresses are distributed efficiently and in accordance with established policies. Examples of RIRs include ARIN (American Registry for Internet Numbers), RIPE NCC (Réseaux IP Européens Network Coordination Centre), and APNIC (Asia-Pacific Network Information Centre). Now, let's address dynamic and static IP addresses. A dynamic IP address is assigned to a device temporarily by a DHCP (Dynamic Host Configuration Protocol) server. Think of it as a hotel room key that's given to you for the duration of your stay. Dynamic IP addresses are practical for devices that frequently join and leave a network, like laptops and smartphones. In contrast, a static IP address is manually configured for a device and remains fixed. It's like having a dedicated parking spot with your name on it. Static IP addresses are typically used for servers or devices that need a consistent address for services like remote access or hosting a website. Now, let's discuss the role of DNS (Domain Name System). DNS acts as the internet's phonebook, translating human-readable domain names (like www.example.com) into IP addresses. It enables us to access websites and services using familiar names instead of numerical IP addresses. Think of DNS as the friendly receptionist who connects your call to the right person in a large office building. Without DNS, navigating the internet would be much more challenging, as we'd have to remember numerical IP addresses for every website we visit. In summary, IP addressing is the backbone of computer networking, providing unique digital addresses to every device connected to the internet. Understanding IP address versions, structure, classes, private vs. public addresses, subnet masks, and the role of DNS is essential for anyone working with networks. As we continue our journey through the world of networking, we'll explore more advanced topics, protocols, and technologies that build upon this foundational knowledge. So, let's keep unraveling the mysteries of computer networks together, one topic at a time. Let's dive into the intricate world of subnetting, a vital skill for network administrators and engineers that enables efficient IP address management. Subnetting is like dividing a large plot of land into smaller, manageable lots to optimize space and resources. In the context of networking, it involves breaking down a larger IP address space into smaller, more manageable subnetworks. Why do we need subnetting, you might wonder? Well, it offers several advantages, such as improving network efficiency, security, and organization. Imagine a sprawling estate with many houses; subdividing it into smaller lots allows for better planning, easier maintenance, and more efficient use of resources. Now, let's get into the fundamentals of subnetting. In IP addressing, each subnet has its unique range of IP addresses. To create subnets, we borrow bits from the host portion of an IP address. Think of it as partitioning a room into separate workspaces; each workspace has its boundaries and resources. The subnet mask, a key element in subnetting, defines which portion of an IP address is the network part and which is the host part. A subnet mask consists of a series of contiguous ones followed by a series of contiguous zeros. The ones indicate the network portion, while the zeros represent the host portion. For example, a subnet mask of "255.255.255.0" means that the first three octets are the network part, and the last octet is the host part. Subnet masks are written in a format like "255.255.255.0," but they can also be represented in CIDR (Classless Inter-Domain Routing) notation, such as "/24." Now, let's discuss IP address classes and subnetting. In traditional IP address classes (A, B, and C), subnetting was somewhat rigid. Each class had a default subnet mask, and subnetting within a class had limitations. But with CIDR, we have greater flexibility. CIDR allows for custom subnetting, breaking free from the constraints of traditional classes. Imagine having the freedom to divide your land into any-sized parcels, not just the predefined ones. Let's dive into an example to demystify subnetting. Suppose you have the IP address "192.168.1.0" with a subnet mask of "255.255.255.0" (or "/24" in CIDR notation). This means you have a Class C address, and the last octet is available for host addresses. If you want to create smaller subnets within this address space, you can borrow bits from the host part. Let's say you want four subnets. To achieve this, you need to borrow two bits from the host portion, converting the subnet mask to "255.255.255.192" (or "/26"). Now you have four subnets: "192.168.1.0/26," "192.168.1.64/26," "192.168.1.128/26," and "192.168.1.192/26." Each subnet can accommodate up to 62 host addresses, as two addresses are reserved for network and broadcast addresses in each subnet. This granular approach allows you to efficiently manage your IP address space, optimizing it for your network's specific needs. And remember, subnetting isn't limited to just dividing an address space into smaller pieces; it can also involve combining smaller address spaces into larger ones. Imagine merging smaller plots of land to create a larger, unified property. This is known as supernetting, and it's the opposite of subnetting. Supernetting simplifies routing by aggregating multiple smaller address spaces into a larger one. For example, if you have four Class C networks, you can create a supernet by combining them into a single network with a Class B address. This reduces the number of routing entries in the network's routing tables, making it more efficient. Now, let's explore Variable Length Subnet Masking (VLSM). VLSM is a technique that allows you to use different subnet masks within the same major network. Think of it as having a neighborhood where each street can have different-sized lots. VLSM is particularly useful when you have varying requirements for subnets within a larger network. For instance, within a Class B address space, you might have departments with different subnet size needs. Using VLSM, you can allocate larger subnets to departments that need more addresses and smaller subnets to those with fewer devices. This flexibility optimizes IP address allocation within your network. To wrap it up, subnetting is a powerful tool in IP address management, enabling efficient use of address space, improved network organization, and enhanced security. It allows you to divide and conquer, whether it's breaking down a large estate into manageable lots or creating a unified property by merging smaller parcels. CIDR notation offers flexibility in subnetting, breaking free from the constraints of traditional IP address classes. Supernetting simplifies routing, while VLSM optimizes IP address allocation within a network. Mastering subnetting is a valuable skill for anyone working with computer networks, ensuring that your network resources are utilized efficiently and effectively. As we continue our journey through the world of networking, we'll delve into more advanced topics, protocols, and technologies that build upon this foundational knowledge. So, let's keep unraveling the mysteries of computer networks together, one subnet at a time.

Chapter 5: Securing Network Communications

Let's explore the fascinating realm of encryption and authentication, two pillars of modern computer security that protect our data and ensure the identities of users and systems. Imagine a secret code that only you and a trusted friend understand; that's the essence of encryption. At its core, encryption transforms readable data into an unreadable format using complex mathematical algorithms. This unreadable data, known as ciphertext, can only be deciphered by someone possessing the correct decryption key. Think of it as sending a letter in a locked box; only the person with the key can open and read it. Encryption plays a pivotal role in securing data during transmission and storage, safeguarding it from prying eyes and potential attackers. Now, let's delve into the different types of encryption. There are two primary categories: symmetric and asymmetric encryption. Symmetric encryption uses a single key for both encryption and decryption. Imagine a shared secret between you and your friend, allowing you to lock and unlock a treasure chest. While symmetric encryption is efficient and fast, it requires a secure method to exchange the secret key. If an eavesdropper intercepts the key during transmission, your data's security is compromised. Asymmetric encryption, on the other hand, employs a pair of keys: a public key for encryption and a private key for decryption. Think of it as a mailbox with two slots—one for sending messages (public key) and one for receiving (private key). You can freely share your public key with anyone, while keeping your private key secure. Messages encrypted with your public key can only be decrypted with your private key. This approach eliminates the need for a secure key exchange, making asymmetric encryption a valuable tool for secure communication over untrusted networks. Now, let's talk about authentication. Authentication is the process of verifying the identity of users, devices, or systems. Imagine showing your ID to a security guard at the entrance of a secure facility; that's authentication in action. Authentication methods can vary widely, from simple username and password combinations to more advanced biometrics like fingerprint or facial recognition. Multi-factor authentication (MFA) adds an extra layer of security by requiring two or more authentication methods. It's like having both your ID card and a biometric scan to access a restricted area. MFA makes it significantly harder for unauthorized individuals to gain access. Now, let's discuss digital certificates. Digital certificates are like digital IDs that verify the authenticity of a person or entity in the online world. They contain information about the certificate holder, their public key, and the certificate's issuer, usually a trusted Certificate Authority (CA). Think of it as an official document with your photo, name, and a notary's stamp, verifying your identity. When you connect to a secure website (with HTTPS), your browser checks the site's digital certificate. If the certificate is issued by a trusted CA and hasn't expired, your browser establishes a secure connection, encrypting data exchanged with the site. Digital certificates are a cornerstone of secure online communication, ensuring that you're connecting to the right server and not an imposter. Now, let's explore Public Key Infrastructure (PKI). PKI is like a digital notary service that manages digital certificates, ensuring their validity and integrity. It includes a hierarchy of CAs, from top-level CAs known as root CAs to intermediate CAs. Think of it as a chain of trust, with each CA vouching for the authenticity of the certificates it issues. PKI provides the framework for secure communication, e-commerce, and various online services.

It's what enables you to confidently enter your credit card information on an e-commerce site, knowing your data is protected. Now, let's talk about secure protocols. Secure communication on the internet relies on protocols like HTTPS, SMTPS, and SFTP. These protocols use encryption and authentication mechanisms to protect data during transmission. Imagine a conversation in a soundproof, sealed room with two people who have shown their IDs to each other; that's secure protocol communication. For example, HTTPS secures web browsing by encrypting data exchanged between your browser and a web server. SMTPS ensures that your email is transmitted securely, and SFTP safeguards file transfers. These protocols rely on encryption algorithms like TLS (Transport Layer Security) and SSL (Secure Sockets Layer) to establish secure connections. Now, let's discuss security tokens. Security tokens are physical or virtual devices that generate one-time codes for authentication. Think of it as a constantly changing combination lock; each time you access a system, the code is different. Tokens can be hardware-based, like a key fob, or software-based, like a mobile app. They add an extra layer of security, as even if an attacker knows your password, they won't have the current token code. This is commonly used in two-factor authentication (2FA) systems. Now, let's touch on biometrics. Biometrics use unique physical or behavioral characteristics to authenticate individuals. Think of it as your fingerprint or face being your password. Biometric systems scan and verify these characteristics to grant or deny access. Fingerprint readers and facial recognition on smartphones are common examples. Biometrics are considered highly secure, as they're difficult to fake. However, they can be less convenient than other authentication methods. In summary, encryption and authentication are the bedrock of modern cybersecurity. Encryption protects our data by rendering it unreadable to unauthorized parties, while authentication ensures that only trusted individuals or systems gain access. Symmetric and asymmetric encryption offer different approaches, with asymmetric encryption eliminating the need for secure key exchange. Authentication methods range from traditional usernames and passwords to advanced biometrics and security tokens. Digital certificates and PKI establish trust in online communication, and secure protocols like HTTPS and SMTPS encrypt and authenticate data in transit. Biometrics add a layer of security by verifying unique physical or behavioral traits. Understanding these concepts is crucial in today's digital landscape, where privacy and security are paramount. As we continue our journey through the world of networking and cybersecurity, we'll explore more advanced topics, techniques, and emerging technologies that keep our digital world safe and secure. So, let's keep unraveling the mysteries of computer security together, one layer at a time. Let's dive into the world of network security best practices, a critical aspect of maintaining the integrity, confidentiality, and availability of your digital assets. Imagine your network as a fortress; network security best practices are like the moat, drawbridge, and guards that protect it from intruders. The first and fundamental principle is access control. Think of access control as the keys to your fortress. Only authorized individuals should have access to your network, systems, and data. Use strong authentication methods, such as complex passwords, biometrics, or multi-factor authentication (MFA), to ensure that only the right people gain entry. Next, consider the principle of least privilege. Imagine giving each person in your fortress only the keys they need to access specific rooms. Apply the same concept to your network. Assign the minimum level of access necessary for users and systems to perform their tasks. This limits the potential damage if a user's credentials are compromised or a system is breached. Now, let's discuss network segmentation. Think of network segmentation as dividing your fortress into different sections with separate defenses. By segmenting your network, you isolate critical assets from less secure areas. This limits the lateral movement of attackers within your network. It's like a medieval castle with multiple layers of walls, making it challenging for invaders to reach the inner sanctum. Regularly update and patch your systems and software. Imagine maintaining the walls and gates of your fortress; neglecting them weakens your defenses. Software updates and patches fix known vulnerabilities that attackers can exploit. Failure to apply them is like leaving a breach in your fortress walls for attackers to walk through. Now, let's talk about intrusion detection and prevention. Intrusion detection is like having watchful guards patrolling your fortress, while intrusion prevention is like having guards who not only detect intruders but also stop them. Use intrusion detection systems (IDS) to monitor network traffic for suspicious activities. Pair them with intrusion prevention systems (IPS) to automatically block or mitigate threats. It's akin to having guards who not only sound the alarm but also take action against intruders. Encrypt your data in transit and at rest. Think of data encryption as placing your treasures in locked chests. Data encryption ensures that even if an attacker gains access to your data, they can't read it without the decryption key. Use secure protocols like HTTPS, VPNs, and encrypted storage to safeguard sensitive information. Now, let's explore the importance of regular security audits and assessments. Imagine hiring a team of expert inspectors to evaluate the security of your fortress. Conduct security audits and assessments to identify vulnerabilities and weaknesses in your network. These assessments can help you proactively address security issues before attackers exploit them. Educate and train your staff in cybersecurity best practices. Think of cybersecurity training as teaching your guards to recognize different attack tactics. Human error is a significant contributor to security breaches. By educating your staff about phishing, social engineering, and safe online behavior, you empower them to be your first line of defense. Implement a robust incident response plan. Imagine having a detailed plan for what to do if your fortress is under attack. Create an incident response plan that outlines how to detect, respond to, and recover from security incidents. This plan should be regularly updated and tested to ensure its effectiveness. Now, let's delve into network monitoring and logging. Network monitoring is like having surveillance cameras throughout your fortress, while logging is like keeping a detailed record of who enters and exits. Use network monitoring tools to continuously observe your network for unusual activities. Simultaneously, maintain comprehensive logs of network traffic, user activities, and system events. These logs can be invaluable for identifying security incidents and investigating their root causes. Implement strong perimeter defenses. Think of your network's perimeter as the outer walls of your fortress. Use firewalls, intrusion detection systems (IDS), and intrusion prevention systems (IPS) to filter incoming and outgoing traffic. Consider implementing a demilitarized zone (DMZ) to segregate public-facing services from your internal network. Regularly back up your data. Imagine making copies of your most valuable treasures and storing them in a secure vault. Regular backups ensure that even in the event of a breach or data loss, you can recover critical information. Store backups in an isolated environment to prevent attackers from compromising them. Now, let's discuss security awareness and culture. Foster a culture of security within your organization. Encourage all employees to take responsibility for cybersecurity. Think of it as instilling a sense of vigilance and caution throughout your fortress. Security awareness programs and regular reminders can help reinforce good security practices. Stay informed about emerging threats. Imagine having scouts who constantly gather information about potential threats outside your fortress. Stay updated on the latest cybersecurity threats and vulnerabilities. Subscribe to security alerts, follow industry news, and participate in information sharing and analysis centers (ISACs). This awareness enables you to adapt your defenses to evolving threats. Now, let's touch on vendor and third-party risk management. Imagine your fortress relying on supplies from external vendors. Evaluate the security practices of third-party vendors and service providers. Ensure that they meet your security standards and don't introduce vulnerabilities into your network. Regularly review and assess their security measures. Lastly, plan for business continuity and disaster recovery. Think of it as having a contingency plan for when unforeseen events threaten your fortress. Develop and test a business continuity and disaster recovery plan to ensure that your network can quickly recover from disruptions. This plan should include backup infrastructure, data recovery procedures, and communication strategies. In summary, network security best practices are the foundation of a robust cybersecurity posture. These practices protect your network, systems, and data from a wide range of threats. By implementing access control, the principle of least privilege, network segmentation, and other security measures, you create a strong defense for your digital assets. Regular updates, intrusion detection and prevention, and encryption enhance security further. Security audits, staff training, and incident response planning prepare you for potential threats. Monitoring, logging, and strong perimeter defenses provide continuous vigilance. Backup and recovery strategies, along with a security-aware culture, ensure resilience. Stay informed about emerging threats and manage third-party risks to maintain a secure network. With these best practices in place, your network becomes a fortress that stands strong against even the most determined attackers. As we continue our journey through the world of networking and cybersecurity, we'll explore advanced topics, emerging technologies, and evolving threats. So, let's keep fortifying our knowledge and defenses, one best practice at a time.

Chapter 6: Wireless Networks and Security

Let's embark on an exploration of wireless network technologies, the invisible threads that connect our devices to the digital world, enabling freedom and mobility. Wireless networks are like the invisible pathways that allow information to flow through the air, connecting our devices without the need for physical cables. Imagine a world where you can access the internet from anywhere in your home, your favorite coffee shop, or even a park; that's the promise of wireless technology. At the heart of wireless networks lies the concept of radio waves. Think of radio waves as the carrier pigeons of the digital age, transporting data between your devices and the network. To achieve this, wireless devices, such as Wi-Fi routers and smartphones, are equipped with radio transmitters and receivers. These devices communicate by sending and receiving radio signals over specific frequencies. Now, let's delve into Wi-Fi, one of the most widely used wireless technologies. Wi-Fi is like the magic portal that connects your laptop to the internet without any physical tether. It stands for "Wireless Fidelity" and is based on the IEEE 802.11 standard. Think of it as a universal language that all Wi-Fi-enabled devices understand. Wi-Fi operates in the 2.4 GHz and 5 GHz frequency bands, with different versions like 802.11n, 802.11ac, and the latest, 802.11ax (Wi-Fi 6). These versions offer varying speeds and capabilities, with Wi-Fi 6 being the fastest and most efficient. The range of a Wi-Fi network depends on factors like the router's power, antenna design, and interference from physical obstacles. Imagine your router as a lighthouse; the farther you are from it, the weaker the signal becomes. To extend the range, you can use Wi-Fi range extenders or mesh networks that create a web of Wi-Fi coverage throughout your home. Now, let's discuss cellular networks. Cellular networks are like the highways of wireless communication, providing mobile devices with internet access on the go. Imagine being able to stream videos, make video calls, and browse the web from your smartphone, all while traveling in a car or on a train; that's the magic of cellular networks. Cellular networks rely on a network of cell towers that transmit and receive signals. These towers are connected to a central hub called the Mobile Switching Center (MSC). When you use your mobile device, it connects to the nearest cell tower, which relays your voice or data to the MSC. The MSC routes your call or data to its destination, whether it's another mobile device, a landline phone, or a website server. Cellular networks use different generations, with 2G, 3G, 4G, and 5G being the most prominent. Each generation offers improvements in speed, capacity, and latency. 5G, the latest generation, promises blazing-fast speeds and low latency, making it suitable for applications like augmented reality and autonomous vehicles. Now, let's explore Bluetooth. Bluetooth is like the invisible thread that connects your wireless earbuds to your smartphone, allowing you to enjoy music without tangled cords. It's a short-range wireless technology designed for connecting devices like headphones, keyboards, and speakers to smartphones, tablets, and computers. Think of it as a digital handshake that two devices perform to establish a connection. Bluetooth operates in the 2.4 GHz frequency band and has different versions, such as Bluetooth 4.0 and Bluetooth 5.0. Bluetooth 5.0 offers improved range and data transfer speeds, making it ideal for connecting smart home devices. Now, let's talk about Zigbee and Z-Wave. Zigbee and Z-Wave are like the secret agents of the smart home world, quietly connecting and controlling your smart devices behind the scenes. These wireless technologies are specifically designed for home automation and the Internet of Things (IoT). They operate in the 2.4 GHz frequency band (Zigbee can also use the 915 MHz band in the United States) and use mesh networking, where each device serves as a relay for other devices, extending the network's range. Imagine your smart lights communicating with a central hub, which then relays commands to other devices like your smart thermostat and locks. This interconnectedness is the magic of Zigbee and Z-Wave. Now, let's touch on NFC (Near Field Communication). NFC is like a digital handshake between your smartphone and a contactless payment terminal, allowing you to make purchases with a tap. It's a short-range wireless technology that operates at very close proximity, typically within a few centimeters. NFC is commonly used for contactless payments, ticketing, and data transfer between devices. Think of it as a virtual business card exchange between smartphones or a digital wallet for your daily coffee purchase. Now, let's discuss satellite communication. Satellite communication is like the celestial radio station that broadcasts signals to your satellite dish, providing internet access in remote areas. It relies on a network of satellites orbiting Earth. These satellites beam signals to and from satellite dishes on the ground. Imagine having high-speed internet access in the middle of a desert or on a ship in the open ocean; that's the power of satellite communication. It's often used in remote and rural areas where traditional wired or cellular networks are impractical. Now, let's explore emerging technologies like Li-Fi. Li-Fi is like the futuristic cousin of Wi-Fi, using light to transmit data instead of radio waves. It operates by modulating LED light sources at high speeds, making it imperceptible to the human eye. Imagine your room's overhead lights not only illuminating the space but also providing high-speed internet access. Li-Fi offers lightning-fast data transfer rates and has the potential to revolutionize wireless communication in environments like hospitals and aircraft. Now, let's discuss the challenges and considerations in wireless network technologies. Wireless networks face challenges like interference, security risks, and limited range. Imagine trying to have a conversation in a crowded room with multiple conversations happening simultaneously; that's similar to the interference wireless networks can experience. To mitigate interference, Wi-Fi routers use different channels within the 2.4 GHz and 5 GHz bands. Security is a significant concern in wireless networks, with threats like eavesdropping and unauthorized access. Encryption protocols like WPA3 (Wi-Fi Protected Access 3) and strong authentication methods help secure wireless communication. Range limitations are another consideration; the farther you are from a wireless access point or cell tower, the weaker the signal. Extenders, mesh networks, and strategic placement of access points can help address range issues. In summary, wireless network technologies have transformed the way we connect and communicate. From Wi-Fi and cellular networks to Bluetooth and IoT protocols like Zigbee and Z-Wave, these technologies empower us to enjoy wireless freedom. As we look to the future with 5G, Li-Fi, and satellite communication, the possibilities for connectivity are boundless. However, challenges like interference, security, and range must be carefully addressed to ensure the reliability and security of wireless communication. So, let's continue to embrace the magic of wireless technologies as they shape our connected world, enabling us to explore new horizons in communication and convenience. Securing Wi-Fi networks is like locking the doors and windows of your digital home, ensuring that only authorized users can enter and protecting your data from prying eyes and cyber threats. Think of your Wi-Fi network as the gateway to your digital world, connecting your devices to the vast landscape of the internet. It's like a bridge that links you to the virtual realm, and just like in the physical world, you want this bridge to be secure.

The first step in securing your Wi-Fi network is changing the default settings. Imagine moving into a new house; you wouldn't keep the default locks and keys that everyone else has, right? Well, it's the same with your Wi-Fi router. Change the default username and password to something unique and strong. This simple step can prevent unauthorized access to your network.

Next, enable WPA3 encryption. WPA3 is like an impenetrable force field around your Wi-Fi network. It ensures that data transmitted between your devices and the router is encrypted, making it nearly impossible for eavesdroppers to intercept and decipher your data. WPA3 is the latest and most secure encryption standard, so make sure your router and devices support it.

Now, let's talk about the importance of strong passwords. Think of your Wi-Fi password as the key to your digital fortress. Create a complex, unique password that combines uppercase and lowercase letters, numbers, and special characters. Avoid using easily guessable passwords like "password123" or "admin." The stronger your Wi-Fi password, the more resilient your network is against brute-force attacks.

Another essential security measure is enabling network segmentation. Network segmentation is like dividing your digital home into separate rooms, each with its own lock and key. Create a guest network for visitors and devices that you don't fully trust. This way, if a guest's device becomes compromised, it won't have access to your main network and sensitive data.

Regularly update your router's firmware. Firmware updates are like security patches for your router, addressing vulnerabilities and improving overall performance. Check for updates on the manufacturer's website or use the router's built-in update feature. Keeping your router's firmware up to date is crucial for staying protected against evolving threats.

Let's discuss MAC address filtering. Every device connected to your network has a unique MAC address, like a digital fingerprint. MAC address filtering allows you to create a whitelist of approved devices that can access your network. Imagine having a guest list for a party; only those on the list are allowed in. While MAC address filtering provides an additional layer of security, it's not foolproof, as MAC addresses can be spoofed. However, it can help deter casual unauthorized users.

Consider hiding your Wi-Fi network's SSID. The SSID is like the nameplate on your digital front door, broadcasting the network's name to anyone in range. When you hide the SSID, it's as if you've removed the nameplate, making your network less visible to potential attackers. While this won't deter determined hackers, it can help reduce the likelihood of casual intrusion.

Implement intrusion detection and prevention systems (IDS/IPS). IDS/IPS are like digital guards that monitor your network for suspicious activities and can automatically block threats. They analyze network traffic patterns and can detect and block intrusions or unauthorized access attempts. Think of them as silent sentinels that keep watch over your network.

Now, let's talk about physical security. Physical security is like locking the doors and windows of your digital home. Ensure that your router is placed in a secure location, and limit physical access to it. If possible, lock it in a cabinet or use a security mount. Physical security measures can prevent unauthorized individuals from tampering with your router.

Regularly review connected devices. Think of it as taking inventory of who's in your digital home. Periodically check the list of devices connected to your network. If you spot any unfamiliar devices, investigate them promptly. It's possible that an unauthorized device has gained access to your network.

Enable two-factor authentication (2FA) for router access. 2FA adds an extra layer of security, requiring not only a password but also a secondary verification method, such as a code sent to your smartphone. Think of it as having a second key to your digital front door. Enabling 2FA for router access can prevent unauthorized individuals from changing your network settings.

Regularly monitor network traffic. Monitoring network traffic is like keeping an eye on who's coming and going from your digital home. Use network monitoring tools to detect unusual activity or unauthorized access. These tools can provide insights into network performance and security, helping you identify and respond to potential threats.

Educate yourself and your household members about online safety. Think of it as teaching your family members to recognize potential dangers in the digital world, just as you would in the physical world. Educate them about phishing scams, social engineering tactics, and safe online behavior. Awareness and vigilance can go a long way in protecting your network.

Consider using a virtual private network (VPN). A VPN is like a secret tunnel that encrypts your internet traffic and routes it through a secure server, providing an extra layer of privacy and security. VPNs are especially useful when connecting to public Wi-Fi networks, as they protect your data from potential eavesdroppers.

Regularly back up your router settings. Backing up your router settings is like creating a spare key for your digital front door. In case your router experiences a failure or you need to reset it, having a backup of your settings can save you time and effort in reconfiguring your network. Check your router's user manual or manufacturer's website for instructions on how to back up and restore settings.

Now, let's touch on the importance of security audits. Security audits are like having a professional inspector assess the safety of your digital home. Consider conducting periodic security audits to identify vulnerabilities and weaknesses in your network. You can use security audit tools or consult with cybersecurity experts for a thorough evaluation.

Finally, keep up to date with the latest security threats and best practices. Think of it as staying informed about new dangers in the digital landscape, just as you would with developments in your neighborhood. Subscribe to security news and updates, follow cybersecurity blogs, and participate in online forums or communities dedicated to network security.

In summary, securing your Wi-Fi network is essential for protecting your digital home and sensitive data from cyber threats. By changing default settings, enabling strong encryption, using complex passwords, and implementing network segmentation, you create a robust defense against unauthorized access. Regularly updating firmware, using MAC address filtering, and considering physical security measures add layers of protection. Intrusion detection and prevention, along with monitoring network traffic, help detect and block threats. Educating yourself and your household members about online safety and using VPNs enhance security. Backing up router settings and conducting security audits are proactive measures. Staying informed about evolving threats and best practices ensures that your Wi-Fi network remains a secure gateway to the digital world. So, let's continue to fortify our digital homes and enjoy the benefits of a secure and reliable Wi-Fi network.

Chapter 7: Introduction to Cybersecurity Threats

Let's delve into the world of cybersecurity and explore some of the common cyber threats that lurk in the digital landscape, like shadows in the night. Just as we take precautions in the physical world to protect our homes and belongings, we must also safeguard our digital assets against a range of threats.

First, there are viruses and malware, which are like digital infections that can spread through your devices. Imagine them as microscopic invaders that can corrupt, steal, or damage your data. Viruses attach themselves to legitimate files, while malware includes a broader category of malicious software, such as Trojans, ransomware, and spyware, each with its own sinister purpose.

Phishing attacks are like cunning scams that attempt to trick you into revealing sensitive information, such as passwords or credit card numbers. Think of them as deceptive ploys, like a charming stranger at your doorstep who turns out to be a con artist. Phishing emails often appear legitimate, but they're designed to steal your personal data or install malware on your device.

Now, let's talk about ransomware, the digital equivalent of a hostage situation. Imagine your files and documents being held captive by malicious actors who demand a ransom for their release. Ransomware encrypts your data, making it inaccessible until you pay a ransom. It's like a digital kidnapper who demands a ransom in exchange for the safe return of your valuable information.

Distributed Denial of Service (DDoS) attacks are like traffic jams on the digital highway. Picture your favorite website suddenly overwhelmed by an army of automated bots and traffic, rendering it inaccessible to legitimate users. DDoS attacks flood a target server or network with traffic, causing disruptions and downtime.

Brute-force attacks are like a relentless burglar attempting to guess the combination to your digital safe. These attacks involve trying every possible combination of passwords until the correct one is found. Think of it as a determined thief who refuses to give up until they crack the code.

Zero-day vulnerabilities are like hidden traps waiting to be discovered. Imagine a secret passage into your castle that only a select few know about. Zero-day vulnerabilities are software flaws that are unknown to the vendor and, therefore, unpatched. Cybercriminals exploit these vulnerabilities before the vendor can release a fix.

Now, let's discuss insider threats, which are like having a spy within your ranks. Insider threats involve individuals within an organization who misuse their access to compromise security. It could be a disgruntled employee leaking sensitive information or an unwitting staff member falling victim to a phishing attack.

Social engineering attacks are like digital manipulations that exploit human psychology. Think of them as digital con artists who use deception and persuasion to trick individuals into divulging confidential information. Social engineering attacks can take various forms, such as pretexting, baiting, or tailgating.

Malvertising is like hidden dangers lurking in plain sight. Imagine clicking on what appears to be a harmless online advertisement, only to be led into a web of malware. Malvertisements are ads that contain malicious code, redirecting users to fraudulent websites or infecting their devices with malware.

Man-in-the-middle (MitM) attacks are like eavesdroppers intercepting your private conversations. These attacks involve a cybercriminal secretly intercepting and possibly altering the communication between two parties. It's like someone secretly listening in on your phone calls or reading your text messages.

Now, let's talk about data breaches, which are like burglaries in the digital realm. Imagine a vault containing sensitive information being cracked open by cybercriminals. Data breaches involve unauthorized access to confidential data, such as personal information, financial records, or intellectual property. These breaches can have severe consequences for individuals and organizations.

SQL injection attacks are like digital pickpockets exploiting vulnerabilities in websites. These attacks manipulate a web application's SQL query to gain unauthorized access to its database. It's like a cunning thief who sneaks into a secure building by exploiting a hidden entrance.

Cross-site scripting (XSS) attacks are like forgeries in the digital world. These attacks inject malicious scripts into websites, which then run on users' browsers. Imagine a crafty forger creating counterfeit documents that appear legitimate but hide malicious intent.

Now, let's discuss drive-by downloads, which are like drive-by shootings in the digital realm. These attacks involve malware being downloaded onto a user's device without their consent or knowledge. It's as if a drive-by attacker fired a digital bullet that infected your device as you innocently browsed the web.

Botnets are like digital armies under the command of a cybercriminal mastermind. Imagine an army of infected devices, from computers to smart refrigerators, all controlled remotely by a single entity. Botnets are networks of compromised devices used for various malicious purposes, such as launching DDoS attacks or sending spam.

Finally, let's touch on identity theft, the digital equivalent of impersonation. Think of it as someone wearing a mask and pretending to be you. Identity theft occurs when cybercriminals steal your personal information, such as Social Security numbers or financial details, to commit fraud or gain unauthorized access to accounts.

In summary, the digital landscape is rife with a myriad of cyber threats, from viruses and malware to phishing attacks and ransomware. These threats are like digital adversaries constantly probing for weaknesses in our defenses. By staying informed, practicing good cybersecurity hygiene, and employing security measures, we can fortify our digital defenses and protect our valuable data and online identities. So, let's continue to navigate the digital world with caution and resilience, just as we do in the physical world, ensuring that our digital homes remain safe and secure.

Let's dive deeper into the world of cybersecurity by exploring attack vectors and methods, the tactics employed by cybercriminals to breach our digital defenses and gain unauthorized access to sensitive information. Think of these attackers as digital adversaries, constantly searching for vulnerabilities in the digital landscape, just as a skilled locksmith might seek weaknesses in a physical lock.

One common attack vector is the exploitation of software vulnerabilities. Imagine your computer's software as a castle wall with hidden cracks. Cybercriminals search for these cracks and exploit them to gain entry. Vulnerabilities can exist in operating systems, applications, or plugins, and cybercriminals exploit them through techniques like buffer overflows or remote code execution.

Another attack vector involves phishing, a deceptive tactic where cybercriminals impersonate legitimate entities to trick individuals into revealing sensitive information. It's like receiving a letter that appears to be from your bank, but it's actually from a clever imposter. Phishing can occur through email, social engineering, or fake websites designed to steal login credentials or financial data.

Social engineering is a crafty attack method that preys on human psychology. Imagine a skilled manipulator who can convincingly impersonate someone you trust. Social engineers use tactics like pretexting (inventing a scenario to obtain information), baiting (enticing victims with an offer), or tailgating (gaining physical access by following an authorized person). These methods exploit human trust and curiosity. Credential stuffing is like using a stolen key to unlock multiple doors. Cybercriminals obtain username and password pairs from one data breach and try them on various online accounts, hoping that victims use the same credentials across multiple sites. It's a numbers game, and if a match is found, the attacker gains unauthorized access.
Man-in-the-middle (MitM) attacks are like eavesdropping on a private conversation. Cybercriminals secretly intercept and possibly alter communication between two parties, often without their knowledge. Think of it as a wiretap on your digital communication, with attackers sitting in the middle, capturing sensitive data or manipulating messages.

Brute-force attacks are a relentless method where attackers systematically try every possible combination of passwords until they find the correct one. Imagine a determined burglar trying every key in the world until one opens your door. Brute-force attacks can be time-consuming, but with powerful computing resources, attackers can crack weak passwords.

Denial of Service (DoS) and Distributed Denial of Service (DDoS) attacks are like digital traffic jams. Cybercriminals flood a target server or network with traffic, overwhelming it and causing disruptions or downtime. Imagine a highway clogged with cars, preventing legitimate users from reaching their destination. DDoS attacks involve multiple devices, making them even more potent.

SQL injection attacks manipulate a web application's SQL query to gain unauthorized access to its database. Think of it as someone sneaking through a hidden passage to access secure information. Attackers insert malicious SQL code into input fields, exploiting vulnerabilities to view, modify, or delete data. It's like a digital heist inside a website's database.

Cross-site scripting (XSS) attacks are like forging a document that appears legitimate but hides malicious intent. Cybercriminals inject malicious scripts into websites, which then run on users' browsers. It's like a crafty forger who manipulates a webpage's content, potentially stealing information or redirecting users to fraudulent sites.

Pharming attacks are deceptive tactics that redirect users from legitimate websites to fraudulent ones without their knowledge. Imagine driving down a familiar road, only to find that the signposts have been changed, leading you to a different destination. Pharming attacks manipulate DNS settings or use malware to reroute users to malicious websites, where their data may be stolen.

Zero-day exploits are like secret keys to locked doors that only a select few know about. These are software vulnerabilities unknown to the vendor and, therefore, unpatched. Cybercriminals exploit these vulnerabilities before the vendor can release a fix, making them especially potent weapons.

Advanced Persistent Threats (APTs) are like covert spies who infiltrate organizations with long-term goals. APTs are highly sophisticated and persistent, often sponsored by nation-states or well-funded groups. They employ a variety of attack vectors and methods, including targeted phishing, zero-day exploits, and advanced malware, to gain access to sensitive information.

Insider threats involve individuals within an organization misusing their access for malicious purposes. Think of it as having a spy within your ranks. Insider threats can be accidental, such as employees falling victim to phishing attacks, or intentional, with employees intentionally leaking sensitive information or compromising security.
Malvertising is like a Trojan horse in the digital world. Malvertisements appear as harmless online ads but contain malicious code. When users click on these ads, they may be redirected to fraudulent websites or unknowingly download malware onto their devices.

Drive-by downloads are like digital infections lurking in unexpected places. Cybercriminals infect legitimate websites with malicious code, and unsuspecting users may inadvertently download malware onto their devices when visiting these compromised sites.

Botnets are like digital armies under the command of a cybercriminal mastermind. Imagine an army of compromised devices, from computers to smart home appliances, all controlled remotely by a single entity. Botnets are used for various malicious purposes, such as launching DDoS attacks, sending spam, or mining cryptocurrencies.
Now that we've explored these attack vectors and methods, it's crucial to understand that cybersecurity is an ongoing

battle. Cybercriminals are continually evolving their tactics, seeking new vulnerabilities to exploit. As responsible digital citizens, we must stay vigilant, keep our software updated, and educate ourselves and our organizations about the latest threats and best practices. By doing so, we can build stronger defenses and protect our digital assets from the ever-present threats in the digital realm. So, let's continue our journey through the world of cybersecurity, armed with knowledge and resilience.

Chapter 8: Malware and Social Engineering Attacks

In our exploration of cybersecurity, one of the critical aspects to understand is the diverse world of malware, which stands as a digital adversary that can infiltrate, disrupt, and compromise our digital lives. Malware, short for malicious software, is like a hidden saboteur lurking in the shadows of the digital realm, waiting for an opportunity to strike.

At the heart of the malware world, we find viruses, a type of malware that behaves like a contagious disease. Just as viruses spread from person to person, computer viruses spread from one device to another. They attach themselves to legitimate files or programs, and when those files are executed, the virus spreads further. Much like the common cold, viruses can be widespread and can cause a range of issues, from minor annoyances to severe system damage.

Trojans, on the other hand, are deceptive in nature. They are like digital trojan horses, masquerading as benign software or files while concealing a hidden malicious payload. When users unknowingly download or execute these trojans, the hidden payload is unleashed, compromising the security of the device. Trojans often serve as a gateway for other malware to enter a system.

Ransomware, a particularly menacing type of malware, operates like a digital extortionist. Imagine your files and documents being held hostage, with a cybercriminal demanding a ransom for their release. Ransomware encrypts your data, rendering it inaccessible until you pay the demanded ransom. It's like a digital kidnapping, with your valuable information as the hostage.

Spyware is akin to digital surveillance, silently observing your online activities without your knowledge or consent. Just as a hidden camera spies on someone's actions, spyware monitors your keystrokes, captures screenshots, and tracks your online behavior. Cybercriminals can use this stolen information for various nefarious purposes, including identity theft and espionage.

Adware, although less harmful, is like a persistent salesperson who constantly bombards you with advertisements. Adware displays unwanted and often intrusive ads on your device. While it may not steal your data or damage your system, adware can be extremely annoying and disruptive to your online experience.

Worms are like digital pests that rapidly spread through networks and devices, replicating themselves without the need for user interaction. Much like the common cold virus spreading from person to person, worms can infect countless devices in a short amount of time. They often exploit vulnerabilities in network protocols to propagate.

Rootkits are stealthy and invasive, much like a burglar who has gained access to your home but remains hidden. These malware types are designed to provide unauthorized and often deep-level access to a device or network, making them challenging to detect and remove. Rootkits can be used to plant backdoors, allowing cybercriminals to maintain control over compromised systems.

Keyloggers are akin to a digital scribe, meticulously recording every keystroke you make. These malware types capture your keyboard input, including usernames, passwords, and sensitive information. Cybercriminals use keyloggers to steal valuable data for various malicious purposes.

Botnets are like a digital army under the control of a cybercriminal mastermind. Imagine a legion of compromised devices, from computers to smart home appliances, all working together toward a common goal. Botnets can be used to launch large-scale attacks, such as Distributed Denial of Service (DDoS) attacks or send spam emails, making them powerful tools in the hands of cybercriminals.

Fileless malware is a cunning type of malware that leaves little to no trace on the victim's device. Unlike traditional malware that relies on files or executables, fileless malware operates in memory, making it difficult to detect and remove. It's like a digital ghost that leaves no physical evidence behind.

Macro viruses target document files, such as those in Microsoft Office, by exploiting macros, which are small programs embedded within these files. When a user opens an infected document and enables macros, the virus is activated. Much like a magician's sleight of hand, macro viruses trick users into unknowingly executing malicious code.

Polymorphic malware is like a shape-shifting creature that constantly changes its appearance to evade detection. This type of malware alters its code each time it infects a new system, making it difficult for traditional antivirus software to recognize and block. It's like a chameleon blending into its surroundings, making it challenging to spot.

File infector viruses attach themselves to executable files, such as program files or applications. When an infected file is executed, the virus spreads to other executable files on the system. It's like a digital vampire, infecting healthy files and turning them into carriers of the virus.

Multipartite malware is a hybrid that combines the characteristics of multiple malware types, making it versatile and challenging to combat. It can infect both files and system areas, using various tactics to compromise a device. Think of it as a multifaceted adversary that adapts to different situations.

Finally, we have mobile malware, specifically designed to target smartphones and tablets. Mobile malware can take various forms, including Trojans, spyware, and adware, and it often disguises itself as legitimate apps. Just as your smartphone is a pocket-sized computer, it can also be vulnerable to digital threats.

Understanding these various malware types is crucial in the ongoing battle against cyber threats. Cybercriminals continually evolve their tactics, creating new strains of malware to exploit vulnerabilities. By staying informed, employing robust security measures, and practicing good cybersecurity hygiene, individuals and organizations can better defend against these digital adversaries. So, let's continue to navigate the ever-changing landscape of cybersecurity, arming ourselves with knowledge and vigilance to protect our digital assets and privacy.

Let's delve into the intriguing world of social engineering, a realm where human psychology meets the art of manipulation, and where cybercriminals use cunning tactics to deceive and exploit individuals and organizations. Imagine social engineering as a digital sleight of hand, where the magician is the cybercriminal, and the audience is you, the potential victim.

One of the most common social engineering techniques is phishing, where cybercriminals send deceptive emails or messages to trick recipients into divulging sensitive information, such as usernames, passwords, or financial details. Picture receiving an email that appears to be from your bank, urgently requesting you to verify your account information by clicking a link. This is a classic phishing attempt, designed to lead you to a fraudulent website that mimics your bank's login page.

Pretexting is another clever tactic, where cybercriminals invent a fabricated scenario to obtain information or gain trust. Think of it as a skilled storyteller crafting a compelling narrative to manipulate your actions. For example, a pretexting scammer might pose as a tech support agent, calling you to resolve a fictitious issue with your computer. By convincing you of their legitimacy, they can coax sensitive information from you.

Baiting is like setting a digital trap. Cybercriminals offer something enticing, such as free software or a tempting download, to lure victims into unknowingly downloading malware onto their devices. Imagine finding a USB drive labeled "Employee Salary Info" lying around your workplace. Curiosity gets the best of you, and you plug it into your computer, unknowingly activating malicious software.

Tailgating is a physical form of social engineering, where an attacker gains unauthorized access to a secure area by following an authorized person. Picture someone holding the door open for you as you enter a restricted office space. You assume they belong there, but in reality, they're exploiting your goodwill to bypass security measures.

Quid pro quo is like a digital exchange where cybercriminals offer something in return for information or access. Imagine receiving a call from a supposed IT technician who promises to fix a computer issue remotely in exchange for your login credentials. In this scenario, you unknowingly trade security for a quick solution.

Impersonation is a tactic where cybercriminals pose as someone you trust or respect. Think of it as a digital masquerade, where the attacker adopts the identity of a colleague, supervisor, or authority figure to manipulate your actions. For instance, an impersonator might pose as your company's CEO, requesting you to urgently transfer funds to a specified account.

Fear and intimidation are powerful tools in the social engineer's arsenal. Cybercriminals may use threats, urgency, or fear to coerce victims into complying with their demands. Imagine receiving a call from someone claiming to be from a government agency, threatening legal action unless you provide personal information or payment immediately. Fearful of the consequences, you might comply without questioning their authenticity.

Influence and persuasion are at the core of social engineering. Think of it as a digital charm offensive, where attackers use flattery, sympathy, or emotional manipulation to gain trust and cooperation. An attacker might contact you, feigning admiration for your work, and then subtly steer the conversation toward extracting sensitive information.

Scarcity is a psychological trigger used in social engineering. Cybercriminals create a sense of urgency or scarcity to manipulate victims into taking hasty actions. Imagine receiving an email claiming you've won a once-in-a-lifetime prize, but you must act quickly to claim it. The fear of missing out may lead you to provide personal information or click on a dubious link.

Authority is another persuasive element in social engineering. Attackers may impersonate figures of authority, such as law enforcement officers or company executives, to gain trust and obedience. Imagine receiving a phone call from someone claiming to be a police officer, demanding immediate payment to resolve a fictitious legal matter. The authority figure's presence can be intimidating and convincing.

Tailoring and personalization make social engineering attacks more convincing. Cybercriminals gather information about their targets, creating tailored messages that appear highly relevant and credible. Imagine receiving an email with your name, job title, and references to recent personal events, all designed to lure you into trusting the sender.

Reverse social engineering is a clever tactic where the victim is convinced to initiate contact with the attacker. Think of it as the cybercriminal playing the role of a helpless victim, making you believe you're providing assistance. For example, you might receive an email from someone claiming to be locked out of their account and requesting your help, but in reality, they're manipulating you into taking action that benefits them.

In essence, social engineering is a psychological game where the cybercriminal seeks to exploit human traits such as trust, curiosity, fear, and empathy. By understanding these techniques and remaining vigilant, individuals and organizations can better protect themselves against the subtle manipulations of social engineers. It's a digital cat-and-mouse game, but with awareness and caution, you can avoid falling into their traps and maintain your digital security. So, let's continue to navigate the digital landscape with a healthy dose of skepticism and a keen eye for the subtle art of social engineering.

Chapter 9: Network Security Best Practices

Let's delve into the realm of security policies and procedures, a vital aspect of safeguarding digital assets and maintaining a secure digital environment. Think of security policies as the rules and guidelines that govern how an organization protects its information and technology infrastructure, much like the rules you set to protect your home or belongings.

Security policies serve as a foundation, establishing the overarching principles that guide an organization's approach to cybersecurity. These policies set the tone for the entire security framework, much like a constitution sets the principles for a nation. They articulate the organization's commitment to security, outlining its goals, objectives, and values in safeguarding information and assets.

Access control policies are like the keys to different rooms in your home. These policies dictate who has access to what information or resources within an organization. They define user roles and permissions, ensuring that individuals can access only the information and systems necessary for their roles. Much like you wouldn't give your house keys to a stranger, access control policies restrict unauthorized access.

Password policies are like the locks on your doors, providing a crucial layer of protection. These policies dictate the rules for creating and managing passwords within an organization. They specify password complexity requirements, expiration periods, and measures to prevent password sharing. Just as you wouldn't leave your doors unlocked, password policies prevent unauthorized access to digital assets.

Encryption policies are like secret codes used to protect sensitive information. These policies mandate the use of encryption techniques to safeguard data during transmission and storage. Encryption scrambles data into unreadable form without the correct decryption key. Think of it as sending a message in a sealed envelope that only the intended recipient can open.

Incident response policies are like emergency procedures for unexpected situations. These policies define how an organization should respond to security incidents, such as data breaches or cyberattacks. They outline the steps to identify, contain, mitigate, and recover from security incidents, ensuring a coordinated and effective response. Much like having a fire escape plan for your home, incident response policies help an organization react swiftly to threats.

Bring Your Own Device (BYOD) policies are like welcoming guests into your home while setting some ground rules. These policies govern the use of personal devices (e.g., smartphones, tablets, or laptops) for work purposes. They establish security measures, such as device encryption and mobile device management, to protect organizational data while allowing employees to use their devices for work-related tasks.

Remote access policies are like allowing trusted individuals to enter your home when you're not there. These policies govern how remote users connect to an organization's network and systems. They define security requirements, such as the use of virtual private networks (VPNs) and multifactor authentication, to ensure secure remote access. Just as you'd want to control who enters your home in your absence, remote access policies control who accesses the organization's systems from remote locations.

Data retention and disposal policies are like cleaning out clutter from your home. These policies outline how long data should be retained and when it should be securely disposed of. They help prevent the accumulation of unnecessary data and ensure that sensitive information is properly disposed of to minimize security risks.

Physical security policies are like the locks, alarms, and security cameras in your home. These policies address the physical protection of an organization's premises, data centers, and equipment. They specify measures like access control systems, surveillance, and visitor management to safeguard physical assets. Just as you'd secure your home with physical barriers, physical security policies protect an organization's physical assets.

Training and awareness policies are like teaching your family members about safety at home. These policies emphasize the importance of educating employees about security best practices. They include cybersecurity training, awareness campaigns, and guidelines for reporting security incidents. Similar to teaching your loved ones about home safety, training and awareness policies empower employees to recognize and respond to security threats.

Vendor and third-party policies are like vetting contractors before allowing them to work on your home. These policies define security requirements for vendors and third-party partners that have access to an organization's systems or data. They ensure that external entities adhere to the same security standards and protocols as the organization itself.

Acceptable use policies are like house rules for the digital world. These policies establish guidelines for how employees should use organizational resources, including computers, email, internet access, and software. They define what is considered acceptable behavior and what activities are prohibited to maintain a secure and productive digital environment.

Privacy policies are like respecting the boundaries of your personal space. These policies address the collection, use, and protection of personal information within an organization. They ensure compliance with privacy laws and regulations and establish transparency regarding how personal data is handled.

Security policies and procedures are the backbone of a robust cybersecurity framework, much like a well-constructed foundation supports a sturdy building. They provide the structure, rules, and guidance necessary to protect digital assets, mitigate risks, and respond effectively to security incidents.

By implementing and adhering to these policies, organizations can create a secure environment that safeguards sensitive information, maintains the trust of stakeholders, and ensures compliance with legal and regulatory requirements. Much like you would feel safer and more secure in a well-protected home, employees, customers, and partners can feel confident in an organization's commitment to cybersecurity when it has strong security policies and procedures in place.

So, let's continue to explore the world of cybersecurity, understanding that security policies and procedures are the building blocks of a resilient and secure digital landscape, ensuring that our digital homes remain safe from intruders and threats.

Let's embark on a journey through the world of continuous monitoring and improvement in the realm of cybersecurity, where the goal is not just to build strong defenses but to evolve and adapt them over time, much like tending to a garden to ensure it thrives and flourishes.

Continuous monitoring is like having vigilant guardians stationed around your digital fortress, constantly watching for signs of intrusion or vulnerabilities. It involves the systematic and ongoing surveillance of an organization's network, systems, and data to identify and respond to security threats in real-time.

Think of it as a watchful sentry who monitors the castle walls for any breaches. Continuous monitoring encompasses a range of activities, including real-time threat detection, vulnerability assessments, and incident response. It's a proactive approach that allows organizations to stay ahead of cyber threats, much like being alert to potential dangers in your surroundings.

One essential component of continuous monitoring is threat detection. Imagine having a digital security system with motion sensors that alert you the moment someone enters your property. In the digital world, threat detection tools and systems continuously analyze network traffic, logs, and data for suspicious activities or anomalies that may indicate a cyberattack.

Much like the keen senses of a guard dog that can detect intruders, these systems use advanced algorithms and machine learning to identify patterns that suggest malicious behavior. When a potential threat is detected, security teams can respond swiftly to investigate and mitigate the risk, preventing or minimizing damage.

Vulnerability assessments are like regularly inspecting the walls of your castle for weak points. Organizations conduct these assessments to identify vulnerabilities, weaknesses, or gaps in their security posture. Vulnerabilities can be software flaws, misconfigurations, or outdated systems that cybercriminals may exploit.

Regular scanning and testing of systems and applications help organizations discover and address vulnerabilities before cybercriminals can take advantage of them. It's akin to fortifying your defenses by reinforcing weak points in your digital fortress to make it less susceptible to attacks.

Incident response is like having a well-drilled team of knights ready to defend the kingdom at a moment's notice. When a security incident occurs, whether it's a data breach, malware infection, or unauthorized access, incident response procedures kick into action. These procedures include a coordinated effort to contain the incident, investigate its scope, and remediate the damage.

Much like responding swiftly to extinguish a fire before it spreads, incident response aims to minimize the impact of a security incident and prevent further harm. It's about learning from the incident to improve security measures and prevent similar attacks in the future.

Continuous improvement is the cornerstone of an effective cybersecurity strategy. Imagine refining your castle's defenses over time, incorporating the latest technologies and strategies to stay one step ahead of potential threats. Continuous improvement involves regularly assessing the effectiveness of security measures and making adjustments based on lessons learned.

For instance, organizations may conduct post-incident reviews to evaluate how well their incident response procedures worked and identify areas for improvement. It's like analyzing the results of a battle to develop better tactics for future conflicts. Continuous improvement ensures that security measures evolve to address emerging threats and changing technology landscapes.

Patch management is an essential aspect of continuous improvement. Just as you'd repair a damaged wall promptly, organizations must apply software patches and updates to address known vulnerabilities. Cybercriminals often target unpatched systems, so keeping software up-to-date is crucial in maintaining a secure digital environment.

Regular training and awareness programs are like honing the skills of your knights through practice and training exercises.

Educating employees about cybersecurity best practices is essential in preventing human errors and social engineering attacks. When employees are aware of potential threats and know how to respond, they become valuable allies in the defense of an organization's digital assets.

Security audits and assessments are akin to having independent inspectors evaluate the integrity of your castle's defenses. Organizations may engage third-party auditors to assess their security posture, ensuring compliance with industry standards and regulations. These audits provide valuable insights and recommendations for enhancing security measures.

Security policies and procedures undergo continuous refinement and adaptation. As new threats emerge and technology evolves, organizations must update their security policies to address these challenges. Think of it as revising the castle's defense strategy to incorporate the latest advancements in warfare.

Regularly reviewing access controls and permissions is like reevaluating who has access to the most critical areas of your fortress. Organizations should conduct periodic reviews to ensure that only authorized individuals have access to sensitive information and systems. This minimizes the risk of insider threats and unauthorized access.

Threat intelligence is like having scouts who provide real-time information about potential threats in the vicinity. Organizations can subscribe to threat intelligence services that offer insights into emerging threats, attack trends, and the tactics used by cybercriminals. This intelligence helps organizations stay one step ahead of cyber threats.

Security awareness campaigns are like rallying the citizens of your kingdom to be vigilant and report any suspicious activities. Encouraging a culture of cybersecurity awareness among employees fosters a collective effort to identify and report security incidents promptly.

Regular tabletop exercises and simulations are like conducting drills to ensure that everyone knows their role in responding to a security incident. These exercises allow organizations to test their incident response plans and identify areas for improvement.

Vendor risk management is akin to evaluating the trustworthiness of allies who provide goods and services to your kingdom. Organizations must assess the security practices of third-party vendors and partners to ensure that they do not introduce vulnerabilities into the organization's ecosystem.

In essence, continuous monitoring and improvement form the backbone of a resilient cybersecurity strategy. It's an ongoing process of vigilance, adaptation, and learning from past experiences. By embracing these practices, organizations can enhance their ability to detect, respond to, and mitigate security threats, much like a well-fortified castle that evolves with the changing tides of warfare.

So, let's continue our journey through the world of cybersecurity, understanding that continuous monitoring and improvement are not just strategies but a way of life in the digital age. With each adjustment and enhancement, we fortify our digital fortresses and stand prepared to defend against the ever-evolving threats that lurk in the digital realm.

Chapter 10: Hands-On Labs: Building a Secure Home Network

Let's embark on the journey of setting up a secure Wi-Fi network, a digital lifeline that connects us to the vast world of information and communication, much like a bridge to the digital realm right from the comfort of our homes.

Begin by choosing a strong and unique Wi-Fi network name, also known as the SSID, that distinguishes your network from others in the vicinity. Think of it as giving your network a distinctive nameplate, making it easily recognizable to your devices and guests.

Now, let's set a robust password for your Wi-Fi network. Think of this password as the key to your digital fortress. It should be long, complex, and include a combination of uppercase and lowercase letters, numbers, and special characters. Avoid using easily guessable information like your name or address.

Enabling WPA3 encryption is like locking your front door with a state-of-the-art security system. WPA3 is the latest and most secure encryption protocol for Wi-Fi networks. It provides robust protection against unauthorized access and eavesdropping. Ensure that your router supports WPA3 and enable it for your network.

Next, consider changing the default login credentials for your router's administrative interface. Just as you wouldn't keep the default key to your castle, it's crucial to change the default username and password to prevent unauthorized access to your router's settings.

Firmware updates are like fortifying your castle walls. Manufacturers release updates to address security vulnerabilities and improve the performance of your router.

Regularly check for firmware updates and apply them to keep your router's defenses up to date.

Now, let's talk about network segmentation, which is like dividing your castle into different sections with distinct access controls. Create separate network segments for devices with varying security needs. For example, you can have one network for your IoT devices, another for guests, and a highly secured network for sensitive data and devices.

Implement MAC address filtering as an additional layer of access control. Think of it as having a guest list for your castle. MAC address filtering allows you to specify which devices are allowed to connect to your network based on their unique MAC addresses. It's an extra step to ensure that only authorized devices gain access.

Consider enabling a guest network for visitors. Just as you'd welcome guests into a separate area of your castle, a guest network isolates guest devices from your primary network, providing them with internet access while keeping your main network secure.

Regularly review and update your Wi-Fi network settings. Think of it as conducting routine maintenance on your castle's defenses. Periodically review your network's security settings, passwords, and access controls to ensure they remain robust and up to date.

Disable remote management of your router if it's not needed. Remote management is like allowing someone to control your castle from afar. Disabling this feature reduces the risk of unauthorized access to your router's settings.

Consider setting up a virtual private network (VPN) for added security, especially when accessing your network remotely. A VPN creates a secure, encrypted tunnel between your device and your home network, protecting your data from eavesdropping while on public Wi-Fi or other untrusted networks.

Regularly monitor your network for unusual activity. Think of it as having guards patrol the castle walls to spot any intruders. Many routers provide logging and alerting features that can help you detect and respond to suspicious activity.

Enable network-level antivirus and malware scanning if your router supports it. This feature acts as a digital gatekeeper, scanning incoming and outgoing data for malicious content and preventing it from entering your network.

Consider using a reputable security solution that offers protection at the network level. These solutions can provide an additional layer of security by identifying and blocking threats before they reach your devices.

Lastly, educate yourself and your family about safe online practices. Just as you'd teach your loved ones about staying safe in your castle, it's essential to teach them about the dangers of phishing, malware, and social engineering attacks.

In summary, setting up a secure Wi-Fi network is like fortifying the defenses of your digital castle. It involves choosing strong passwords, enabling robust encryption, updating firmware, segmenting your network, and staying vigilant for potential threats.

By following these steps and best practices, you can create a secure Wi-Fi network that protects your digital assets and ensures a safe and reliable online experience for you and your family. Much like safeguarding your physical home, securing your Wi-Fi network is an essential step in today's digital age, where connectivity and security go hand in hand. So, let's continue to explore the digital landscape with confidence, knowing that our digital fortresses are well-guarded and fortified.

Let's dive into the world of firewall configuration and monitoring, a crucial aspect of cybersecurity that acts as a digital gatekeeper, shielding your network from potential threats and unauthorized access, much like a vigilant guardian at the entrance of your digital fortress.

Firewalls are like the sentinels of your digital realm, standing between your network and the vast, sometimes treacherous landscape of the internet. They serve as a protective barrier, allowing safe and authorized traffic to pass while blocking or scrutinizing suspicious or harmful data packets.

Firewall rules are like the instructions given to the sentinels at the gate. These rules define what is allowed and what is denied in terms of network traffic. For example, you can create rules that permit web traffic on port 80 while blocking traffic on port 22 used for SSH, a secure shell protocol. This fine-tuning of rules ensures that your firewall only permits legitimate traffic.

Intrusion detection and prevention systems (IDS/IPS) work alongside firewalls, acting as digital watchmen who patrol the perimeter for any signs of unusual or suspicious activity. These systems can detect and block malicious traffic, helping to fortify your network's defenses.

Setting up a firewall often involves creating access control lists (ACLs), which are like the guest list to an exclusive event. ACLs specify which IP addresses, ports, or protocols are allowed or denied access to your network. By carefully configuring ACLs, you can control who can enter your digital realm.

Application-layer filtering is akin to inspecting the contents of packages before allowing them inside. Some firewalls offer deep packet inspection at the application layer, allowing them to analyze the data payload of network packets. This enables the firewall to identify and block specific applications or content, such as instant messaging or social media, based on predefined policies.

Firewall policies are like the code of conduct within your digital kingdom. These policies define the security rules and expectations for your network. For instance, you may establish a policy that blocks all incoming traffic from certain countries to reduce exposure to known sources of cyber threats.

Stateful inspection, a core feature of modern firewalls, is like remembering who is allowed inside your castle. This technique keeps track of the state of active connections and ensures that incoming traffic is part of a legitimate, established session. If it doesn't match an existing session, the firewall scrutinizes it closely.

Port forwarding is like creating a special pathway to a hidden chamber within your castle. This feature allows you to redirect incoming traffic from a specific port to a designated internal device or service. For example, you can set up port forwarding to direct incoming web traffic to a web server within your network.

Network Address Translation (NAT) is like assigning aliases to your castle's residents. NAT allows multiple devices on your internal network to share a single public IP address. It disguises the internal IP addresses, enhancing security and conserving public IP addresses.

Logging and monitoring are like keeping a detailed journal of all the activities within your castle. Firewalls provide logs that record traffic events, rule violations, and other activities. Monitoring these logs allows you to detect and investigate potential security incidents.

Regularly updating your firewall is like fortifying your castle walls with stronger materials. Firewall manufacturers release updates to address vulnerabilities and improve security. It's essential to keep your firewall's firmware and rule sets up to date to ensure optimal protection.

Firewall testing is like conducting security drills to ensure your digital fortress is well-prepared for potential attacks. Organizations often perform penetration tests to assess the effectiveness of their firewall and identify vulnerabilities that need addressing.

User authentication is like requiring identification at the castle gates. Implementing user authentication for remote access to your network ensures that only authorized individuals can enter. This can involve using multifactor authentication (MFA) for an extra layer of security.

Firewall redundancy is like having multiple gateways to your digital kingdom. High-availability setups involve deploying multiple firewalls to ensure uninterrupted protection in case one fails. Redundancy ensures that your network remains secure even during hardware or software failures.

Firewall performance optimization is like enhancing your sentinels' agility and alertness. To ensure that your firewall can handle the traffic demands of your network, it's crucial to optimize its performance by adjusting settings, hardware, or configurations as needed.

Firewall rules review is like periodically inspecting your guards' gear to ensure it's in good condition. Regularly reviewing and updating firewall rules helps maintain an effective security posture and adapt to changing threats.

Advanced threat intelligence integration is like giving your sentinels access to a network of informants. Some firewalls can integrate threat intelligence feeds to stay updated on emerging threats and automatically block malicious IPs or domains.

Application of security policies is like enforcing laws within your digital realm. Firewall policies should align with your organization's security objectives and legal requirements, ensuring that your network operates within established guidelines.

Firewall management platforms are like having a command center to oversee your sentinels. These platforms provide a centralized interface to configure, monitor, and manage multiple firewalls, streamlining administrative tasks.

Regular security audits and assessments are like inviting experienced knights to evaluate your castle's defenses. Organizations often engage third-party security experts to assess their firewall configurations, ensuring compliance with best practices and industry standards.

Security awareness and training for your network users are like educating the citizens of your digital kingdom. Teaching employees about security best practices, including recognizing and reporting suspicious activities, enhances overall cybersecurity.

In summary, firewall configuration and monitoring are essential pillars of your digital defense strategy. Firewalls act as vigilant sentinels, enforcing security policies, and protecting your network from potential threats and unauthorized access. By configuring your firewall thoughtfully, monitoring it diligently, and staying up to date with the latest security practices, you can maintain a strong defense for your digital realm.

So, let's continue our journey through the intricate world of cybersecurity, knowing that our firewall is a trustworthy guardian, diligently protecting our digital assets and ensuring a secure and resilient network.

BOOK 2
UNDERSTANDING NETWORK ATTACKS
INTERMEDIATE TECHNIQUES AND COUNTERMEASURES

ROB BOTWRIGHT

Chapter 1: Types and Anatomy of Network Attacks

Let's explore the realm of cybersecurity and delve into the common categories of network attacks, those digital adversaries that lurk in the shadows of the internet, waiting for an opportunity to breach our digital defenses and compromise our valuable data and resources.

First, there are the Denial-of-Service (DoS) attacks, which are like a traffic jam on the digital highway. In a DoS attack, cybercriminals flood a network, server, or website with an overwhelming volume of traffic, rendering it inaccessible to legitimate users. Think of it as a protest blocking the entrance to a castle, preventing anyone from entering.

A variation of DoS attacks is Distributed Denial-of-Service (DDoS) attacks, where an army of compromised devices, often called a botnet, simultaneously bombard a target. It's like an entire village staging a protest at the castle gates, overwhelming the defenses.

Network intrusion attacks are like covert spies infiltrating your castle. In these attacks, cybercriminals gain unauthorized access to a network, system, or application, often by exploiting vulnerabilities or using stolen credentials. Once inside, they can steal sensitive information, disrupt operations, or even establish a persistent presence.

Malware attacks are akin to a hidden plague sweeping through your digital realm. Malware, short for malicious software, includes viruses, Trojans, worms, and ransomware. These programs infiltrate systems, infect files, and execute malicious actions. Think of them as digital diseases that can corrupt, steal, or encrypt your data.

Phishing attacks are like crafty con artists trying to trick you into revealing your castle's secrets. Phishing emails or messages impersonate legitimate entities, such as banks or trusted organizations, to deceive recipients into providing sensitive information like passwords or credit card details. It's essential to be vigilant and verify the authenticity of such communications.

Man-in-the-Middle (MitM) attacks are like eavesdroppers intercepting your private conversations. In MitM attacks, cybercriminals position themselves between two parties, often without their knowledge, to intercept and manipulate communications. They can eavesdrop on sensitive information or even alter the content of messages.

SQL injection attacks are like cunning spies exploiting weak points in your castle's defenses. In these attacks, cybercriminals inject malicious SQL (Structured Query Language) code into input fields of web applications, exploiting vulnerabilities to gain unauthorized access to databases. They can access, modify, or steal sensitive data.

Cross-Site Scripting (XSS) attacks are like secret messages hidden within your castle's walls. Cybercriminals inject malicious scripts into web pages viewed by other users, often tricking them into executing harmful actions. These attacks can steal data or hijack user sessions.

Password attacks are like thieves attempting to pick the lock to your castle. These attacks involve trying to guess or crack passwords to gain unauthorized access to accounts or systems. Brute force attacks, dictionary attacks, and credential stuffing are common techniques used by cybercriminals.

Packet sniffing attacks are like spies intercepting your mail. Cybercriminals use network monitoring tools to capture and analyze network traffic, potentially revealing sensitive information, including login credentials and unencrypted data.

Zero-Day exploits are like vulnerabilities that only a few know about but haven't been patched yet. Cybercriminals target software vulnerabilities that are unknown to the software vendor, giving them an advantage until the vulnerability is discovered and patched.

Social engineering attacks are like manipulation tactics used to gain the trust of your castle's residents. These attacks rely on psychological manipulation to trick individuals into divulging confidential information or performing actions that compromise security. Techniques include pretexting, baiting, and tailgating.

Insider threats are like trusted castle residents who turn against you. These threats come from individuals within an organization who misuse their access to data, systems, or resources. Insider threats can be intentional or accidental, making them a challenging category to manage.

Advanced Persistent Threats (APTs) are like highly skilled infiltrators who patiently study your castle for a long time. APTs are sophisticated and targeted attacks by well-funded and determined adversaries. They often employ multiple attack vectors and can persist undetected for extended periods, making them challenging to combat.

Botnet attacks are like armies of automated soldiers marching towards your castle. Cybercriminals use networks of compromised devices, called botnets, to carry out various malicious activities, such as DDoS attacks, sending spam, or stealing data.

Drive-by downloads are like hidden traps scattered along the paths leading to your castle. These attacks occur when users visit compromised or malicious websites that automatically download malware onto their devices without their consent or knowledge.

Ransomware attacks are like digital kidnappers holding your castle's assets hostage. Ransomware encrypts files or systems, rendering them inaccessible. Cybercriminals demand a ransom payment in exchange for the decryption key to unlock the data.

Brute force attacks are like persistent attackers trying every possible key to open your castle's locks. These attacks involve repeatedly attempting various combinations of passwords until the correct one is found. They can be time-consuming but, when successful, provide unauthorized access.

DNS spoofing attacks are like misdirecting travelers on their way to your castle. Cybercriminals manipulate DNS (Domain Name System) servers to redirect users to malicious websites, often used in phishing or malware distribution.

Eavesdropping attacks are like spies secretly listening to your conversations within your castle. In these attacks, cybercriminals intercept and monitor network communications to gather sensitive information or gain unauthorized access to confidential data.

Now that we've explored these common categories of network attacks, it's essential to remember that cybersecurity is an ongoing battle. Staying informed about emerging threats, implementing robust security measures, and fostering a culture of cybersecurity awareness are vital steps in protecting your digital realm.

So, let's continue our journey through the ever-evolving landscape of cybersecurity, remaining vigilant and prepared to defend our digital fortresses against these cunning adversaries. By understanding these attack categories and taking proactive steps to safeguard our networks and data, we can navigate the digital world with confidence and resilience.

Let's embark on a journey through the intricate landscape of network attacks, exploring the anatomy of these digital threats that lurk in the shadows, seeking vulnerabilities in our digital fortresses and aiming to breach our defenses, much like cunning adversaries in a strategic game.

At the heart of a network attack lies the attacker's motive, a driving force that compels them to target a specific network or system. Motives can range from financial gain to ideological beliefs or even personal vendettas, shaping the attacker's objectives and tactics.

The attacker's arsenal includes an array of tools and techniques, much like a crafty thief with a toolkit. These tools can include malware, exploit kits, social engineering tactics, and even advanced persistent threats (APTs), each designed to achieve specific goals.

The reconnaissance phase is akin to the attacker scouting the perimeter of a castle, looking for weaknesses. During reconnaissance, attackers gather information about the target network, such as its structure, vulnerabilities, and potential entry points. This phase can involve scanning for open ports, identifying services running on them, and probing for vulnerabilities.

Exploitation is like the moment the attacker finds a crack in the castle's walls and exploits it. This phase involves taking advantage of vulnerabilities discovered during reconnaissance. Attackers may use known exploits, zero-day vulnerabilities, or social engineering tactics to gain unauthorized access to the network or system.

The delivery of malware is like planting a hidden trap within the castle. Attackers use various methods, such as email attachments, malicious websites, or infected software updates, to deliver malware to target devices. Once the malware is executed, it can carry out its malicious actions, such as data theft or system disruption.

Privilege escalation is like the attacker climbing higher within the castle, gaining access to more critical areas. In this phase, attackers attempt to elevate their privileges within the compromised system or network, often by exploiting additional vulnerabilities or weaknesses. Privilege escalation enables them to perform more destructive actions.

Maintaining persistence is like the attacker leaving a hidden backdoor in the castle. Attackers aim to ensure ongoing access to the compromised network or system, even after being discovered or removed. They may install rootkits, create new user accounts, or employ other techniques to maintain their presence.

Exfiltration is like the attacker smuggling out treasures from the castle. In this phase, cybercriminals steal valuable data or resources from the compromised network. This stolen information can include sensitive documents, financial records, or intellectual property.

The command and control (C2) phase is like the attacker's hidden communication channel within the castle. Attackers establish a means of controlling compromised devices remotely, enabling them to issue commands, update malware, or exfiltrate data without direct access to the target network.

Covering tracks is like the attacker erasing their footprints within the castle. To avoid detection, cybercriminals attempt to remove traces of their activities, such as logs, event records, or malware artifacts. This makes it more challenging for defenders to trace their actions.

The aftermath of a successful network attack often includes data breaches, service disruptions, financial losses, and reputational damage. Organizations must respond swiftly, much like a castle owner fortifying their defenses after an intrusion, to contain the incident, mitigate damage, and prevent future attacks.

Network attacks can vary in complexity and sophistication, from opportunistic attacks targeting poorly protected systems to highly orchestrated APTs aimed at specific high-value targets. It's essential to understand that no network is entirely immune to attacks, and cybersecurity requires constant vigilance and adaptation.

Defenders employ various security measures, including firewalls, intrusion detection systems, and security patches, to protect their networks. They also invest in cybersecurity awareness training for employees and establish incident response plans to mitigate the impact of potential attacks.

In this ever-evolving digital landscape, understanding the anatomy of network attacks is essential for individuals and organizations alike. By recognizing the motives, tools, and phases involved in these attacks, we can better prepare ourselves to defend against them.

Ultimately, cybersecurity is a continuous effort, much like the ongoing maintenance of a castle's defenses. As technology advances, attackers become more sophisticated, and the digital landscape evolves, defenders must adapt, learn, and stay one step ahead of those who seek to breach our digital fortresses.

So, let's continue our journey through the world of cybersecurity, equipped with knowledge and awareness, as we navigate the complex terrain of network attacks, safeguarding our digital realms and ensuring a secure and resilient digital future.

Chapter 2: Network Vulnerabilities and Exploitation Techniques

Let's delve into the intriguing world of identifying network vulnerabilities, a critical aspect of cybersecurity that involves uncovering weaknesses and potential entry points within your digital fortress, much like inspecting the walls and gates of a medieval castle for hidden cracks and vulnerabilities.

One primary method for identifying vulnerabilities is vulnerability scanning, which is similar to sending scouts to examine the castle walls. Vulnerability scanning tools systematically scan your network, devices, and applications for known vulnerabilities and misconfigurations. They compile a list of potential weaknesses that require further investigation.

Penetration testing, on the other hand, is like hiring skilled knights to launch controlled attacks on your castle. In penetration testing, ethical hackers, often referred to as "white hat" hackers, simulate real-world attacks to identify vulnerabilities from an attacker's perspective. They attempt to breach your network's defenses and report their findings for remediation.

Red teaming takes penetration testing a step further, akin to orchestrating a siege on your castle. Red teams are specialized groups that conduct comprehensive assessments of your network's security. They employ advanced tactics and techniques to identify vulnerabilities that may be challenging to detect using traditional methods.

Network logs and monitoring systems act as your castle's watchtowers, continuously scanning the surroundings for any signs of suspicious activity. Analyzing network logs can reveal anomalies, such as repeated login failures or unusual traffic patterns, which may indicate a potential breach or vulnerability.

Regularly applying security patches and updates is like maintaining the structural integrity of your castle. Software vendors release patches to address known vulnerabilities and improve security. Failure to apply these patches promptly can leave your network exposed to exploitation.

Asset management is like keeping an inventory of your castle's assets, knowing where each valuable item is located. In the digital realm, asset management involves identifying and cataloging all devices and software running on your network. This helps ensure that nothing goes unnoticed, reducing the risk of unpatched or forgotten systems becoming vulnerabilities.

Network segmentation is like dividing your castle into sections with distinct security levels. By segmenting your network, you isolate sensitive systems or data from less secure areas. This limits the potential impact of a breach, making it harder for attackers to move laterally within your network.

Regular security audits are like hiring inspectors to assess the castle's condition. Organizations often conduct security audits to evaluate their network's adherence to security policies and best practices. Audits can uncover vulnerabilities and weaknesses that need to be addressed.

Password policies are like setting strong locks on your castle doors. Implementing robust password policies, such as requiring complex passwords and enforcing regular password changes, enhances security by reducing the risk of unauthorized access due to weak or compromised passwords.

User training and awareness are like educating the castle's residents about security practices. Providing employees with cybersecurity training helps them recognize potential threats, such as phishing attempts or social engineering tactics. Educated users become a valuable layer of defense against network vulnerabilities.

Configuration management ensures that your digital castle's defenses are properly configured. It involves reviewing and fine-tuning settings for network devices, servers, and software to align with security best practices. Misconfigurations can introduce vulnerabilities, so it's crucial to maintain strict control over configurations.

Bastion hosts, similar to the heavily fortified towers of a castle, are highly secured systems that act as gateways to sensitive areas of your network. Implementing bastion hosts adds an extra layer of protection by controlling and monitoring access to critical resources.

Web application security testing is like inspecting the integrity of your castle's drawbridge. Web applications are common targets for attackers, so regularly testing their security can uncover vulnerabilities, such as injection flaws or cross-site scripting (XSS) vulnerabilities, which can be exploited.

Firewalls act as the guards stationed at your castle gates, monitoring and controlling incoming and outgoing traffic. Properly configured firewalls can filter out malicious traffic and block unauthorized access attempts, helping to prevent network vulnerabilities.

Patch management is like maintaining the castle's walls and structures. It involves keeping all software and systems up to date with the latest security patches and updates. Neglecting patch management can leave your network vulnerable to known exploits.

Zero-day vulnerability monitoring is like having scouts constantly on the lookout for hidden paths into your castle. Security teams and researchers actively monitor for zero-day vulnerabilities, which are unknown to vendors and have no available patches. Promptly addressing these vulnerabilities is crucial to prevent exploitation.

Security information and event management (SIEM) systems are like having a team of vigilant sentinels patrolling your castle grounds. SIEM systems collect and analyze logs from various network devices and applications, helping to detect and respond to security incidents in real time.

Threat intelligence feeds are like receiving reports about potential threats in the kingdom surrounding your castle. Threat intelligence provides valuable information about emerging threats, including new vulnerabilities and attack techniques. Integrating threat intelligence into your security strategy can help you stay one step ahead of attackers.

Regular vulnerability assessments are like conducting routine inspections of your castle's defenses. Organizations often perform vulnerability assessments to identify weaknesses and potential entry points within their network. These assessments provide a comprehensive view of your network's security posture.

Security policies and procedures are like the laws and rules governing your castle. Establishing clear and comprehensive security policies ensures that everyone within your organization understands their roles and responsibilities in maintaining network security.

Intrusion detection and prevention systems (IDS/IPS) are like having watchful sentries guarding your castle's gates. These systems monitor network traffic for suspicious activity and can automatically block or alert on potential threats, helping to protect against vulnerabilities.

Encryption, much like the secret codes and ciphers used in medieval times, ensures that sensitive data remains unreadable to unauthorized parties. Implementing encryption for data at rest and in transit adds an extra layer of protection against potential vulnerabilities.

Regular vulnerability management is like conducting regular maintenance on your castle's defenses. It involves continuously monitoring for new vulnerabilities, prioritizing their remediation based on their severity, and applying patches and updates promptly.

Risk assessments are like evaluating the potential threats and vulnerabilities that your castle faces. Conducting risk assessments helps organizations prioritize their security efforts and allocate resources effectively to address the most critical vulnerabilities.

Now that we've explored the multifaceted world of identifying network vulnerabilities, it's clear that cybersecurity is a dynamic and ongoing endeavor. Just as a vigilant castle owner must continuously inspect, maintain, and fortify their stronghold, organizations and individuals must remain proactive in their efforts to safeguard their digital assets.

By embracing best practices, employing the right tools and techniques, and fostering a culture of cybersecurity awareness, we can strengthen our digital fortresses, protecting them from potential vulnerabilities and ensuring a secure and resilient digital realm.

So, let's continue our journey through the realm of cybersecurity, equipped with the knowledge and tools needed to identify and mitigate network vulnerabilities, ensuring that our digital castles stand strong against the ever-evolving threats of the digital age.

Let's explore the intriguing realm of techniques for exploiting vulnerabilities, a subject that delves into the tactics and methods that attackers employ to breach digital fortresses and capitalize on weaknesses, much like cunning adversaries seeking the perfect moment to storm a castle's gates.

One common technique employed by attackers is known as "Buffer Overflow," akin to a sly infiltrator sneaking past a castle's guards by exploiting a weak point in the gate. In a buffer overflow attack, an attacker sends more data than a program's buffer can handle, causing it to overflow and potentially execute malicious code, gaining unauthorized access.

"SQL Injection" is another technique used by cyber adversaries, similar to a spy infiltrating the castle by manipulating hidden passages. In this attack, attackers inject malicious SQL code into input fields or queries, exploiting vulnerabilities to access, modify, or steal data from a database.

"Cross-Site Scripting (XSS)" attacks are like leaving secret messages within the castle's walls, as attackers inject malicious scripts into web applications. When other users access these compromised web pages, the scripts execute on their devices, potentially stealing sensitive information or hijacking user sessions.

"Privilege Escalation" is much like an infiltrator climbing the castle walls to reach more critical areas. In this technique, attackers aim to elevate their privileges within a compromised system, gaining additional access rights that allow them to perform more destructive actions.

"Social Engineering" attacks are similar to clever manipulation tactics used to gain trust within the castle's walls. Attackers employ psychological tricks to deceive individuals into divulging confidential information or performing actions that compromise security.

"Zero-Day Exploits" are akin to vulnerabilities only a select few know about, much like hidden passages into the castle that haven't been discovered yet. Cyber adversaries target software vulnerabilities that are unknown to the vendor, giving them an advantage until the vulnerability is detected and patched.

"Man-in-the-Middle (MitM)" attacks are like eavesdroppers intercepting secret conversations within the castle. In MitM attacks, attackers position themselves between two parties, often without their knowledge, intercepting and potentially altering communications.

"Password Attacks" are like persistent attackers trying every possible key to open the castle's locks. These attacks involve repeatedly attempting various combinations of passwords to gain unauthorized access to accounts or systems.

"Phishing" attacks are similar to con artists tricking castle residents into revealing secrets. Phishing emails or messages impersonate trusted entities to deceive recipients into providing sensitive information like passwords or credit card details.

"Malware" attacks are akin to hidden plagues sweeping through the castle, as these malicious programs infiltrate systems, infect files, and execute harmful actions, such as data theft or disruption.

"Distributed Denial-of-Service (DDoS)" attacks are like an army of attackers overwhelming the castle gates, as they employ a network of compromised devices to flood a target with an overwhelming volume of traffic, rendering it inaccessible to legitimate users.

"Web Application Attacks" are similar to infiltrators exploiting hidden vulnerabilities within the castle's architecture. Attackers target web applications to exploit vulnerabilities like injection flaws, broken authentication, or security misconfigurations.

"Insider Threats" are like trusted castle residents turning against their fellow inhabitants. These threats come from individuals within an organization who misuse their access to data, systems, or resources, posing a challenge to detect and mitigate.

"Advanced Persistent Threats (APTs)" are like highly skilled infiltrators patiently studying the castle for a prolonged period. APTs are sophisticated and targeted attacks by well-funded adversaries who often employ multiple attack vectors, persisting undetected for extended periods.

"Ransomware" attacks are like digital kidnappers holding castle assets hostage, as they encrypt files or systems, demanding a ransom for the decryption key.

"Drive-By Downloads" are similar to hidden traps scattered along the paths leading to the castle, as users unwittingly download malware from compromised or malicious websites.

"Brute Force Attacks" are like relentless attackers trying every key to open the castle doors, involving repeated attempts to guess or crack passwords.

"DNS Spoofing" attacks are akin to misdirecting travelers on their way to the castle, as attackers manipulate DNS servers to redirect users to malicious websites, often used in phishing or malware distribution.

"Eavesdropping" attacks are like spies secretly listening to conversations within the castle, as cyber adversaries intercept and monitor network communications to gather sensitive information or gain unauthorized access.

"Botnet Attacks" are like armies of automated soldiers marching towards the castle, as attackers use networks of compromised devices to carry out various malicious activities.

In our digital age, understanding these techniques for exploiting vulnerabilities is essential, much like recognizing the strategies employed by adversaries who seek to breach our digital fortresses.

Defenders must remain vigilant, employing security measures such as firewalls, intrusion detection systems, security patches, and user training to protect their networks.

Recognizing the methods attackers use allows organizations and individuals to bolster their defenses and respond effectively to potential threats.

Just as castle owners fortify their strongholds against invaders, we must strengthen our digital fortresses by staying informed, implementing security best practices, and fostering a culture of cybersecurity awareness.

So, let's continue our journey through the complex landscape of cybersecurity, armed with knowledge about these exploitation techniques, as we work together to safeguard our digital realms from cunning adversaries and emerging threats.

Chapter 3: Intermediate-Level Malware Analysis

Welcome to the fascinating world of malware analysis tools and methods, a realm where digital detectives, much like Sherlock Holmes, dissect and decipher the inner workings of malicious software to uncover its secrets and protect our digital realms.

One of the primary tools in a malware analyst's arsenal is the "sandbox," a virtual environment where suspicious files or programs can be executed safely, akin to a controlled laboratory for studying dangerous substances. Sandboxes isolate malware from the host system, allowing analysts to observe its behavior without risking infection.

"Dynamic Analysis" is like watching a play unfold within the sandbox, as analysts run malware and observe its actions in real-time. This method involves monitoring system calls, file changes, network traffic, and registry modifications to understand how the malware operates.

"Static Analysis," on the other hand, is akin to examining the script of a play before it's performed, as analysts inspect the code and structure of malware without executing it. Static analysis can reveal valuable information about the malware's logic and potential capabilities.

"Reverse Engineering" is like taking apart a complex puzzle to understand its pieces and how they fit together. In malware analysis, reverse engineers dissect the code to understand its functionality, revealing its secrets layer by layer.

"Debuggers" are the magnifying glasses of malware analysis, enabling analysts to inspect and manipulate the execution of a program, much like closely examining a suspect's actions.

Debuggers allow analysts to step through code, set breakpoints, and observe how malware behaves.

"Packet Capture and Analysis" is like intercepting and decoding secret messages sent by the malware, as analysts capture and analyze network traffic generated by the malware to uncover its communication with command and control servers.

"Memory Analysis" is akin to examining a crime scene for hidden clues, as analysts inspect the contents of a system's memory to identify running processes, injected code, and potential indicators of compromise.

"YARA Rules" are like search queries for identifying specific characteristics or patterns within malware code, allowing analysts to create custom rules to detect known malware or unique variants.

"Signature-Based Detection" is similar to recognizing a suspect's distinctive fingerprint, as analysts compare malware samples against known signatures to identify previously identified threats.

"Heuristic Analysis" is like profiling a suspect based on their behavior, as analysts use heuristics to identify potentially malicious behavior patterns within code, even if the malware's signature is not known.

"Machine Learning" is akin to having a trained detective who can recognize patterns and anomalies in large datasets, as machine learning models are employed to detect and classify malware based on learned patterns.

"Sandnet" environments are like virtual neighborhoods where malware samples are exposed to various scenarios, allowing analysts to observe their behavior in more realistic settings.

"Decompilers" are like translators for malware code, as they convert compiled code back into a higher-level programming language, making it more readable and understandable.

"Disassemblers" are like decrypting a secret message, as they convert machine code into assembly language, enabling analysts to review and understand the malware's instructions.

"Hex Editors" are like digital surgeons who can dissect and manipulate the very bytes of a program's code, allowing analysts to examine and modify malware binaries.

"File Analysis" is akin to examining the contents of a suspect's briefcase, as analysts inspect file metadata, headers, and contents to understand their purpose and potential threats.

"Behavioral Analysis" is like observing a suspect's actions in various scenarios, as analysts analyze how malware behaves in different environments and situations.

"Code Emulation" is akin to creating a digital replica of the suspect's hideout, as analysts use emulators to run malware in a controlled environment, mimicking the target system's architecture.

"Threat Intelligence Feeds" are like receiving updates from informants about known criminals, as analysts leverage threat intelligence to identify and categorize malware based on known threats and attack patterns.

"Memory Forensics" is akin to analyzing a crime scene for hidden evidence, as analysts examine the contents of a computer's memory to uncover artifacts left behind by malware.

"Pattern Recognition" is like identifying recurring patterns in a suspect's behavior, as analysts use pattern recognition techniques to detect anomalies and potential threats.

"YARA Rules" are like search warrants for digital investigations, as they allow analysts to define criteria for identifying specific malware characteristics.

"Packers and Crypters" are like disguises worn by suspects, as they are used to obfuscate malware code, making it more challenging to analyze.

"Network Analysis Tools" are like listening devices placed in a suspect's hideout, as they capture and analyze network traffic to identify communication patterns and potential threats.

"Malware Sandboxes" are like sterile laboratories where suspicious code can be safely examined, isolated from the host environment.

"API Monitoring" is akin to observing a suspect's interactions with the outside world, as analysts track how malware communicates with external servers and services.

"Registry Analysis" is like searching for hidden compartments within a suspect's dwelling, as analysts examine the Windows Registry for traces of malware activity.

"Payload Analysis" is akin to studying the contents of a suspect's package, as analysts dissect the payload delivered by malware to understand its intended actions.

"Timeline Analysis" is like reconstructing a suspect's activities over time, as analysts create timelines of events to trace the progression of a malware infection.

"Indicators of Compromise (IoCs)" are like identifying characteristics of a suspect, as analysts use IoCs to detect and respond to potential threats.

In the realm of cybersecurity, these tools and methods serve as the detective's toolkit, helping analysts uncover the mysteries of malware and protect our digital domains. With a combination of dynamic and static analysis, reverse engineering, and various specialized tools, analysts work tirelessly to dissect, understand, and defend against the ever-evolving landscape of malware threats.

Just as Sherlock Holmes used deductive reasoning and keen observation to solve intricate cases, malware analysts employ their expertise and tools to unravel the complexities of malicious software, safeguarding our digital world from potential threats.

So, let's continue our journey through the intricate realm of cybersecurity, armed with knowledge about malware analysis tools and methods, as we work together to protect our digital realms from cunning cyber adversaries.

Welcome to the captivating world of analyzing malware behavior, a realm where cybersecurity investigators, much like detectives in a thrilling mystery, unravel the actions and intentions of malicious software to protect our digital landscapes.

Imagine you're a cybersecurity sleuth, and you've just stumbled upon a suspicious file. Your first step is to place it in a controlled environment, like a digital laboratory, where it can't harm your computer. This environment, often called a sandbox, allows you to observe the file's every move without endangering your system.

As you watch the malware execute within the sandbox, it's like witnessing a suspect's behavior in a secure interrogation room. You carefully monitor the malware's actions, recording its every move to understand what it's up to.

One of the things you're keenly interested in is the malware's interaction with the operating system. It's as if you're observing how a suspect navigates a complex web of corridors and rooms within a building. The malware may attempt to make changes to files, modify the system's registry, or open network connections.

As you continue your investigation, you're essentially dissecting the malware's behavior, like a forensic scientist analyzing evidence at a crime scene. You look for clues about its purpose and capabilities. Does it try to steal sensitive data, communicate with a remote server, or launch other malicious activities?

To gain a deeper understanding of the malware's behavior, you use specialized tools, much like a detective relies on forensic equipment. These tools help you examine the malware's code, inspect its memory usage, and analyze its network communication.

You pay close attention to any attempts by the malware to contact external servers, almost as if you're eavesdropping on secret conversations between the suspect and their associates. This communication can reveal crucial information about the malware's command and control infrastructure.

Just as a detective collects evidence, you gather information about the malware's files and processes. You want to know if it creates or modifies files on the system, disguises itself by using deceptive file names, or employs encryption techniques to hide its activities.

The malware's persistence is another critical aspect you investigate. You want to determine if it tries to maintain a foothold on the system, like a persistent intruder who keeps finding ways back into a building. Does it create hidden autostart entries or scheduled tasks to ensure it runs every time the system boots?

Much like a detective considers a suspect's behavior under different circumstances, you analyze how the malware behaves in various environments. You may observe its actions in a controlled lab setting as well as in real-world scenarios, such as on a live network.

Throughout your investigation, you document your findings meticulously, just as a detective maintains a detailed case file. Your notes include information about the malware's actions, the files it touches, the registry keys it modifies, and the network traffic it generates.

To complement your behavioral analysis, you might also conduct static analysis, examining the malware's code and structure, much like scrutinizing a suspect's background and history. This helps you understand the malware's logic and potential vulnerabilities.

You often encounter malware that uses evasion techniques, attempting to avoid detection, much like a fugitive trying to stay one step ahead of the law. These evasion techniques can include anti-analysis tricks, like checking for the presence of virtual environments or security tools.

While analyzing malware behavior, you're essentially building a profile of the suspect, gaining insight into its motives and tactics. You identify its attack vectors, the vulnerabilities it exploits, and the data it targets.

As you delve deeper into the investigation, you consider the broader threat landscape. You explore whether the malware is part of a larger campaign or if it's a standalone threat. This contextual analysis helps you understand the malware's role in the grand scheme of cyber threats.

To aid your analysis, you rely on threat intelligence, just as a detective might consult informants or sources within the criminal underworld. Threat intelligence provides you with valuable information about known threats, attack patterns, and the tactics, techniques, and procedures (TTPs) employed by cybercriminals.

Throughout your work, you remain vigilant, much like a detective who stays alert for any unexpected developments in a case. You're prepared to adapt your analysis techniques as new malware variants emerge and cyber threats evolve.

Your ultimate goal is to uncover the malware's secrets, much like a detective aims to solve a complex case. You want to understand its behavior, motives, and capabilities so that you can mitigate its impact and protect your digital domain.

In the world of cybersecurity, analyzing malware behavior is an ongoing and essential task. Just as detectives tirelessly investigate crimes to maintain law and order, cybersecurity professionals work diligently to dissect and understand malicious software, safeguarding our digital world from threats.

So, let's continue our journey through the intricate landscape of cybersecurity, equipped with the knowledge of how to analyze malware behavior, as we strive to protect our digital landscapes from cunning adversaries and evolving threats.

Chapter 4: Web Application Security: Threats and Countermeasures

Welcome to the dynamic world of web application vulnerabilities, a realm where web developers, security experts, and digital defenders collaborate to identify, understand, and fortify against potential weaknesses in the software that powers the internet.

Think of web applications as the doors and windows of the digital world, allowing users to interact with websites, conduct online transactions, and access a multitude of services. These applications are everywhere, from e-commerce platforms to social media sites, and they're designed to make our online experiences seamless and enjoyable.

However, just as physical doors and windows can be vulnerable to break-ins, web applications can have vulnerabilities that cybercriminals can exploit. These vulnerabilities are essentially weaknesses in the code or design of the application that can be manipulated to compromise data, steal information, or dlsrupt services.

One common web application vulnerability is the "Injection Attack," where malicious code is injected into input fields, much like slipping a forged document through a mail slot. This injected code can exploit vulnerabilities in the application's handling of input data, potentially leading to data breaches or unauthorized access.

Another vulnerability is the "Cross-Site Scripting (XSS)" attack, which is like a digital graffiti artist defacing a website. In an XSS attack, attackers inject malicious scripts into web pages, which are then executed by unsuspecting users, potentially compromising their data or sessions.

Similarly, the "Cross-Site Request Forgery (CSRF)" vulnerability is akin to a digital puppeteer manipulating a user's actions. In CSRF attacks, attackers trick users into performing actions without their consent or knowledge, potentially leading to unintended actions or data changes.

"SQL Injection" is like a crafty spy infiltrating an organization through hidden passages. In this type of attack, attackers manipulate SQL queries to gain unauthorized access to a database, potentially exposing sensitive information.

"Security Misconfigurations" are akin to leaving the keys to your house under the doormat. These vulnerabilities occur when developers fail to configure security settings properly, allowing attackers to exploit default settings or access sensitive information.

"Broken Authentication" is like an imposter using someone else's ID to gain access to a secure building. This vulnerability allows attackers to bypass authentication mechanisms, potentially gaining unauthorized access to user accounts.

"Sensitive Data Exposure" is akin to leaving confidential documents in an unlocked drawer. In this scenario, sensitive data is inadequately protected, making it susceptible to theft or unauthorized access.

"XML External Entity (XXE) Injection" is like a Trojan horse sneaking into a well-guarded castle. Attackers exploit XML parsing vulnerabilities to execute malicious actions or extract sensitive data.

"Insecure Deserialization" is akin to unwrapping a seemingly harmless gift that contains a hidden trap. Attackers exploit vulnerabilities in deserialization processes to execute arbitrary code or gain unauthorized access.

"Using Components with Known Vulnerabilities" is like installing a security system that hasn't been updated in years. When web applications use outdated or vulnerable components, attackers can exploit known weaknesses to compromise the system.

"Unvalidated Redirects and Forwards" are akin to misleading road signs, as attackers trick users into visiting malicious websites or performing unintended actions.

These vulnerabilities are not hypothetical scenarios; they represent real risks that web applications face daily. Developers and security professionals work tirelessly to identify and mitigate these vulnerabilities, much like locksmiths fortifying doors and windows against burglars.

Security measures include input validation, where data is checked and sanitized before processing, and output encoding to prevent XSS attacks. Developers also use secure authentication and access controls to protect against unauthorized access, and they regularly update and patch their applications to address known vulnerabilities.

Furthermore, organizations conduct regular security assessments, like penetration testing and code reviews, to identify and remediate vulnerabilities. These assessments are like security audits, helping ensure that web applications remain resilient against potential threats.

In the ever-evolving landscape of web application vulnerabilities, collaboration is key. Developers, security experts, and users all play essential roles in identifying, addressing, and mitigating vulnerabilities. Users can practice good cybersecurity hygiene, like using strong passwords and being cautious about clicking on suspicious links.

Security researchers and ethical hackers also contribute to the collective effort by responsibly disclosing vulnerabilities to organizations, allowing them to fix issues before cybercriminals exploit them.

In essence, the world of web application vulnerabilities is a dynamic ecosystem where vigilance, collaboration, and continuous improvement are essential. Just as a neighborhood watches out for signs of trouble and works together to keep their community safe, the digital world relies on individuals and organizations to identify and address vulnerabilities to ensure a secure online environment.

So, let's continue our journey through the complex landscape of cybersecurity, equipped with knowledge about web application vulnerabilities, as we work together to fortify the doors and windows of the digital realm against potential threats and intruders.

Welcome to the world of mitigating web application threats, a journey where cybersecurity defenders deploy strategies and tactics to protect the digital landscape from the lurking dangers that threaten our online experiences.

Imagine web applications as bustling marketplaces, where users and businesses interact, share information, and conduct transactions. These digital marketplaces are essential to our online lives, powering everything from e-commerce websites to social media platforms.

However, like any bustling marketplace, web applications can attract not only legitimate users but also malicious actors looking to exploit vulnerabilities for personal gain or to sow chaos. These malicious actors may attempt to steal sensitive data, disrupt services, or compromise the integrity of the application.

To defend against these threats, cybersecurity experts employ a multifaceted approach, much like a team of guards and security measures safeguarding a bustling market. Let's explore the key strategies and tactics used to mitigate web application threats:

Secure Coding Practices: Just as a skilled architect designs a sturdy building, developers follow secure coding practices to build web applications with robust defenses. They adhere to coding standards and best practices that prevent vulnerabilities at the source.

Input Validation: Think of input validation as a vigilant gatekeeper checking visitors' credentials before they enter the marketplace. It ensures that data received from users is safe and within expected parameters, preventing injection attacks like SQL injection or XSS.

Output Encoding: Much like ensuring that the goods displayed in a shop window are clean and safe, output encoding ensures that data displayed to users is properly sanitized, mitigating XSS attacks.

Authentication and Authorization: These are like bouncers and access passes for our marketplace. Authentication ensures that users are who they claim to be, while authorization controls what actions they can perform within the application, preventing unauthorized access.

Session Management: Session management is akin to providing secure lockers for visitors in our marketplace. It ensures that user sessions are securely established, maintained, and terminated, preventing session hijacking.

Data Encryption: Imagine data encryption as a secure vault where sensitive information is stored. It protects data both in transit and at rest, ensuring that even if malicious actors gain access to it, they cannot decipher the contents.

Security Headers: These are like security banners displayed in the marketplace, informing everyone about security policies. They help prevent common web attacks and enhance overall security.

Security Patching and Updates: Much like maintaining and upgrading marketplace infrastructure, regularly applying security patches and updates to web applications is essential. This addresses known vulnerabilities and keeps the application resilient.

Web Application Firewalls (WAFs): Think of WAFs as vigilant security guards patrolling the marketplace's entrances, detecting and blocking malicious traffic and requests before they can harm the application.

Incident Response Plans: Just as a marketplace has contingency plans for emergencies, web applications need incident response plans. These plans outline how to react when a security incident occurs, helping to minimize damage.

Security Testing: Similar to hiring a security audit team to inspect the marketplace's infrastructure, web applications undergo security testing, including penetration testing and code reviews, to identify vulnerabilities proactively.

User Education: Educating users about safe online practices is like encouraging responsible shopping in our marketplace. Users are informed about creating strong passwords, recognizing phishing attempts, and being cautious with their data. Threat Intelligence: Gathering threat intelligence is akin to having informants who provide information about potential threats in the digital realm. This information helps defenders stay ahead of emerging risks.

Continuous Monitoring: Just as security cameras monitor the marketplace around the clock, web applications undergo continuous monitoring to detect and respond to suspicious activities in real-time. Content Security Policies: These policies are like rules that define what content is allowed in the marketplace. They prevent malicious content, such as scripts from untrusted sources, from executing within the application. Rate Limiting and DDoS Mitigation: Similar to managing crowd flow in the marketplace, rate limiting and DDoS mitigation strategies ensure that the application can handle sudden traffic spikes and deter malicious attacks.

Code Signing and Integrity Checks: These measures are like verifying the authenticity of products in the marketplace.

Code signing ensures that the application code hasn't been tampered with, maintaining its integrity.

Zero Trust Security: Zero trust is the approach of treating every user and device as untrusted until proven otherwise, much like thoroughly inspecting everyone entering our marketplace.

Security Headers: These headers are like digital signage that provides instructions on how web browsers should behave when rendering the application, enhancing security.

Red Teaming and Bug Bounty Programs: Red teaming is like hiring a group of undercover security experts to actively attempt to breach the application's security, while bug bounty programs invite ethical hackers to find and report vulnerabilities.

In this ever-evolving landscape of web application threats, a layered and proactive defense is essential. Security is not a one-time effort but an ongoing process. Much like a vigilant marketplace that adapts to new challenges and threats, web applications must continually adapt and strengthen their defenses.

Together, developers, security experts, and users can maintain the integrity of our digital marketplaces, ensuring that they remain safe and secure spaces for online interactions. Just as a community comes together to keep its physical marketplace thriving, the digital world relies on collaboration to mitigate web application threats and provide secure online experiences.

So, let's continue our journey through the intricate realm of cybersecurity, well-equipped with the knowledge of mitigating web application threats, as we work together to fortify the digital marketplaces that power our online lives against potential dangers and intrusions.

Chapter 5: Intermediate Intrusion Detection and Prevention

Welcome to the world of Intrusion Detection Systems, where we'll unravel the intricacies of safeguarding digital domains from unseen threats, much like vigilant security personnel keeping watch over a bustling city.

Think of an Intrusion Detection System as a network of surveillance cameras placed strategically throughout a city. These cameras continuously scan the environment, looking for any suspicious activities or potential threats.

In the digital realm, an IDS serves a similar purpose. It monitors network traffic, system activities, and various digital interactions to detect unauthorized access attempts, malicious activities, or deviations from normal behavior.

Imagine it as a watchful guardian for your computer network or system, tirelessly patrolling and scanning for any signs of trouble.

An IDS operates on a principle similar to a vigilant security guard who knows the layout of a building like the back of their hand. It has a baseline understanding of what normal network and system activities should look like and alerts when something seems amiss.

Now, let's delve deeper into the world of IDS:

Types of IDS: Just as there are different security personnel for various locations, there are different types of IDS. Network-based IDS (NIDS) monitors network traffic, while host-based IDS (HIDS) focuses on activities within a single host or system.

Signature-Based Detection: This method is akin to identifying troublemakers based on known characteristics. Signature-based IDS uses predefined patterns or signatures to match against observed network or system activities.

Anomaly-Based Detection: Think of this as spotting unusual behavior in a crowd. Anomaly-based IDS establishes a baseline of normal activities and raises alarms when deviations from this baseline occur.

Hybrid Approaches: Like a security team combining different strategies, some IDS solutions use a mix of signature-based and anomaly-based detection to provide comprehensive protection.

Real-Time Monitoring: IDS continuously monitors network traffic and system activities in real-time, much like a security guard staying vigilant around the clock.

Alerts and Notifications: When IDS detects suspicious activities, it generates alerts or notifications, much like a vigilant security guard contacting authorities when spotting potential trouble.

Logs and Reporting: Much like documenting incidents for future reference, IDS systems maintain logs and reports of detected activities, aiding in post-incident analysis and forensic investigations.

Response Actions: In some cases, IDS can trigger automated response actions, such as blocking certain IP addresses or isolating compromised systems, similar to a security guard taking immediate action to mitigate threats.

Tuning and Customization: Just as a security team tailors their approach to the specific needs of their location, IDS systems can be tuned and customized to suit the unique requirements of a network or system.

False Positives and Negatives: Similar to a security guard occasionally mistaking a harmless visitor for a threat, IDS can generate false positives (incorrectly identifying normal activities as threats) or false negatives (failing to detect actual threats).

Scalability: IDS solutions can scale to accommodate the size and complexity of networks, ensuring that both small and large organizations can benefit from intrusion detection.

Integration with SIEM: Much like a city's security personnel collaborate with law enforcement agencies, IDS often integrates with Security Information and Event Management (SIEM) systems, allowing for centralized monitoring and analysis of security events.

Threat Intelligence: IDS can benefit from threat intelligence feeds, similar to law enforcement agencies receiving information about potential threats. These feeds provide real-time data on emerging threats and attack techniques.

Continuous Updates: IDS systems must be regularly updated, much like security personnel receiving training to stay up-to-date with the latest security threats and tactics.

Compliance and Regulations: Just as security measures in a city must adhere to regulations, organizations often deploy IDS solutions to meet compliance requirements and industry standards.

Ethical Hacking: Some organizations employ ethical hackers or penetration testers to simulate attacks and assess the effectiveness of their IDS systems, much like stress-testing security measures in a city.

In the ever-evolving landscape of cybersecurity, Intrusion Detection Systems play a crucial role in identifying and responding to potential threats. They act as the digital guardians of our networks and systems, tirelessly scanning for signs of trouble and raising alarms when necessary.

Much like a well-trained security team, IDS systems are an essential part of an organization's overall cybersecurity strategy. They work hand in hand with other security measures, such as firewalls and antivirus software, to create a robust defense against digital threats.

So, as we navigate the complex terrain of cybersecurity, let's remember the diligent work of Intrusion Detection Systems, continuously monitoring our digital landscapes and alerting us to potential dangers, ensuring that our online experiences remain safe and secure.

Welcome to the world of configuring Intrusion Detection and Prevention, where we'll explore the essential steps to set up and fine-tune these vital security systems, much like crafting a customized security plan for your home.

Imagine you're fortifying your house against potential threats. You wouldn't just install locks; you'd configure them to suit your needs. Similarly, configuring Intrusion Detection and Prevention (IDP) systems is about tailoring security measures to your network's unique requirements.

Let's dive into the intricate process of configuring IDP systems:

System Deployment: Begin by selecting the appropriate IDP system for your network, much like choosing the right security measures for your home. Consider factors such as network size, traffic volume, and specific security needs.

Placement: Decide where to deploy IDP sensors within your network. This is similar to strategically placing security cameras in your home to cover vulnerable areas.

Network Segmentation: Much like securing different sections of your home, segment your network to isolate critical assets from less secure areas. This limits the scope of potential threats.

Rule Creation: Configure IDP rules to match your network's security policies. These rules specify what traffic is allowed and what should trigger alerts or actions, similar to setting access rules for your home.

Traffic Analysis: IDP systems continuously analyze network traffic, much like an alarm system monitoring movement around your property. Fine-tune the system to recognize normal traffic patterns and distinguish them from anomalies. Thresholds and Alerts: Set thresholds for alerts. These are like configuring your home alarm to trigger when certain conditions are met, such as multiple failed login attempts.

Response Actions: Decide what actions IDP should take when it detects suspicious activity. Options may include alerting administrators, blocking traffic, or taking predefined actions, much like instructing a security service on how to respond to an incident.

Tuning: Regularly review and adjust IDP rules and configurations, similar to fine-tuning your home security measures based on changing circumstances.

Signature Updates: Keep IDP signatures up to date, much like ensuring your home security system is equipped with the latest threat intelligence.

Logging and Reporting: Configure IDP to generate logs and reports, similar to having a record of security events at your home. These logs are valuable for incident investigation and compliance.

Integration: Integrate IDP with other security systems, such as firewalls and SIEM solutions, to create a unified defense, similar to coordinating security measures in different areas of your property.

Testing and Validation: Regularly test IDP configurations to ensure they are effective, much like conducting security drills at home to verify your response plans.

User Training: Educate network users about IDP and its capabilities, much like teaching your family members how to use your home security system.

Policy Enforcement: IDP can enforce security policies, just as you might enforce rules within your home. Ensure that policies are consistent and aligned with your organization's security objectives.

Scalability: Plan for future growth and scalability, much like considering security measures that can adapt to changes in your family or property.

Compliance: Align IDP configurations with industry regulations and compliance requirements, much like adhering to local laws and regulations for home security.

Backup and Redundancy: Implement backup IDP systems and redundancy measures to ensure continuous protection, similar to having backup security measures in place at home.

Monitoring and Incident Response: Continuously monitor IDP alerts and respond promptly to incidents, just as you would be vigilant and responsive to security incidents at home.

Documentation: Maintain detailed documentation of IDP configurations and changes, similar to keeping records of your home security measures.

Audit and Review: Regularly audit IDP configurations and review security logs, much like conducting periodic security assessments of your home.

Intrusion Detection and Prevention systems are the guardians of your network, tirelessly monitoring and protecting it from potential threats. Properly configuring and maintaining these systems is crucial for your network's security, just as securing your home is essential for your family's safety.

Remember that configuring IDP is an ongoing process. As your network evolves and new threats emerge, your configurations may need adjustments. Think of it as continuously improving the security of your home to keep your loved ones safe.

So, let's embark on this journey of configuring Intrusion Detection and Prevention systems, armed with the knowledge to create a robust security posture for your network, similar to fortifying your home against potential threats, ensuring a safe and secure digital environment.

Chapter 6: Advanced Firewall Configuration and Management

Welcome to the world of firewalls, where we'll explore the different types and features of these digital guardians that protect our networks, much like having various security measures in place to safeguard our homes.

Imagine a firewall as a security gatekeeper, standing at the entrance of your network like a vigilant sentry. Its primary mission is to allow authorized traffic in and out while blocking unauthorized access and potentially harmful data.

Now, let's delve into the fascinating realm of firewalls:

Network-Based Firewalls: Think of these as the main gatekeepers for your entire network, examining incoming and outgoing traffic at the network level. They decide which packets are allowed or denied based on predefined rules, similar to screening visitors at your front door.

Host-Based Firewalls: These are like individual room locks within your home. Host-based firewalls run on individual computers or devices, providing an additional layer of protection by controlling traffic specifically for that host.

Stateful Inspection: Much like a vigilant guard remembering who entered and ensuring they leave when the time comes, stateful inspection firewalls keep track of the state of active connections to make informed decisions.

Proxy Firewalls: These are like having an intermediary guide for visitors. Proxy firewalls act as intermediaries between clients and servers, making requests on behalf of clients and returning responses, which helps hide internal network details.

Application Layer Firewalls (ALGs): Think of these as highly specialized guards with deep knowledge of specific applications. ALGs operate at the application layer, making them proficient at filtering traffic for particular applications or services.

Packet Filtering: This is akin to allowing or denying visitors based on a set of predefined characteristics, such as source IP addresses, destination ports, and protocols.

Stateless Packet Filtering: Stateless firewalls inspect packets individually, making decisions based solely on packet headers, similar to checking visitors' ID cards without considering their previous interactions.

Deep Packet Inspection (DPI): Much like thoroughly inspecting the contents of packages, DPI firewalls analyze the payload of packets, looking for patterns or anomalies to identify threats.

Intrusion Detection and Prevention (IDP) Integration: Some firewalls integrate IDP functionality, actively identifying and mitigating known threats, much like having a team of investigators and enforcers on standby.

Virtual Private Network (VPN) Support: Firewalls can facilitate secure remote access through VPNs, much like securely granting access to trusted visitors.

Access Control Lists (ACLs): ACLs are like guest lists for exclusive events. They specify which devices or users are allowed to access specific network resources.

Content Filtering: This is similar to having strict rules about what's allowed inside your home. Content filtering firewalls block or allow traffic based on content categories, helping enforce security policies.

User Authentication: Like checking IDs at the entrance, user authentication ensures that only authorized individuals or devices can access the network.

Logging and Reporting: Firewalls maintain logs and generate reports, similar to recording who enters your home and when. These logs are essential for monitoring and incident investigation.

Application Control: Much like managing who is allowed to use certain rooms in your home, application control firewalls manage which applications can access the network.

Geo-IP Filtering: This is like allowing or denying access based on a visitor's country of origin. Geo-IP filtering restricts traffic from specific geographical regions.

High Availability (HA): HA configurations ensure that even if one firewall fails, another takes over seamlessly, ensuring uninterrupted protection, similar to having a backup security guard on standby.

Scalability: Firewalls can be scaled to accommodate the size and complexity of your network, just as you might increase security measures for a larger property.

Zero Trust Security: This modern approach treats every device and user as untrusted until proven otherwise, similar to verifying the identity of every visitor.

Threat Intelligence Integration: Firewalls can benefit from threat intelligence feeds, similar to receiving information about potential threats in your neighborhood. These feeds provide real-time data on emerging threats and attack techniques.

Security Policies: Security policies define the rules and behaviors of the firewall, similar to outlining the rules and regulations of your home.

Port Forwarding: Like having specific mail or package delivery instructions, port forwarding directs traffic from specific ports to designated internal resources.

Denial-of-Service (DoS) Protection: Firewalls can include DoS protection measures to safeguard against overwhelming traffic, similar to managing crowd control during a large event.

Encryption Inspection: This is like inspecting packages for hidden threats. Firewalls can decrypt and inspect encrypted traffic to detect and mitigate threats hidden within.

Security Information and Event Management (SIEM) Integration: Firewalls often integrate with SIEM systems, providing centralized monitoring and analysis of security events, much like coordinating security measures with law enforcement.

Regular Updates: Firewalls must be regularly updated with the latest threat intelligence and security patches, similar to staying informed about potential threats in your neighborhood.

Compliance: Align firewall configurations with industry regulations and compliance requirements, much like ensuring your home security measures comply with local laws and regulations.

Testing and Validation: Regularly test and validate firewall configurations to ensure they are effective, much like conducting security drills to verify response plans.

Firewalls are the first line of defense for your network, much like locks and security systems protect your home. Properly configuring and maintaining these digital guardians is essential for your network's security and integrity.

Remember that firewall configuration is an ongoing process. As your network evolves and new threats emerge, your configurations may need adjustments. Think of it as continuously improving the security of your home to keep your loved ones safe.

So, let's embark on this journey of understanding firewall types and features, well-equipped to make informed decisions about securing your digital domain, similar to fortifying your home against potential threats, ensuring a safe and secure online environment.

Welcome to the advanced realm of firewall rule management, where we'll explore the intricacies of crafting and managing rules to protect your network with the finesse of an experienced curator arranging priceless artifacts in a museum.

Imagine your firewall rules as the security policies for your network, akin to the guidelines you set for guests in your home. These rules determine what is allowed to enter or exit your network, making them a critical component of your overall security strategy.

Now, let's delve into the art of advanced firewall rule management:

Rule Organization: Much like arranging items in your home for easy access, organize firewall rules logically. Group related rules together to streamline management.

Rule Naming Conventions: Establish clear and consistent naming conventions for rules, similar to labeling items in your home to quickly find what you need.

Rule Prioritization: Assign priorities to rules, ensuring that critical security measures take precedence, much like prioritizing essential tasks in your daily routine.

Rule Commenting: Add comments to rules for clarity, similar to writing notes to remind yourself of the purpose of each item in your home.

Deny by Default: Implement a "deny by default" policy, allowing only explicitly permitted traffic, much like locking your doors by default and granting access to trusted visitors.

Rule Decommissioning: Regularly review and decommission outdated rules, similar to decluttering your home and getting rid of items you no longer need.

Rule Testing: Before implementing new rules, test them in a controlled environment to ensure they work as intended, much like trying out new furniture arrangements in your home before finalizing them.

Rule Logging: Enable logging for specific rules to monitor traffic and potential security incidents, similar to keeping a record of activities in your home.

Rule Versioning: Maintain version control for rules, allowing you to track changes and roll back to previous configurations if needed, much like keeping records of your home's renovation projects.

Rule Time-Based Controls: Implement time-based rules to control access during specific hours or days, similar to setting timers for lights and appliances in your home.

Rule Geo-Location Controls: Restrict traffic based on geographic location, similar to allowing or denying access to certain areas of your home to different individuals.

Rule User-Based Controls: Define rules based on user identities, ensuring that only authorized users can access specific resources, much like granting access to different parts of your home based on family members' roles.

Rule Bandwidth Controls: Allocate bandwidth to specific applications or services, ensuring fair usage and optimal network performance, similar to managing the allocation of resources in your home.

Rule Threat Intelligence Integration: Integrate threat intelligence feeds into your rules to proactively block traffic associated with known threats, similar to staying informed about potential dangers in your neighborhood.

Rule Quarantine and Isolation: Create rules that automatically quarantine or isolate compromised devices to prevent further damage, much like isolating a sick family member to prevent the spread of illness.

Rule Redundancy: Implement redundant rules and failover configurations to ensure continuous protection, similar to having backup security measures in your home.

Rule Audit and Review: Regularly audit and review rules to ensure they align with your security policies and compliance requirements, much like conducting periodic home security assessments.

Rule Compliance: Ensure that rules comply with industry regulations and standards, similar to adhering to local laws and regulations for home security.

Rule Reporting: Generate reports on rule activity and security events for analysis and compliance purposes, similar to keeping records of activities in your home.

Rule Troubleshooting: Develop a troubleshooting process for diagnosing and resolving rule-related issues, much like addressing household maintenance problems.

Rule Documentation: Maintain comprehensive documentation of rules, configurations, and changes, similar to keeping records of your home's maintenance history.

Rule Education: Educate network administrators and users about the purpose and impact of specific rules, much like explaining house rules to your family members and guests.

Rule Collaboration: Collaborate with other teams and departments to ensure that rules align with the organization's overall objectives, similar to coordinating household rules with family members.

Rule Change Control: Implement a change control process to carefully manage rule modifications and ensure that they do not introduce vulnerabilities, much like planning home renovations with attention to safety and security.

Rule Simulation: Use simulation tools to test the impact of rule changes before implementing them in a production environment, similar to using design software to plan home improvements.

Rule Backup and Recovery: Establish a backup and recovery strategy for rules to quickly restore configurations in case of unexpected issues, much like having contingency plans for emergencies in your home.

Advanced firewall rule management is an art that requires precision, organization, and adaptability. Just as a skilled curator ensures that every piece of art in a museum is protected and displayed to its best advantage, advanced firewall rule management safeguards your network while optimizing its performance.

Remember that rule management is an ongoing process. As your network evolves, security threats change, and compliance requirements shift, your rules may need adjustments. Think of it as continuously fine-tuning your home's security measures to adapt to changing circumstances.

So, let's embark on this journey of mastering advanced firewall rule management, armed with the knowledge to create a robust security posture for your network, similar to curating a museum that showcases the beauty of your digital domain while safeguarding it from potential threats.

Chapter 7: Data Encryption and Secure Communication

Welcome to the fascinating world of encryption algorithms and protocols, where we'll uncover the intricate mechanisms that safeguard your data in transit and at rest, much like storing your most precious belongings in a secure vault.

Imagine encryption as a secret language that only you and your trusted recipient understand, rendering your messages indecipherable to prying eyes. It's the digital equivalent of sending a letter in a locked box that only the intended recipient can open.

Now, let's embark on our journey into the realm of encryption algorithms and protocols:

Encryption Fundamentals: At its core, encryption is about transforming plaintext data into ciphertext using complex mathematical algorithms, making it unreadable without the proper decryption key.

Symmetric Encryption: Think of this as having a shared secret key between you and your recipient. Symmetric encryption uses the same key for both encryption and decryption, ensuring confidentiality but requiring secure key exchange.

Asymmetric Encryption: Much like a pair of unique keys—one to lock and another to unlock—a public key encrypts data, while a private key decrypts it. Asymmetric encryption solves the key exchange challenge, enhancing security.

Key Management: Managing encryption keys is crucial. It's like safeguarding the keys to your vault with utmost care, ensuring that only authorized parties have access to them.

Data at Rest Encryption: This is akin to storing your valuables in a secure safe. Data at rest encryption protects information when it's stored on devices, servers, or databases.

Data in Transit Encryption: Imagine your data as a confidential message passed between couriers. Data in transit encryption ensures that information is secure as it travels across networks, much like an envelope sealed and locked during delivery.

Secure Sockets Layer (SSL)/Transport Layer Security (TLS): These are the protocols that secure your online transactions, similar to the trusted handshake between individuals before exchanging information.

Public Key Infrastructure (PKI): PKI is the infrastructure that manages digital certificates and public-private key pairs, much like a trusted certification authority verifying your identity.

Digital Certificates: These are like digital IDs, issued by trusted authorities to validate the authenticity of websites and individuals, ensuring secure communication.

Secure File Storage: Think of this as a digital safe deposit box for your files. Secure file storage ensures that sensitive documents remain protected even when stored in the cloud.

End-to-End Encryption: Just as only you and your intended recipient can understand a handwritten letter, end-to-end encryption ensures that only the sender and receiver can decrypt messages, even service providers cannot access the content.

Homomorphic Encryption: This advanced encryption technique allows for computations on encrypted data without revealing the underlying information, much like securely outsourcing a task without disclosing details.

Quantum Encryption: Quantum encryption leverages the principles of quantum mechanics to create unbreakable encryption, akin to using unbreakable locks for your digital valuables.

Perfect Forward Secrecy: This feature ensures that even if a single encryption key is compromised, past and future communications remain secure, similar to changing locks after a lost key.

Zero-Knowledge Proofs: Much like proving your identity without revealing your name, zero-knowledge proofs allow verification of information without disclosing the data itself.

Homomorphic Encryption: Think of this as performing calculations on sensitive data without seeing the actual information, ensuring privacy even during analysis.

Multi-factor Authentication (MFA): MFA is like having multiple layers of security before accessing a vault. It combines something you know (password), something you have (device), and something you are (biometrics) for enhanced security.

Secure Messaging Apps: These apps use encryption to protect your messages and calls, ensuring that only you and your intended recipients can access the content, similar to a private conversation in a sealed room.

Email Encryption: Much like sending a confidential letter in a locked box, email encryption protects the content of your emails from unauthorized access during transmission.

Secure Browsing: Secure browsing uses encryption to protect your online activities, ensuring that your sensitive information remains confidential, much like a private conversation in a soundproof room.

VPN Encryption: VPNs use encryption to create secure tunnels for your internet traffic, much like a secret passageway that shields your data from prying eyes.

Blockchain Encryption: Blockchain employs encryption to secure transactions and data, ensuring the integrity and immutability of the ledger, similar to sealing each entry in an unalterable record.

Encryption Key Rotation: Regularly changing encryption keys is essential, similar to changing the locks on your doors to enhance security continually.

Zero Trust Security: This modern approach treats every device and user as untrusted until proven otherwise, much like verifying the identity of every visitor to your digital domain.

Data Loss Prevention (DLP): DLP solutions monitor and prevent the unauthorized transfer of sensitive data, similar to preventing valuables from leaving your premises without permission.

Regulatory Compliance: Ensuring that encryption practices align with industry regulations and compliance requirements is akin to adhering to local laws and regulations for security measures.

Continuous Monitoring: Regularly monitoring encrypted traffic and security configurations is crucial, much like having security cameras in your vault to detect any suspicious activity.

Incident Response: Developing an incident response plan for encryption-related incidents is similar to having a well-defined protocol for responding to security breaches.

User Education: Educating users about the importance of encryption and secure practices is essential, much like teaching family members to safeguard your home.

Encryption is the guardian of your digital world, much like locks and safes protect your physical possessions.

Welcome to the realm of secure communication channels, where we'll unravel the techniques and strategies to ensure that your digital conversations remain private, akin to having a confidential discussion behind closed doors.

Imagine secure communication channels as virtual meeting rooms with encrypted walls, where you can discuss sensitive matters without the fear of eavesdroppers. These channels serve as the backbone of secure online interactions, much like private conversations in a secluded area.

Now, let's dive into the world of implementing secure communication channels:

Confidential Conversations: Just as you would lower your voice in a private room, secure communication channels ensure that your conversations are confidential, protected from prying eyes.

Secure Socket Layer (SSL) and Transport Layer Security (TLS): Think of SSL/TLS as the locked doors and windows of your virtual meeting room, ensuring that data travels securely between you and your counterpart.

End-to-End Encryption: Much like speaking in a secret code known only to you and your trusted companion, end-to-end encryption guarantees that only you and your recipient can decipher the messages, even service providers are in the dark.

Secure Video Conferencing: Secure video conferencing is akin to having a secure, virtual meeting room with video feeds encrypted from end to end, ensuring that your visual interactions are confidential.

Secure Messaging Apps: Imagine these apps as private, encrypted chat rooms where your messages are shielded from unauthorized access, similar to hushed conversations in a closed-off space.

Voice Encryption: Voice encryption ensures that your spoken words remain confidential during phone calls, similar to speaking in a soundproof room.

Email Security: Implementing email security measures is like sealing your letters in envelopes before sending them, ensuring that only the intended recipient can access the content.

Secure File Sharing: Secure file sharing is akin to safely exchanging confidential documents in your virtual meeting room, ensuring that only authorized parties can access the files.

Virtual Private Networks (VPNs): VPNs create private, encrypted tunnels for your internet traffic, much like a secret passage that shields your data from prying eyes during transmission.

Secure Cloud Storage: Secure cloud storage is like storing your valuable possessions in a digital safe deposit box, ensuring that your data is protected even when stored remotely.

Secure Browsing: Secure browsing uses encryption to protect your online activities, much like ensuring that your digital footprint remains hidden from snoopers.

Secure Social Media: Secure social media platforms ensure that your posts and interactions are private, similar to having a closed-door gathering with trusted friends.

Multi-Factor Authentication (MFA): MFA adds extra layers of security to your access, similar to requiring multiple forms of identification to enter a secure facility.

Blockchain Security: Blockchain employs cryptographic techniques to secure transactions and data, much like sealing each entry in an unalterable ledger.

Secure Collaboration Tools: These tools are like collaborative workspaces with fortified walls, ensuring that your shared projects remain confidential.

Zero Trust Security: Zero Trust treats every device and user as untrusted until proven otherwise, much like scrutinizing each visitor to your digital space before granting access.

Incident Response Plan: Much like having a well-rehearsed plan for unexpected events, an incident response plan ensures a swift and effective response to security incidents.

User Training: Educating users about secure communication practices is essential, similar to teaching individuals the etiquettes of holding confidential conversations.

Data Classification: Just as you categorize your belongings for added organization, classifying data helps in identifying what requires extra layers of protection.

Data Loss Prevention (DLP): DLP tools monitor and prevent unauthorized data transfers, similar to guards ensuring that valuables aren't taken from your premises without permission.

Security Audits: Regular security audits are like conducting thorough inspections of your virtual meeting rooms to check for any potential vulnerabilities.

Compliance and Regulations: Ensuring that secure communication practices comply with industry regulations is akin to adhering to local laws and regulations for privacy.

Continuous Monitoring: Much like having security cameras in your virtual meeting rooms, continuous monitoring detects any suspicious activities in your digital space.

Backup and Recovery: Having a robust backup and recovery strategy is similar to having contingency plans for unexpected events, ensuring that your conversations can be restored if needed.

Encryption Key Management: Managing encryption keys is crucial for maintaining the security of your communication channels, similar to safeguarding the keys to your virtual meeting rooms.

Public Key Infrastructure (PKI): PKI manages digital certificates and keys, much like a trusted authority ensuring the authenticity of your virtual meeting rooms.

Threat Intelligence Integration: Integrating threat intelligence feeds into your secure communication channels is akin to staying informed about potential risks and threats in your digital environment.

User Privacy: Respecting user privacy is vital, similar to respecting the confidentiality of those who enter your virtual meeting rooms.

Regulatory Compliance: Ensuring that secure communication practices align with industry regulations is akin to adhering to local laws and regulations for privacy.

Secure communication channels are the foundation of a private and trusted digital space, similar to having an exclusive meeting room where confidential discussions remain shielded from eavesdroppers. Remember that maintaining the security of these channels is an ongoing effort, much like regularly inspecting and fortifying the walls of your virtual meeting rooms.

Chapter 8: Incident Response and Forensics

Welcome to the world of incident response frameworks, where we'll explore the structured approaches and methodologies that organizations use to effectively manage and mitigate cybersecurity incidents, similar to having a well-organized emergency response plan for unexpected events.

Think of an incident response framework as a well-thought-out playbook that guides you through the steps to take when a security breach occurs. It's like having a fire drill procedure in place to ensure that everyone knows what to do in case of a fire.

Now, let's delve into the intricacies of incident response frameworks:

Preparation Phase: Just as you prepare for emergencies by having fire extinguishers and alarms in place, the preparation phase of an incident response framework involves establishing the necessary resources, policies, and procedures to respond effectively to incidents.

Incident Identification: Imagine a security incident as a fire in a building; the first step is to detect it. Incident identification involves recognizing abnormal activities or security alerts that indicate a potential breach.

Classification and Initial Assessment: Once you've identified an incident, it's essential to classify it based on its severity and impact, similar to assessing the scale of a fire to determine the level of response required.

Incident Escalation: Escalation is like calling the fire department when a fire exceeds the capabilities of in-house firefighting. Incident escalation involves notifying the appropriate personnel and management about the incident.

Containment and Eradication: Just as firefighters work to contain and extinguish a fire, incident responders aim to contain the incident to prevent further damage and then eradicate the root cause.

Communication: Effective communication during an incident is crucial, much like alerting building occupants about a fire. Incident responders need to keep stakeholders informed, including management, legal, and public relations teams.

Recovery: After a fire is extinguished, recovery efforts begin, such as rebuilding damaged areas. In cybersecurity, recovery involves restoring systems and services to normal operation and ensuring that lessons learned are applied to prevent future incidents.

Lessons Learned: Much like conducting a post-fire analysis to understand what went wrong and how to prevent future fires, incident responders perform a post-incident analysis to identify weaknesses in security measures and improve the incident response process.

Documentation and Reporting: Detailed documentation of the incident and response actions is essential, similar to filing a report after a fire. This documentation helps in legal and regulatory compliance and supports future incident analysis.

Legal and Regulatory Compliance: Just as building safety codes and regulations must be followed, incident response frameworks often involve legal and regulatory requirements that organizations must adhere to when responding to incidents.

Forensic Analysis: Much like fire investigators determine the cause of a fire, incident responders often engage in forensic analysis to identify the source and extent of a security breach.

Incident Closure: Closure is like marking the end of a fire incident when it's completely resolved. In cybersecurity, incident closure involves ensuring that all affected systems are secure, and normal operations are restored.

Continuous Improvement: Incident response is an ongoing process, much like regularly conducting fire drills to improve emergency preparedness. Organizations continually refine their incident response frameworks based on lessons learned from previous incidents.

Incident Response Teams: Just as firefighters are a specialized team trained to handle fires, organizations often have dedicated incident response teams with specialized skills and expertise.

Incident Severity Levels: Incidents are categorized by severity, similar to how fires are classified as small, medium, or large. Incident response frameworks often define severity levels to guide response efforts.

Notification and Coordination: Incident response often involves coordinating with external parties, such as law enforcement or third-party security vendors, similar to calling for external help during a fire emergency.

Public Relations: When a fire occurs in a public place, public relations efforts are crucial to manage public perception. In cybersecurity, incident responders may work with PR teams to communicate with the public and stakeholders.

Incident Simulation and Training: Just as firefighters undergo regular training exercises, incident response teams conduct simulations and training to ensure they are well-prepared for real incidents.

Incident Response Playbooks: Playbooks are like step-by-step guides for incident response, ensuring that responders follow a structured approach when handling incidents.

Threat Intelligence Integration: Threat intelligence feeds provide information about emerging threats and vulnerabilities, similar to monitoring fire risk factors in a building.

Incident Response Automation: Automation tools can help streamline incident response processes, similar to using automated fire suppression systems in buildings.

Business Continuity Planning: Incident response is closely tied to business continuity planning, ensuring that critical business functions can continue even during and after a security incident.

Incident Recovery Testing: Testing recovery processes is essential, similar to fire drill exercises, to ensure that systems can be restored efficiently.

Incident Response in Cloud Environments: With the shift to cloud computing, incident response frameworks must also address incidents in cloud environments, much like ensuring fire safety in modern buildings.

Incident Response Metrics: Metrics and Key Performance Indicators (KPIs) are used to assess the effectiveness of incident response efforts, similar to evaluating the efficiency of firefighting procedures.

Incident Response Policy Review: Incident response policies are regularly reviewed and updated, similar to revising building safety policies to reflect changing regulations and technologies.

Crisis Communication Plans: Like having communication plans for fire emergencies, organizations develop crisis communication plans for cybersecurity incidents to ensure that stakeholders are informed promptly and accurately.

Post-Incident Legal Actions: Just as investigations may follow a fire incident, legal actions and regulatory investigations may follow a cybersecurity incident, requiring organizations to cooperate fully.

Incident Response Challenges: Incident response can be complex, similar to addressing challenges like determining the extent of data breaches and managing the reputational impact of incidents.

In essence, incident response frameworks are the strategic plans that guide organizations through the chaotic moments of a cybersecurity incident, ensuring a structured and effective response, much like well-practiced fire drills that save lives in emergencies.

Welcome to the realm of digital forensics, where we embark on a journey into the fascinating world of uncovering digital evidence and solving cyber mysteries, much like modern-day digital detectives.

Digital forensics is akin to peering through a digital magnifying glass to examine the hidden details within electronic devices and data, helping us understand the who, what, when, where, and how of cyber incidents.

Now, let's explore the tools and techniques that make digital forensics a crucial discipline in today's interconnected world:

Data Recovery Tools: Think of data recovery tools as the digital equivalent of search and rescue missions, helping retrieve lost or deleted data from storage devices, much like recovering precious items from the depths of a lake.

Disk Imaging: Disk imaging is like creating a digital copy of a crime scene; it involves capturing a complete snapshot of a storage device to preserve its current state for analysis.

File Carving: Imagine extracting puzzle pieces from a jumbled box; file carving involves reconstructing files from fragmented or partially overwritten data, helping in the recovery of digital evidence.

Memory Forensics: Memory forensics is akin to examining a suspect's immediate thoughts; it involves analyzing the volatile memory (RAM) of a system to uncover information about running processes and activities.

Timeline Analysis: Much like piecing together the sequence of events in a crime, timeline analysis helps investigators reconstruct a chronological order of digital activities, aiding in understanding the progression of incidents.

Hashing: Hashing is like creating a digital fingerprint for files; it generates unique codes (hashes) for files, ensuring their integrity and helping detect tampering.

Keyword Searching: Keyword searching is similar to using a search warrant to find specific evidence in a physical location; it involves searching digital storage for specific words or phrases related to an investigation.

Email Forensics: Email forensics is akin to analyzing a suspect's correspondence; it involves examining email headers, content, and attachments to gather evidence related to a case.

Internet History Analysis: Internet history analysis is like flipping through a suspect's diary; it involves examining web browser history to uncover online activities and visited websites.

Mobile Device Forensics: Mobile device forensics is similar to investigating a suspect's phone; it involves extracting data from smartphones and tablets to gather evidence.

Network Forensics: Network forensics is akin to analyzing the communication between suspects; it involves monitoring and analyzing network traffic to identify patterns and potential threats.

Forensic Analysis Tools: Forensic analysis tools are like digital laboratories; they provide investigators with a range of functionalities for examining digital evidence, including file viewing, keyword searching, and timeline analysis.

Forensic Virtual Machines: Forensic virtual machines are isolated environments where investigators can safely analyze digital evidence without altering the original data, similar to a controlled crime scene.

Database Forensics: Database forensics is akin to examining the records in a suspect's ledger; it involves analyzing database systems to extract information related to a case.

Registry Analysis: Registry analysis is like sifting through a suspect's personal documents; it involves examining the Windows Registry to gather information about system settings and user activities.

Artifacts Analysis: Artifacts are digital traces left behind by user activities, much like fingerprints at a crime scene; analyzing these artifacts can provide valuable insights into digital behavior.

Steganography Detection: Steganography detection is similar to uncovering hidden messages; it involves identifying and decoding concealed information within files or images.

Encryption Analysis: Encryption analysis is like deciphering a secret code; it involves decrypting encrypted data to access its contents, which can be crucial in digital investigations.

Data Authentication: Data authentication techniques help ensure the integrity and authenticity of digital evidence, much like verifying the authenticity of physical documents.

Malware Analysis: Malware analysis is akin to dissecting a suspicious object to understand its inner workings; it involves examining malicious software to identify its behavior and impact.

Volatility Analysis: Volatility analysis is like studying the behavior of a fleeting suspect; it involves analyzing volatile memory to gather information about currently running processes.

Chain of Custody: Chain of custody procedures ensure the integrity of digital evidence throughout an investigation, similar to maintaining a secure chain of evidence for physical items.

Reporting: Reporting is like compiling a comprehensive case file; it involves documenting findings, analysis, and conclusions in a clear and organized manner for legal and investigative purposes.

Expert Testimony: Expert testimony in court is similar to presenting evidence to a judge and jury; digital forensic experts may testify about their findings and methods during legal proceedings.

Data Preservation: Data preservation is like securing a crime scene; it involves ensuring that digital evidence is properly handled, stored, and protected to maintain its integrity.

Data Acquisition: Data acquisition is akin to collecting physical evidence; it involves gathering digital evidence from various sources, such as computers, mobile devices, and network logs.

Forensic Analysis Challenges: Just as physical investigations face challenges like weather and contamination, digital forensics encounters obstacles such as encryption and anti-forensic techniques.

Legal and Ethical Considerations: Like respecting individuals' rights and privacy during investigations, digital forensics must adhere to legal and ethical guidelines.

Continuous Learning: Digital forensics is a constantly evolving field, much like staying updated on the latest investigative techniques and tools.

In essence, digital forensics is the art and science of uncovering the digital trail left behind by cyber actors, similar to piecing together clues at a crime scene. It's a field where investigators leverage advanced tools and techniques to decipher the intricate web of digital interactions, ultimately shedding light on cyber incidents and contributing to the pursuit of justice in the digital age.

Chapter 9: Wireless Network Attacks and Defenses

Imagine the air around us buzzing with invisible signals, connecting us to the digital world; that's the beauty of wireless networks, offering us convenience and mobility, much like the magic of radio waves carrying music to our ears.

However, in this world of wireless wonders, there also lurk malicious actors who seek to exploit vulnerabilities and compromise our digital sanctuaries, much like unseen burglars breaking into our homes.

In this chapter, we'll embark on a journey through the realm of common wireless network attacks, where we'll explore the techniques and tactics employed by these digital miscreants.

Eavesdropping: Picture someone secretly listening to your private conversations; eavesdropping in wireless networks involves intercepting and monitoring wireless communications without authorization, potentially revealing sensitive information.

Rogue Access Points: Think of rogue access points as fake doorways; attackers can set up unauthorized wireless access points to lure unsuspecting users into connecting, allowing them to intercept and manipulate data.

Man-in-the-Middle (MitM) Attacks: MitM attacks are like having a third party intercepting your phone calls; attackers position themselves between a victim's device and the network, capturing and altering data passing through.

Denial-of-Service (DoS) and Distributed Denial-of-Service (DDoS) Attacks: Imagine someone repeatedly ringing your doorbell or flooding your mailbox with junk; DoS and DDoS attacks overwhelm wireless networks or devices with excessive traffic, rendering them inaccessible.

Password Cracking: Password cracking is akin to attempting to pick a lock; attackers use various methods to guess or crack wireless network passwords, gaining unauthorized access.

Deauthentication and Disassociation Attacks: These attacks are similar to evicting someone from a party; attackers send deauthentication or disassociation packets to force users off a network, disrupting their connectivity.

Evil Twin Attacks: Think of an evil twin as your doppelgänger trying to impersonate you; attackers create a fraudulent Wi-Fi hotspot with a similar name to a legitimate one, tricking users into connecting to the rogue network.

WEP and WPA/WPA2 Cracking: Cracking WEP or WPA/WPA2 encryption is like decoding a secret message; attackers exploit weaknesses in these security protocols to gain access to protected networks.

MAC Spoofing: MAC spoofing is like using a disguise; attackers change their device's MAC address to impersonate an authorized device on the network.

WPS Vulnerabilities: Think of Wi-Fi Protected Setup (WPS) as a backdoor; attackers exploit WPS vulnerabilities to gain access to a network using a PIN or brute force attacks.

Packet Injection: Packet injection is similar to slipping fake letters into someone's mailbox; attackers inject malicious or unauthorized packets into the wireless traffic stream to disrupt or manipulate communication.

Sniffing and Data Interception: Sniffing is like reading someone's mail; attackers use tools to capture and analyze wireless traffic, potentially intercepting sensitive data.

Bluetooth Attacks: Bluetooth attacks are like tampering with your wireless headphones; attackers exploit Bluetooth vulnerabilities to gain unauthorized access or control over Bluetooth-enabled devices.

Near Field Communication (NFC) Attacks: NFC attacks are akin to pickpocketing digital wallets; attackers exploit NFC vulnerabilities to steal data from nearby devices or initiate unauthorized transactions.

War Driving: War driving is like cruising the neighborhood looking for unlocked doors; attackers drive around searching for vulnerable wireless networks to compromise.

Jamming: Jamming is like blasting loud noise to disrupt a conversation; attackers transmit interference signals to disrupt wireless communications and render networks or devices unusable.

Karma Attacks: Karma attacks are like a hypnotic spell; attackers exploit the "Karma" feature in some routers to trick devices into connecting to a rogue network.

Honeypots and Deception: Honeypots are like digital bait; attackers set up fake networks or services to lure unsuspecting users, monitoring their actions or attempting to compromise their devices.

Credential Theft: Credential theft is akin to stealing someone's keys; attackers target wireless networks to steal login credentials or sensitive information.

Zero-Day Exploits: Zero-day exploits are like secret keys to locked doors; attackers discover and exploit previously unknown vulnerabilities in wireless devices or protocols.

Wireless Phishing: Wireless phishing is similar to email phishing; attackers create fake login pages or captive portals on rogue networks to trick users into revealing their credentials.

Hijacking Sessions: Session hijacking is like sneaking into a theater without a ticket; attackers steal or hijack established user sessions on a wireless network to gain unauthorized access.

Password Spraying: Password spraying is akin to trying a few keys on multiple locks; attackers attempt common passwords across multiple accounts to gain access.

Brute Force Attacks: Brute force attacks are like trying every possible combination on a combination lock; attackers systematically try all possible passwords until they find the correct one.

Social Engineering: Social engineering is like convincing someone to give you their house keys; attackers manipulate users into revealing sensitive information or performing actions that compromise network security.

Countermeasures and Defense: Much like fortifying your home with security measures, organizations and individuals can implement security measures such as strong encryption, network monitoring, and intrusion detection systems to protect against wireless attacks.

Awareness and Education: Just as vigilant neighbors can prevent neighborhood crime, raising awareness and educating users about wireless security best practices can help prevent attacks.

Regulatory Compliance: Regulatory compliance is like having laws that govern home security standards; organizations may need to adhere to wireless security regulations to protect sensitive data.

Incident Response: Similar to calling the authorities during a break-in, having an incident response plan in place can help organizations effectively respond to wireless network attacks.

In essence, understanding common wireless network attacks is crucial in safeguarding our digital lives, much like knowing the types of threats that can target our homes. By staying informed about these attack techniques and employing robust security measures, we can fortify our digital fortresses and enjoy the benefits of wireless connectivity with confidence.

Welcome to the world of wireless network security, where we embark on a journey to ensure the safety and privacy of our digital interactions, much like fortifying the walls of our virtual castles.

Securing wireless networks is akin to safeguarding your home against intruders, as it involves implementing measures to protect your data and communications from unauthorized access and potential threats.

Now, let's dive into the realm of securing wireless networks and explore the strategies and best practices that can help you establish a strong digital defense.

Encryption: Think of encryption as sealing your messages in an impenetrable envelope; it scrambles data into an unreadable format that can only be deciphered by those with the right decryption key.

Wi-Fi Protected Access (WPA3): WPA3 is like an advanced lock for your Wi-Fi network; it offers stronger encryption and protection against brute force attacks, enhancing the security of your wireless communications.

Complex Passwords: Creating a complex password is similar to installing a robust lock on your front door; it's essential to choose strong, unique passwords for your Wi-Fi network to deter unauthorized access.

Network Segmentation: Network segmentation is like having separate rooms in your house; it involves dividing your network into separate segments to limit access and contain potential threats.

Guest Networks: Guest networks are like providing a separate entrance for visitors; they allow guests to access the internet without exposing your main network to potential security risks.

Change Default Credentials: Changing default credentials is similar to changing the locks when you move into a new house; it's crucial to replace default usernames and passwords on your networking equipment.

Firmware Updates: Think of firmware updates as fixing security vulnerabilities in your home's foundation; keeping your router's firmware up to date is essential to patch known security flaws.

Firewalls: Firewalls act like a security gate for your network; they filter incoming and outgoing traffic, blocking malicious or unauthorized access attempts.

Intrusion Detection Systems (IDS): IDS is like having a vigilant security guard; it monitors network traffic for suspicious activity and alerts you to potential threats.

Intrusion Prevention Systems (IPS): IPS is akin to a security guard who not only alerts you but also takes action to block threats; it actively prevents unauthorized access and attacks.

Wireless Isolation: Wireless isolation is like having soundproof walls between rooms; it prevents wireless devices on the same network from communicating with each other, adding an extra layer of security.

MAC Filtering: MAC filtering is similar to allowing only authorized individuals into your home; it restricts network access to devices with specific MAC addresses.

Hidden SSID: Hiding your SSID is like having an unlisted phone number; it makes your network less visible to potential attackers, although it's not a foolproof security measure.

Regular Audits: Regularly auditing your network is like inspecting your home for vulnerabilities; it involves scanning for open ports, unsecured devices, and potential weaknesses.

Access Control: Access control is like having a guest list for your home; it ensures that only authorized devices and users can connect to your network.

Security Protocols: Using secure network protocols is akin to communicating through an encrypted radio frequency; it ensures that data transmission between devices is secure.

Physical Security: Just as you lock your doors, physical security measures such as placing your router in a secure location and using cable locks can prevent unauthorized physical access.

Security Awareness: Security awareness is like teaching your family members about home safety; educating users about best practices and potential risks can help maintain a secure network.

Backup and Recovery: Backup and recovery strategies are like having insurance for your digital assets; they ensure that you can recover your network's configuration and data in case of a breach.

Multi-Factor Authentication (MFA): MFA is similar to requiring both a key and a fingerprint to enter a secure room; it adds an extra layer of authentication to protect network access.

Regular Monitoring: Regularly monitoring your network is like having security cameras installed; it allows you to detect and respond to potential threats in real-time.

Incident Response Plan: Having an incident response plan is akin to having a fire evacuation plan for your home; it ensures that you know what to do in case of a security breach.

Compliance with Regulations: Similar to adhering to building codes, compliance with wireless security regulations is essential for organizations to protect sensitive data and avoid legal issues.

Penetration Testing: Penetration testing is like hiring a security expert to test your home's vulnerabilities; it involves ethical hackers simulating attacks to identify weaknesses.

Vendor Security Recommendations: Following vendor security recommendations is like following a manufacturer's maintenance guidelines for your home appliances; it ensures that you're using your networking equipment optimally and securely.

Wireless Security Audits: Wireless security audits are like conducting regular home inspections; they help identify vulnerabilities and assess the overall security of your network.

Security Updates for Devices: Ensuring that all your devices are up to date with the latest security patches is similar to checking your home's smoke detectors regularly; it's vital for maintaining a secure environment.

User Training: Providing user training is like teaching your family how to lock doors and windows; it empowers users to make informed decisions and recognize potential security threats.

Adaptive Security Measures: Much like adjusting your home security based on changing circumstances, adapting security measures to evolving threats is crucial to staying protected.

In essence, securing wireless networks is not unlike fortifying your home; it requires a combination of protective measures, user education, and vigilant monitoring to ensure a safe and secure digital environment. By implementing these strategies and staying informed about the latest security developments, you can build a strong defense against potential threats and enjoy the benefits of wireless connectivity with confidence.

Chapter 10: Developing Effective Network Defense Strategies

As we navigate the ever-evolving landscape of technology and connectivity, it's essential to understand that risks and challenges are an inherent part of our digital journey, much like the uncertainties we face in everyday life. Just as we take precautions to protect our homes from potential hazards, it's crucial to assess and mitigate risks in the digital realm to ensure a secure and resilient environment.

Risk assessment is like conducting a thorough inspection of your home to identify potential vulnerabilities and hazards. It involves evaluating various aspects of your digital landscape, including networks, systems, data, and processes, to determine the likelihood and impact of potential threats. This process allows you to prioritize risks and develop effective mitigation strategies.

One of the fundamental elements of risk assessment is identifying assets. Think of assets as the valuable possessions in your home. In the digital world, assets can be data, hardware, software, intellectual property, or even the reputation of your organization. Understanding what you need to protect is the first step in assessing risks.

Once you've identified your assets, it's essential to evaluate the threats they may face. These threats can be compared to the potential risks your home might face, such as burglary, fire, or natural disasters. In the digital domain, threats can take various forms, including cyberattacks, data breaches, malware infections, and even human errors.

The next aspect of risk assessment involves assessing vulnerabilities. Vulnerabilities can be likened to weak points in your home's security, such as unlocked doors or windows.

In the digital context, vulnerabilities can be software flaws, misconfigurations, outdated systems, or inadequate security measures that could be exploited by threats.

Now, let's talk about the likelihood and impact of risks. Imagine you're assessing the risk of a burglary in your neighborhood. You would consider factors like the crime rate, the presence of security measures, and the value of your possessions. Similarly, in risk assessment, you need to evaluate how likely it is for a threat to exploit a vulnerability and what the potential consequences would be.

Assessing the likelihood and impact of risks allows you to prioritize them. You can focus your resources and efforts on addressing the most critical risks, much like securing the most valuable possessions in your home first. This prioritization ensures that you allocate your resources effectively and efficiently.

Once you've identified and prioritized risks, it's time to develop mitigation strategies. Mitigation is like installing security systems, fire alarms, and locks in your home to reduce the risk of burglary and fire. In the digital realm, mitigation strategies involve implementing security controls, policies, and procedures to reduce the likelihood and impact of potential threats.

Security controls can be thought of as the locks, alarms, and security cameras of your digital environment. They include firewalls, intrusion detection systems, encryption, access controls, and antivirus software, among others. These controls are designed to safeguard your assets and protect them from various threats.

Policies and procedures are like the rules and guidelines you set for your home. In the digital world, they define how employees and users should handle data, access systems, and respond to security incidents. Well-defined policies and procedures are essential for maintaining a secure and compliant environment.

Risk mitigation is an ongoing process, much like the regular maintenance and updates you perform in your home. It's essential to continuously monitor your digital landscape, assess emerging threats, and adapt your mitigation strategies accordingly. This proactive approach helps you stay ahead of potential risks and vulnerabilities.

Now, let's delve into some common risk mitigation practices:

Patch Management: Regularly updating software and systems is like fixing a leaky roof in your home. Patch management involves applying security patches and updates to address known vulnerabilities and ensure that your digital environment remains secure.

User Training and Awareness: Educating users about security best practices is akin to teaching your family members how to use security systems in your home effectively. Well-informed users are less likely to fall victim to social engineering attacks and more likely to contribute to a secure environment.

Incident Response Planning: Having an incident response plan is like having a fire evacuation plan for your home. It ensures that you have a structured approach to detecting, responding to, and recovering from security incidents.

Regular Audits and Assessments: Conducting regular security audits and assessments is like periodically inspecting your home for potential issues. These assessments help you identify vulnerabilities and weaknesses that may need immediate attention.

Data Backups: Think of data backups as creating duplicates of your valuable documents and storing them in a secure location. Regular backups ensure that you can recover your data in case of data loss or ransomware attacks.

Access Control: Implementing access control measures is like installing locks on specific rooms in your home. It restricts access to sensitive data and systems to authorized users only.

Encryption: Encrypting sensitive data is akin to placing valuable items in a locked safe. It ensures that even if data is intercepted, it remains unreadable without the encryption key.

Vendor Security Evaluation: Evaluating the security practices of third-party vendors is like vetting contractors before hiring them to work on your home. It ensures that your partners meet security standards and won't introduce risks into your environment.

Business Continuity Planning: Developing a business continuity plan is like having a backup generator for your home. It ensures that your organization can continue operations in the face of disruptions, including security incidents.

Compliance with Regulations: Compliance with industry-specific regulations is like adhering to building codes in construction. It ensures that your organization meets legal and regulatory requirements related to security and privacy.

In summary, risk assessment and mitigation are essential components of maintaining a secure and resilient digital environment, much like securing and maintaining your home. By identifying, prioritizing, and addressing risks through security controls, policies, and procedures, you can protect your assets and enjoy the benefits of technology with confidence. Just as you take steps to protect your physical space, taking measures to safeguard your digital world is crucial in today's interconnected landscape. Embarking on the journey of security policy development is akin to crafting a set of rules and guidelines for your home to ensure the safety and well-being of your family. Much like creating house rules that govern behavior and protect against potential risks, security policies establish a framework for safeguarding your digital assets and maintaining a secure and compliant environment.

Security policies are the foundation of your organization's security posture, much like the blueprint of a well-constructed house. These policies define the principles, practices, and responsibilities that guide your organization's approach to security. They serve as a roadmap for decision-making and help establish a culture of security awareness and compliance.

The first step in security policy development is to understand your organization's unique needs and objectives, much like considering the specific needs and lifestyle of your family when setting household rules. To do this, you must conduct a thorough assessment of your organization's assets, risks, and compliance requirements.

Assets, in the context of security policies, can be compared to the valued possessions in your home. They encompass data, intellectual property, hardware, software, and even the reputation of your organization. Identifying these assets is crucial as it forms the basis for determining what needs protection.

Next, you must assess the risks your organization faces, much like evaluating potential hazards in your home. Risks in the digital realm include threats such as cyberattacks, data breaches, insider threats, and compliance violations. Evaluating the likelihood and potential impact of these risks helps prioritize security efforts.

Compliance requirements are similar to local building codes or safety regulations that dictate certain standards for your home. Depending on your industry and location, your organization may need to adhere to specific regulations, such as GDPR, HIPAA, or industry-specific standards like PCI

DSS. Understanding these requirements is essential for aligning your security policies with legal and industry standards.

With a clear understanding of your organization's needs, risks, and compliance requirements, you can begin crafting security policies that address these factors. Think of these policies as the house rules that establish the framework for a secure and compliant environment.

Acceptable Use Policy: This policy is like setting guidelines for how family members can use household resources. It defines acceptable and unacceptable behaviors related to the use of technology and digital resources within the organization.

Password Policy: Much like requiring family members to have their own keys to the house, a password policy dictates the rules for creating and managing passwords. It ensures that access to systems and data is protected by strong, unique passwords.

Data Classification and Handling Policy: Data classification is similar to categorizing items in your home based on their value and importance. This policy outlines how different types of data should be classified, handled, and protected based on their sensitivity.

Access Control Policy: Access control policies are like deciding who has access to different parts of your home. They specify how access to systems, data, and physical locations is granted, monitored, and revoked.

Incident Response Plan: Much like having a plan for emergencies at home, an incident response plan outlines how the organization should respond to security incidents. It includes procedures for detecting, reporting, and mitigating security breaches.

Security Awareness and Training Policy: Just as you might educate family members about safety measures at home, this policy ensures that employees receive training and education on security best practices.

Remote Work and Bring Your Own Device (BYOD) Policy: These policies are akin to setting rules for guests or housemates in your home. They establish guidelines for remote work and the use of personal devices within the organization while maintaining security standards.

Encryption Policy: Encryption policies are like locking valuable items in a safe. They specify when and how encryption should be applied to protect sensitive data.

Vendor Management Policy: This policy is similar to vetting contractors before allowing them to work on your home. It defines the criteria and processes for evaluating and managing third-party vendors' security practices.

Physical Security Policy: Physical security policies are like setting up security systems in your home. They outline measures to protect physical assets, including access control, surveillance, and security personnel.

Compliance Policy: Compliance policies are akin to ensuring your home complies with local regulations. They detail how the organization will meet legal and regulatory requirements related to security and privacy.

Privacy Policy: Privacy policies are like respecting the privacy of family members in your home. They define how personal information is collected, stored, and used, ensuring compliance with data protection laws.

Asset Management Policy: Asset management policies are akin to keeping an inventory of valuable items in your home. They establish procedures for tracking and managing digital assets, including hardware, software, and data.

Business Continuity and Disaster Recovery Policy: These policies are like having a contingency plan for emergencies in your home. They outline strategies for ensuring business continuity in the face of disruptions, including data backups and recovery procedures.

Audit and Monitoring Policy: Audit and monitoring policies are akin to installing security cameras and alarms in your home. They define how the organization will monitor and audit systems, networks, and user activities to detect and respond to security threats.

Security policies, much like the house rules you establish, should be communicated, understood, and followed by all members of your organization. Regular updates and reviews are essential to ensure that policies remain effective in addressing emerging threats and changing business needs.

In summary, security policy development is a vital aspect of maintaining a secure and compliant digital environment, much like creating and enforcing household rules to ensure the well-being of your family. By crafting policies that align with your organization's unique needs, risks, and compliance requirements, you establish a strong foundation for security and foster a culture of awareness and compliance. Just as a well-protected home provides a sense of security and peace, robust security policies offer protection and confidence in the digital world.

BOOK 3
ADVANCED NETWORK DEFENSE STRATEGIES MITIGATING SOPHISTICATED ATTACKS

ROB BOTWRIGHT

Chapter 1: Evolving Threat Landscape: Recognizing Advanced Attacks

In the ever-evolving landscape of cyberspace, it's crucial to be aware of the constantly emerging cyber threats, much like staying vigilant for new and unexpected challenges in our daily lives. These evolving threats pose risks to individuals, organizations, and even nations, underscoring the need for proactive and adaptive cybersecurity measures. Imagine navigating a busy city where you encounter new traffic patterns, construction zones, and potential hazards regularly. Similarly, the digital world presents a dynamic environment where cyber threats continuously adapt, innovate, and exploit vulnerabilities. As we explore these emerging cyber threats, it's essential to be equipped with knowledge and strategies to mitigate the risks effectively.

One of the prominent emerging threats in recent years is the rise of sophisticated and targeted cyberattacks, akin to encountering skilled and strategic adversaries in a competitive sport. These attacks often leverage advanced techniques, such as zero-day exploits, which target vulnerabilities unknown to the public or the organization affected. To defend against such threats, organizations must maintain a robust patch management process and stay informed about the latest security updates.

Another concerning trend is the proliferation of ransomware attacks, much like dealing with hostage situations in real life. Ransomware is malicious software that encrypts a victim's data and demands a ransom for decryption. These attacks have become more prevalent, and cybercriminals have adopted double-extortion tactics, threatening to leak sensitive data if the ransom is not paid. Protection against ransomware requires a combination of robust backup strategies, security awareness training, and endpoint protection.

In the interconnected digital world, supply chain attacks have emerged as a significant threat, much like safeguarding the integrity of the products you purchase. Cybercriminals target the software and hardware supply chain to compromise products before they even reach end-users. Defending against supply chain attacks involves thorough vetting of suppliers, monitoring for suspicious activities, and implementing robust access controls.

The Internet of Things (IoT) has brought convenience to our lives, but it has also introduced new vulnerabilities and attack vectors, similar to using smart devices in our homes. Insecure IoT devices can become entry points for cybercriminals into home and corporate networks. Protecting against IoT threats entails proper device management, segmentation of IoT networks, and regular security updates.

As organizations increasingly adopt cloud services for their data storage and computing needs, cloud security has become a top concern, much like safeguarding valuable assets stored in a remote location. Misconfigurations and inadequate security practices can expose sensitive data to the public or unauthorized users. Effective cloud security involves proper configuration, monitoring, and access control within cloud environments.

Phishing attacks have evolved beyond generic email scams, similar to deceptive tactics used by con artists in various scenarios. Spear phishing, for instance, targets specific individuals or organizations, often with highly tailored and convincing messages. Staying vigilant against phishing threats requires security awareness training, email filtering, and multi-factor authentication.

The digital world is not limited to traditional computing devices; it now includes mobile devices, which have become a primary target for cyberattacks, much like safeguarding personal belongings in a crowded public space. Mobile malware, malicious apps, and unsecured Wi-Fi networks can put sensitive data at risk. Mobile security measures include regular updates, app vetting, and secure network usage.

The use of artificial intelligence (AI) and machine learning in cyberattacks is a growing concern, similar to facing adversaries who employ advanced tactics and strategies. Cybercriminals can use AI to automate attacks, evade detection, and personalize their threats. Protecting against AI-driven attacks involves deploying AI-powered defenses and continuously improving threat detection capabilities.

Deepfakes, which involve the manipulation of audio and video content to create realistic but fabricated media, pose a unique challenge, much like distinguishing between genuine and counterfeit items. Deepfakes can be used for identity theft, misinformation, and social engineering attacks. Defending against deepfakes requires media authentication tools and critical thinking.

The convergence of cyber and physical threats, known as cyber-physical attacks, is another emerging concern, similar to addressing threats that have real-world consequences. These attacks can target critical infrastructure, autonomous vehicles, and industrial control systems. Mitigating cyber-physical risks demands robust security measures, including network segmentation and intrusion detection.

As we navigate this evolving landscape of emerging cyber threats, it's essential to adopt a proactive and adaptive cybersecurity posture, much like developing a keen awareness of potential risks in our daily lives. This includes continuous monitoring of the threat landscape, regular security assessments, and the implementation of best practices and technologies to protect against evolving threats.

In summary, the digital world presents a dynamic and ever-changing environment where cyber threats continually evolve and adapt. Being aware of these emerging threats and taking proactive measures to protect against them is essential for individuals, organizations, and society as a whole. By staying informed, implementing effective cybersecurity measures, and fostering a culture of security awareness, we can navigate this digital landscape with confidence and resilience, much like we do in our everyday lives.

Advanced attacks in the realm of cybersecurity possess distinct characteristics that set them apart from common threats, much like skilled artisans who employ unique techniques to create exceptional works of art. Understanding these characteristics is crucial for organizations and individuals to enhance their defense strategies and protect their digital assets effectively.

First and foremost, advanced attacks are characterized by their sophistication and complexity, much like intricate puzzles or challenging riddles that demand creative problem-solving. These attacks often involve multiple stages, intricate coding, and the use of advanced techniques to evade detection. Cybercriminals behind these attacks are akin to master craftsmen who meticulously plan and execute their strategies.

One hallmark of advanced attacks is their ability to remain covert and stealthy, similar to a skilled magician who performs tricks without revealing the secrets behind them. Attackers often employ techniques to blend in with legitimate network traffic, making it challenging for security teams to detect their presence. This stealthiness allows them to stay undetected for extended periods, increasing the potential damage they can inflict.

Advanced attacks also exhibit adaptability and resilience, much like seasoned athletes who adjust their strategies in response to changing game conditions. When confronted with security measures or countermeasures, attackers may alter their tactics, switch to new attack vectors, or change their attack infrastructure. This adaptability makes it difficult for defenders to predict and mitigate these attacks effectively.

Another characteristic of advanced attacks is their use of zero-day vulnerabilities, which are akin to secret weapons in a spy's arsenal. Zero-day vulnerabilities are flaws in software or hardware that are unknown to the vendor or have not yet been patched. Attackers exploit these vulnerabilities to gain unauthorized access or compromise systems, often with devastating consequences. The term "zero-day" refers to the fact that there are zero days of protection against such vulnerabilities until a patch is released.

Advanced attacks often involve meticulous reconnaissance, much like intelligence agents gathering information before executing a mission. Attackers conduct thorough research to gather information about their target's infrastructure, vulnerabilities, and security measures. This reconnaissance phase helps them tailor their attacks for maximum impact and evasion.

Social engineering is another hallmark of advanced attacks, similar to skilled persuaders who can influence others with their words and actions. Attackers use social engineering tactics to manipulate individuals into divulging sensitive information or performing actions that compromise security. These tactics can range from phishing emails to sophisticated spear-phishing campaigns that target specific individuals.

Many advanced attacks are financially motivated, much like elaborate heists or embezzlement schemes in the physical world. Cybercriminals seek financial gain by stealing sensitive data, conducting fraudulent transactions, or extorting victims through tactics like ransomware. The monetary incentives drive them to continuously refine their attack techniques and find new vulnerabilities to exploit.

Advanced attacks often employ encryption and obfuscation techniques, similar to coded messages that only the intended recipient can decipher. Attackers use encryption to hide their malicious activities and evade detection by security solutions. Decrypting these communications requires advanced threat detection capabilities and the ability to analyze encrypted traffic without compromising privacy.

These attacks are not limited by geography or borders, much like global espionage operations that transcend international boundaries. Cybercriminals can launch advanced attacks from anywhere in the world, making it challenging to track and apprehend them. This global reach enables attackers to target organizations and individuals regardless of their location.

The motivation behind advanced attacks varies, much like the diverse motivations that drive individuals in the physical world. While some attacks are financially motivated, others may be politically driven, ideologically motivated, or intended to disrupt critical infrastructure. Understanding the attackers' motivations is essential for predicting their behavior and mitigating potential threats.

In summary, advanced attacks in the realm of cybersecurity possess unique characteristics that distinguish them from common threats. These attacks are characterized by their sophistication, stealthiness, adaptability, use of zero-day vulnerabilities, meticulous reconnaissance, social engineering tactics, financial motivation, encryption and obfuscation techniques, global reach, and diverse motivations. Recognizing these characteristics is crucial for developing effective defense strategies and safeguarding digital assets against the ever-evolving landscape of advanced cyber threats.

Chapter 2: Threat Intelligence and Proactive Defense

Understanding and leveraging threat intelligence sources is like having a reliable network of informants in the world of cybersecurity, providing critical insights and early warnings about potential threats. These sources are essential for organizations and individuals looking to enhance their cybersecurity posture by staying ahead of emerging threats.

Imagine threat intelligence sources as a vast library filled with valuable information about cyber threats. This information comes from various channels, including government agencies, cybersecurity firms, open-source communities, and industry-specific organizations. These sources collect, analyze, and disseminate data on known threats, emerging vulnerabilities, and malicious actors.

One primary source of threat intelligence is government agencies and law enforcement organizations, much like law enforcement agencies sharing information about criminal activity. These entities often gather intelligence on cyber threats with a focus on national security and public safety. They share this information with other government agencies and private-sector organizations to enhance overall cybersecurity.

Cybersecurity firms and vendors play a significant role in threat intelligence, similar to experts in a specific field sharing their knowledge. These companies monitor global cyber threats, conduct research on malware, vulnerabilities, and attack techniques, and provide regular updates to their customers. Subscribing to threat intelligence services from these firms can help organizations proactively defend against threats.

The open-source community contributes valuable threat intelligence, much like volunteers who collaborate to solve common challenges. Open-source threat intelligence platforms and communities share information about known threats, malware signatures, and detection techniques. These resources are freely available and can be a valuable asset for organizations with limited resources.

Industry-specific organizations and information sharing and analysis centers (ISACs) provide sector-specific threat intelligence, much like industry experts sharing insights with their peers. These organizations collect data on threats targeting specific industries, such as finance, healthcare, or energy. Participating in ISACs allows organizations to receive tailored threat intelligence relevant to their sector.

Dark web monitoring is another crucial source of threat intelligence, similar to undercover agents gathering intelligence from the criminal underworld. The dark web is a hidden part of the internet where cybercriminals conduct illicit activities, such as selling stolen data, hacking tools, and services. Monitoring the dark web can provide early warnings about potential threats and data breaches.

Open-source intelligence (OSINT) is a valuable resource for threat intelligence, much like investigative journalists uncovering hidden information. OSINT involves collecting and analyzing publicly available information from various sources, including social media, forums, and websites. This information can help identify potential threats and malicious actors.

Collaborative threat intelligence sharing platforms bring together organizations to share threat information and collaborate on defense strategies, much like a neighborhood watch program. These platforms enable participating organizations to exchange threat data and benefit from collective knowledge, helping them respond to threats more effectively.

Threat intelligence feeds are automated sources of threat data, much like automated sensors detecting environmental changes. These feeds provide real-time information on known threats, such as malicious IP addresses, domains, and file hashes. Integrating threat intelligence feeds into security solutions allows organizations to block known threats proactively.

Threat intelligence platforms (TIPs) are comprehensive tools that facilitate the collection, analysis, and dissemination of threat intelligence, much like a command center coordinating responses to emergencies. TIPs help organizations centralize threat data, automate analysis, and share intelligence with relevant stakeholders. They play a crucial role in managing and operationalizing threat intelligence.

Machine learning and artificial intelligence (AI) are increasingly used to analyze and derive insights from threat intelligence data, much like data scientists uncover patterns in vast datasets. These technologies can identify trends, anomalies, and potential threats more efficiently than manual analysis. They are valuable assets in the proactive defense against emerging threats.

Threat intelligence can also be derived from internal sources within an organization, such as logs, incident reports, and security alerts, much like a detective investigating a crime scene. Analyzing internal data can help organizations identify suspicious activities and potential threats originating from within their network.

In summary, leveraging threat intelligence sources is a crucial aspect of modern cybersecurity. These sources, including government agencies, cybersecurity firms, open-source communities, industry-specific organizations, dark web monitoring, OSINT, collaborative sharing platforms, threat intelligence feeds, TIPs, machine learning, AI, and internal data sources, provide valuable insights and early warnings about cyber threats. By harnessing these sources and integrating threat intelligence into their security strategies, organizations can proactively defend against emerging threats and enhance their overall cybersecurity posture.

Proactive defense strategies in the realm of cybersecurity are like setting up a strong perimeter and employing vigilant guards to deter potential intruders from entering your castle. These strategies focus on taking preemptive measures to prevent cyberattacks and minimize their impact, rather than merely reacting to incidents as they occur.

Think of proactive defense as an early warning system that helps you anticipate and prepare for threats before they materialize. It involves several key components, each contributing to a robust cybersecurity posture.

One fundamental aspect of proactive defense is threat intelligence, akin to receiving timely information about potential dangers in your vicinity. Threat intelligence sources, which include government agencies, cybersecurity firms, open-source communities, and industry-specific organizations, provide valuable insights into emerging threats, vulnerabilities, and malicious actors. By staying informed through threat intelligence, organizations can proactively identify and address potential risks.

Vulnerability management is another critical component of proactive defense, much like inspecting the walls and gates of your castle for weak points. Regular vulnerability assessments and penetration testing help organizations discover and patch security flaws before cybercriminals can exploit them. This proactive approach reduces the attack surface and strengthens the overall security posture.

Access control and privilege management are essential for proactive defense, similar to controlling who has access to certain areas within your castle. Implementing strong authentication mechanisms, role-based access controls, and the principle of least privilege ensures that only authorized individuals can access sensitive data and systems. This reduces the risk of unauthorized access and data breaches.

Proactive defense also involves continuous monitoring and anomaly detection, much like having guards patrolling your castle grounds for any unusual activities. Security information and event management (SIEM) systems, intrusion detection systems (IDS), and user behavior analytics (UBA) tools help organizations detect suspicious activities and potential threats in real-time. Early detection allows for swift response and mitigation.

Education and awareness training are crucial components of proactive defense, similar to instructing the inhabitants of your castle on security protocols and how to recognize potential threats. Cybersecurity awareness programs educate employees about safe online practices, social engineering tactics, and the importance of reporting suspicious activities. Well-informed employees are an organization's first line of defense.

Regular security audits and compliance assessments are proactive measures that ensure adherence to security policies and regulations, much like conducting regular safety inspections in your castle. These audits help organizations identify gaps in their security controls, assess compliance with industry standards, and make necessary improvements to maintain a strong defense.

Incident response planning is a critical part of proactive defense, akin to having a well-defined emergency protocol in case of an attack. Organizations should develop comprehensive incident response plans that outline the steps to take when a security incident occurs. These plans include communication strategies, containment procedures, and recovery processes to minimize the impact of an incident.

Data encryption and data loss prevention (DLP) measures are proactive defenses that protect sensitive information, similar to safeguarding valuable treasures within your castle's vault. Encrypting data at rest and in transit ensures that even if it falls into the wrong hands, it remains unreadable. DLP technologies help organizations prevent the unauthorized sharing or leakage of sensitive data.

Security by design is a proactive approach that integrates security considerations into the development of software and systems, much like designing a castle with security in mind from the beginning. By implementing secure coding practices, conducting code reviews, and performing security testing during the development lifecycle, organizations can create more resilient and less vulnerable applications.

Regular security awareness training is vital for proactive defense, similar to providing ongoing training for the guards protecting your castle. Security teams must stay up-to-date with the latest threats, attack techniques, and security best practices. Continuous training helps security professionals make informed decisions and adapt to evolving threats.

Collaboration and information sharing with industry peers are proactive measures that help organizations collectively defend against common threats, much like neighboring castles sharing intelligence to protect the region. Industry-specific information sharing and analysis centers (ISACs) facilitate the exchange of threat intelligence and best practices among organizations within the same sector.

In summary, proactive defense strategies in cybersecurity involve a multifaceted approach to preventing and mitigating cyber threats. These strategies encompass threat intelligence, vulnerability management, access control, monitoring, education, security audits, incident response planning, data encryption, security by design, continuous training, and collaboration with industry peers. By adopting a proactive mindset and implementing these measures, organizations can significantly enhance their ability to defend against cyberattacks and safeguard their digital assets.

Chapter 3: Advanced Intrusion Detection and Prevention Systems

Imagine intrusion detection systems (IDS) and intrusion prevention systems (IPS) as vigilant guards stationed at the entrances and throughout the corridors of your digital castle, tirelessly monitoring for signs of unauthorized access or suspicious activities. These technologies play a pivotal role in modern cybersecurity, helping organizations identify and thwart potential threats in real-time.

Let's start with intrusion detection systems (IDS), which are like sentries patrolling your castle walls, keeping a watchful eye for any unusual movements. IDS are security tools that monitor network traffic and system activities for signs of unauthorized access, attacks, or anomalies. Their primary function is to detect and alert security teams to potential security incidents. Think of IDS as your digital security sentinels, always on the lookout for suspicious behavior.

Intrusion detection systems operate using two primary methods: signature-based and anomaly-based detection. Signature-based detection is akin to recognizing specific patterns or behaviors that are known to be indicative of attacks. Much like recognizing the banner of a rival kingdom's army approaching your castle, IDS with signature databases identify known attack patterns and trigger alerts when they match.

Anomaly-based detection, on the other hand, is more like having guards who notice when something seems out of place within the castle grounds. IDS using anomaly detection algorithms establish a baseline of normal network or system behavior. When they detect deviations from this baseline, they raise alarms. This approach is particularly useful for identifying new or previously unknown threats.

Now, let's talk about intrusion prevention systems (IPS), which are like those same vigilant guards, but with the added capability to take immediate action to stop threats in their tracks. IPS builds upon IDS by not only detecting suspicious activities but also actively blocking or mitigating them. Think of IPS as your digital knights who can spring into action when a threat is identified.

IPS employs various techniques to prevent or mitigate attacks. One common method is signature-based blocking, which is similar to recognizing known attack patterns and immediately blocking traffic associated with them. It's like your knights swiftly intercepting the enemy at the gates and preventing them from entering the castle.

Another technique used by IPS is anomaly-based blocking, much like guards responding when they notice something unusual. IPS with anomaly detection capabilities can take action when deviations from the baseline are detected, helping to stop potentially harmful activities before they cause damage.

In addition to signature and anomaly-based methods, IPS can use reputation-based blocking. This is akin to knowing the reputations of travelers approaching your castle and allowing or denying them entry based on their history. IPS can assess the reputation of IP addresses, domains, or files and block those with a bad reputation.

Now, consider intrusion detection and prevention as a well-coordinated team of guards and knights working together to protect your castle. This combination of IDS and IPS, often referred to as intrusion detection and prevention systems (IDPS), provides a comprehensive defense against a wide range of threats. IDPS can operate at various levels within your network, from the perimeter to internal segments, just like assigning guards and knights to different areas of your castle. Some IDPS are network-based, monitoring network traffic and activities, while others are host-based, focusing on individual systems and endpoints.

A critical aspect of IDS and IPS is their ability to generate alerts and reports, much like guards and knights reporting incidents and activities to the castle's leadership. These alerts provide security teams with valuable information about potential threats, allowing them to investigate and respond promptly. Additionally, IDPS can log events for forensic analysis and compliance purposes, ensuring that any security incidents are thoroughly documented.

Intrusion detection and prevention systems are not static; they evolve to keep pace with emerging threats, much like your castle's defenses adapting to new siege tactics. Regular updates to signature databases and detection algorithms are essential to ensure that IDS and IPS can effectively identify and mitigate the latest threats.

To implement IDS and IPS effectively, organizations must consider factors such as the placement of sensors (the locations where monitoring occurs), the tuning of detection rules (to reduce false positives), and the response strategies (how and when to take action). It's like strategically positioning guards and knights, training them to recognize friend from foe, and defining rules of engagement.

In summary, IDS and IPS technologies are like the vigilant guards and knights defending your digital castle. IDS detects and alerts security teams to potential threats, while IPS takes immediate action to block or mitigate those threats. Together, they form a dynamic defense that helps organizations protect their networks and systems from cyberattacks. Just as a well-trained and coordinated team of guards and knights is essential for the security of a medieval castle, IDS and IPS are crucial components of modern cybersecurity, safeguarding digital assets from intruders and threats.

Fine-tuning intrusion detection and prevention (IDP) systems is like meticulously adjusting the sensitivity and response capabilities of your castle's guards and knights to ensure optimal security without unnecessary disruptions. This process involves optimizing the settings and configurations of your IDP systems to strike a balance between robust threat detection and minimizing false alarms.

Imagine you have a team of castle guards tasked with monitoring the castle's perimeter. Initially, they may be a bit too alert, raising alarms at every rustling leaf or distant noise. This hyper-vigilance can lead to a flood of false alarms, causing confusion and reducing the effectiveness of the guard team.

In a similar way, when setting up an IDP system, it's essential to strike the right balance between sensitivity and accuracy. The sensitivity of an IDP system determines how closely it scrutinizes network traffic and system activities for potential threats. A highly sensitive IDP system may flag a wide range of behaviors as suspicious, while a less sensitive one might only detect the most obvious threats. Fine-tuning begins with understanding your network and its normal behavior patterns. It's akin to the castle's guards getting to know the routine activities within the castle walls, such as when merchants arrive, when the gates open, and when residents move about. In the context of an IDP system, this means establishing a baseline of what constitutes normal network and system behavior.

To create this baseline, you'll need to analyze historical network traffic and system logs, much like studying the castle's daily activities over time. By identifying what is typical and expected, you can define parameters that help the IDP system differentiate between normal and abnormal behavior.

Once you've established a baseline, it's time to fine-tune the IDP system's detection rules, much like instructing the guards on which behaviors to pay special attention to. Detection rules are specific criteria or patterns that the IDP system uses to identify potential threats. These rules can range from simple signature-based rules, which look for known attack patterns, to more complex behavior-based rules that detect deviations from the established baseline. Think of detection rules as guidelines for your guards on what to watch out for: unauthorized access attempts, unusual data transfer patterns, or suspicious user behavior. Fine-tuning these rules involves adjusting their parameters to reduce false positives (incorrectly identifying normal behavior as a threat) and false negatives (failing to detect actual threats).

Fine-tuning also entails configuring the response actions that the IDP system should take when it identifies a potential threat, similar to defining how your knights should respond to different types of intrusions. Response actions can include blocking network traffic associated with the threat, generating alerts for security teams, or logging the event for further analysis.

While it's crucial to optimize sensitivity and detection rules, you should also consider the impact of response actions on your network's functionality and performance. Blocking legitimate traffic or generating excessive alerts can disrupt normal operations, much like overzealous guards causing inconvenience to residents and visitors of the castle.

Regular monitoring and review of the IDP system's performance are essential, much like evaluating the effectiveness of your guards' adjustments over time. By analyzing the system's alerts and responses, you can identify areas where further fine-tuning may be needed. This iterative process ensures that the IDP system remains aligned with the evolving threat landscape and network dynamics. Furthermore, collaboration and knowledge sharing within your organization and with industry peers are valuable resources in fine-tuning your IDP system. Just as knights in neighboring castles might exchange information about new siege tactics, cybersecurity professionals can benefit from insights and best practices shared within the cybersecurity community.

In summary, fine-tuning intrusion detection and prevention systems is a critical aspect of cybersecurity, much like ensuring your castle's guards and knights are finely attuned to the threats they face. It involves balancing sensitivity, optimizing detection rules, and carefully configuring response actions to enhance threat detection while minimizing false alarms. Regular monitoring and collaboration with industry peers ensure that your IDP system remains effective in safeguarding your digital assets from evolving threats. Much like the well-adjusted and vigilant guards and knights, a finely tuned IDP system plays a pivotal role in the overall security posture of your organization.

Chapter 4: Security Information and Event Management (SIEM)

Let's delve into the world of Security Information and Event Management, or SIEM, which is like having a skilled and attentive scribe in your medieval castle, diligently recording every event, no matter how small or significant, to maintain a comprehensive record of all activities within the kingdom.
Imagine your castle as a bustling hub of activity, with knights patrolling the walls, guards monitoring the gates, and residents going about their daily lives. There's a lot happening, and it's crucial to keep track of everything to maintain order and security.

In the digital realm, organizations face a similar challenge. Networks are constantly in motion, with data flowing in and out, devices connecting, and users interacting. It's vital to have a way to capture, analyze, and interpret this vast amount of data to ensure the security and integrity of the digital kingdom.
This is where SIEM comes into play. SIEM solutions are like the diligent scribes of the digital age, tasked with collecting, organizing, and analyzing the vast amount of security-related data generated by various systems, devices, and applications within an organization's network.
SIEM systems are designed to aggregate data from multiple sources, much like our medieval scribe compiling information from various scrolls and parchments. These sources include firewalls, antivirus software, intrusion detection systems, and more. SIEM centralizes this data, creating a unified view of the organization's security posture.

Now, think of your scribe carefully examining each piece of information, identifying patterns, and noting any anomalies or suspicious activities. SIEM solutions perform a similar function by analyzing the collected data to detect security incidents, policy violations, or potential threats.

To achieve this, SIEM systems use various techniques, including correlation, which is like your scribe connecting related events to uncover hidden insights. Correlation in SIEM involves identifying patterns and relationships between seemingly unrelated events to uncover potential security threats.

For example, if a SIEM system detects multiple failed login attempts from different IP addresses followed by an unusually large data transfer, it might correlate these events to recognize a potential brute-force attack and generate an alert.

In addition to correlation, SIEM solutions also employ real-time monitoring, which is akin to our diligent scribe keeping an eye on current events within the kingdom. Real-time monitoring allows SIEM systems to detect and respond to security incidents as they happen, providing organizations with the ability to take immediate action to mitigate threats.

As data is continuously collected and analyzed, SIEM systems generate alerts and reports, much like the scribe documenting noteworthy events and creating records. These alerts are sent to security teams, enabling them to investigate and respond to potential security incidents promptly.

SIEM solutions also play a crucial role in compliance and reporting, similar to how the scribe maintains records for historical and legal purposes. Many organizations are subject to regulatory requirements that mandate the monitoring and reporting of security-related events. SIEM systems provide the necessary tools to generate compliance reports and demonstrate adherence to security standards.

Now, imagine your diligent scribe not only recording events but also providing insights and recommendations based on the information gathered. SIEM solutions offer advanced features such as threat intelligence integration, which is like your scribe consulting with experts to stay updated on the latest developments. Threat intelligence feeds provide SIEM systems with information about emerging threats and vulnerabilities, enhancing their ability to detect and respond to new attack techniques.

Another crucial aspect of SIEM is the ability to create custom rules and policies, much like instructing your scribe to pay special attention to specific types of events or activities. Organizations can define their own rules and policies within the SIEM system to tailor it to their unique security requirements.

SIEM solutions are highly versatile and can be scaled to meet the needs of organizations of all sizes. Whether you have a small digital kingdom or a vast digital empire, SIEM can be customized to align with your specific security objectives.

In summary, Security Information and Event Management (SIEM) solutions are like diligent scribes in the digital age, tasked with collecting, analyzing, and interpreting vast amounts of security-related data to maintain the security and integrity of the digital kingdom. SIEM centralizes data from multiple sources, performs correlation and real-time monitoring, generates alerts, and facilitates compliance reporting. With the ability to integrate threat intelligence and customize rules, SIEM systems are essential tools in the ongoing battle to protect digital assets and ensure the safety of the digital realm. Much like a skilled and attentive scribe, SIEM solutions provide invaluable insights and support to security teams in their mission to safeguard the organization's digital infrastructure.

Let's embark on a journey into the realm of SIEM implementation and optimization, a process akin to constructing a fortified castle that not only defends against external threats but also stands resilient against the test of time.

Picture yourself as the lord of a digital fortress, determined to safeguard your kingdom's treasures and secrets. Just as a castle requires careful planning, skilled craftsmen, and strategic fortifications, implementing a Security Information and Event Management (SIEM) system demands a thoughtful approach and expert guidance.

The first step in SIEM implementation is defining your objectives, much like establishing the purpose and goals of your castle. What do you aim to achieve with your SIEM system? Are you primarily focused on threat detection, compliance, or both? These goals will shape your SIEM strategy and help you select the right tools and resources.

Next, consider the architecture of your digital fortress. SIEM systems can be deployed on-premises, in the cloud, or in a hybrid environment, similar to deciding whether to build your castle on a hill, in a valley, or a combination of both. The choice depends on your organization's infrastructure, scalability requirements, and compliance considerations.

Once you've settled on the architectural design, it's time to assemble the right team of experts, just as a castle requires skilled craftsmen and architects. SIEM implementation is a complex endeavor, and having a knowledgeable team is essential. This team may include security analysts, network engineers, and SIEM administrators who will work together to design, deploy, and manage the system.

As you begin building your digital fortress, think of data sources as the eyes and ears of your castle's guards. SIEM systems rely on data from various sources, such as firewalls, antivirus software, intrusion detection systems, and logs. You'll need to configure these sources to send their data to the SIEM, similar to instructing your guards to report any unusual activities.

Integration is a critical aspect of SIEM implementation, much like ensuring that the drawbridge, gates, and walls of your castle work seamlessly together. Your SIEM system should integrate with existing security tools, allowing for a holistic view of your digital kingdom's security posture.

Once the data starts flowing into your SIEM, it's time to configure the system's detection rules and correlation policies. These are the rules of engagement for your digital guards, specifying what behaviors and events should trigger alerts and investigations. Much like knights being briefed on their duties, your SIEM system needs clear instructions to identify threats accurately.

Consider your SIEM system's dashboards and reporting capabilities as the watchtowers and battlements of your digital fortress. Security analysts will rely on these interfaces to monitor and respond to alerts, similar to guards surveying the castle walls for potential threats.

Training and education are crucial for the success of your SIEM implementation, just as knights undergo rigorous training to defend the castle. Ensure that your security team is well-versed in using the SIEM system and interpreting its alerts.

Continuous refinement and optimization are essential aspects of SIEM deployment. Much like maintaining and fortifying your physical castle over time, your SIEM system requires ongoing attention. Regularly review and update detection rules, correlation policies, and reporting mechanisms to adapt to evolving threats.

Think of compliance requirements as the laws and regulations governing your digital kingdom. Your SIEM system should assist in compliance efforts by providing the necessary reports and documentation, much like keeping meticulous records to satisfy the kingdom's authorities.

Optimizing your SIEM system involves fine-tuning its performance, enhancing its detection capabilities, and reducing false positives. This process is akin to reinforcing your castle's defenses and training your knights to be even more vigilant.

Integration with threat intelligence feeds is a valuable strategy, similar to receiving intelligence reports about potential threats from neighboring kingdoms. Threat intelligence enriches your SIEM's ability to detect emerging threats and vulnerabilities.

Consider leveraging automation and orchestration capabilities within your SIEM system. Automation is like adding mechanical traps and defenses to your castle, allowing for rapid response to threats without manual intervention.

Regular audits and assessments of your SIEM implementation are like security inspections of your castle's defenses. These reviews help identify vulnerabilities and areas for improvement.

In summary, SIEM implementation and optimization are critical for building a resilient digital fortress that can withstand modern cyber threats. Just as a castle requires careful planning, skilled craftsmen, and ongoing maintenance, a SIEM system demands a thoughtful approach, expert guidance, and continuous refinement. By defining objectives, assembling a skilled team, integrating data sources, configuring detection rules, and staying vigilant against emerging threats, organizations can harness the power of SIEM to defend their digital kingdoms effectively. Much like the lord of a well-fortified castle, those who implement and optimize SIEM systems are better equipped to safeguard their digital assets and maintain the security and integrity of their domains.

Chapter 5: Application Layer Security: Protecting Critical Services

Let's explore the fascinating world of Application Layer Attacks, a topic that's akin to unraveling the intricacies of a magician's sleight of hand. In the realm of cybersecurity, the Application Layer is where the digital magic happens, but it's also where adversaries may attempt to deceive, disrupt, or exploit vulnerabilities.

Think of the Application Layer as the topmost layer of the OSI model, much like the performer's stage where the magic tricks are showcased. This layer deals with the communication between software applications and services running on different devices across a network. It's where web browsers interact with websites, email clients send and receive messages, and where you access various online services.

Now, consider the applications and services within this layer as the main acts of our digital magic show. These applications are designed to provide valuable functionality to users, such as web browsing, email communication, and file sharing. However, they also represent a potential target for attackers who aim to exploit weaknesses in the code or the way these applications interact with users and other systems.

One common form of Application Layer Attack is the infamous Distributed Denial of Service (DDoS) attack, which is like a magician creating a diversion to draw the audience's attention away from the real trick. In a DDoS attack, a flood of malicious traffic is directed at a web server or application, overwhelming it and causing it to become unavailable to legitimate users. It's a diversionary tactic, diverting the focus from the real objective of the attacker, which may be to steal sensitive data or compromise the server's security.

Cross-Site Scripting (XSS) is another type of Application Layer Attack, akin to a magician secretly planting a message in the audience's minds. In XSS attacks, malicious scripts are injected into web applications, which then execute these scripts on the browsers of unsuspecting users. This can result in the theft of sensitive information, such as login credentials or personal data, or the manipulation of website content seen by users.

SQL Injection is like a magic trick where the magician manipulates the order of cards in a deck. In SQL Injection attacks, malicious SQL queries are inserted into web application inputs, taking advantage of poor input validation and allowing attackers to access, modify, or delete database information. It's a clever sleight of hand, as the attacker gains unauthorized access to valuable data.

Imagine an attacker masquerading as an audience member who infiltrates the backstage of a magic show; this is similar to what happens in a Man-in-the-Middle (MitM) attack at the Application Layer. In a MitM attack, the attacker intercepts and possibly alters the communication between two parties, often without either party realizing it. This can lead to eavesdropping, data manipulation, or even the theft of sensitive information.

Brute-Force attacks in the Application Layer are like attempting to guess the magician's secrets through sheer persistence. Attackers use automated tools to repeatedly guess passwords or access codes, hoping to gain unauthorized entry into a system or account. It's a straightforward but often effective approach for attackers.

Consider Clickjacking as a digital illusion where the magician deceives the audience into clicking on something they didn't intend to. Clickjacking involves disguising a malicious action as something benign or enticing, tricking users into clicking on elements on a web page without their knowledge. This can lead to unintended actions, such as liking a social media post or unknowingly making a purchase.

File Upload attacks are like the magician switching out a prop with a look-alike during a performance. In these attacks, malicious files are uploaded to web applications that allow user-generated content. Once uploaded, these files may contain malware or execute malicious code, compromising the security of the hosting server.

Credential Stuffing is akin to an attacker trying different keys to open a magical lock. In this type of attack, attackers use stolen username and password combinations obtained from previous data breaches to gain unauthorized access to user accounts on various websites and services. It relies on the unfortunate habit of many users who reuse passwords across multiple platforms.

As we unravel the secrets of Application Layer Attacks, it becomes clear that defending against these digital deceptions requires a combination of vigilant monitoring, robust security measures, and user education. Organizations must implement strong security practices, such as input validation, encryption, and access controls, to protect their applications. Additionally, user awareness and education play a crucial role in preventing attacks like phishing and Clickjacking.

Much like a magician who constantly refines their tricks to stay ahead of their audience's expectations, cybersecurity professionals must stay informed about the latest attack techniques and evolving threats. By understanding the intricacies of Application Layer Attacks, organizations can better defend their digital assets and ensure that the magic of the digital world remains safe and secure for all.

Let's delve into the fascinating world of implementing application security controls, where we embark on a journey akin to fortifying a medieval castle against relentless attackers. In the digital age, applications are the lifeblood of organizations, serving as gateways to critical data and services. However, just as castles require robust defenses, so do these applications, which often face a barrage of threats.

Imagine your organization's applications as the crown jewels within a castle's treasury, brimming with value and significance. The responsibility of safeguarding these digital gems falls upon your shoulders, and the first step is to understand the nature of the threats they face.

Consider the threat landscape as a treacherous terrain surrounding your castle. Threats may come from various directions, ranging from malicious actors seeking to exploit vulnerabilities to insider threats that could compromise security from within. It's crucial to conduct a comprehensive risk assessment to identify potential weaknesses and prioritize security efforts.

Much like a castle's moat and drawbridge act as primary defenses, implementing secure coding practices is the first line of defense for your applications. Developers must follow coding standards and guidelines, perform regular code reviews, and use secure libraries to prevent vulnerabilities from creeping into the application's foundation.

Authentication mechanisms are like the castle's gates, controlling who is allowed entry. Implementing strong authentication, such as multi-factor authentication (MFA), helps ensure that only authorized users gain access to the application. User credentials are the keys to the kingdom, and protecting them is paramount.

Authorization controls act as the interior chambers of the castle, determining who can access specific areas. Role-based access control (RBAC) and least privilege principles limit users' access to only what is necessary for their roles, reducing the risk of unauthorized data exposure or manipulation.

Encryption is akin to the castle's secret vault, where sensitive information is stored securely. Implementing encryption protocols like SSL/TLS for data in transit and encryption at rest ensures that even if attackers breach the perimeter, the data remains unintelligible to them.

Web Application Firewalls (WAFs) serve as the castle's guards stationed along the walls, monitoring incoming traffic for suspicious activity. These security appliances filter out malicious requests, helping to protect against attacks like SQL injection and Cross-Site Scripting (XSS).

Intrusion Detection and Prevention Systems (IDS/IPS) are like vigilant sentinels on the lookout for any signs of intrusion. These systems analyze network and application traffic to detect and block suspicious behavior, much like guards identifying and thwarting threats at the castle's gates.

Application Security Testing is the equivalent of regularly inspecting and maintaining the castle's defenses. Techniques such as static application security testing (SAST) and dynamic application security testing (DAST) help identify vulnerabilities and weaknesses in the application's code and configuration.

Secure file upload and handling is like inspecting goods and supplies entering the castle to ensure they are not hiding any threats. Proper validation and sanitization of user-uploaded files prevent malicious content from infiltrating the application.

Cross-Site Request Forgery (CSRF) protection is akin to guarding against treacherous attempts to trick users into taking unauthorized actions. Implementing anti-CSRF tokens ensures that requests to the application are legitimate and not forged by attackers.

Secure session management is like ensuring that the keys to the castle are never misplaced. Robust session management controls prevent session hijacking and ensure that users are securely authenticated throughout their interaction with the application.

Secure logging and monitoring are the watchful eyes and attentive ears within the castle, recording events and detecting anomalies. By implementing comprehensive logging and real-time monitoring, organizations can identify and respond to security incidents swiftly.

Incident Response Planning is like having a well-organized plan to defend the castle during an attack. Establishing an incident response team, defining procedures, and conducting regular drills help organizations react effectively when security incidents occur.

API security is akin to ensuring that secret passages and tunnels within the castle are well-guarded. Application Programming Interfaces (APIs) must be protected against abuse, unauthorized access, and data leakage.

Supply Chain Security is equivalent to scrutinizing the merchants and traders who enter the castle. Ensuring the security of third-party components and dependencies used in the application is crucial to prevent supply chain attacks.

Security awareness training for personnel is like educating the inhabitants of the castle about the importance of vigilance and caution. Users and employees should be trained to recognize and report security threats.

Security updates and patch management are similar to reinforcing and repairing weak points in the castle's defenses. Regularly applying security patches and updates to the application and its dependencies is essential to fix known vulnerabilities.

Penetration testing is like hiring a team of expert infiltrators to assess the castle's defenses from an attacker's perspective. This practice helps identify vulnerabilities that might be missed through other testing methods.

Now, imagine that the implementation of these security controls is not a one-time endeavor but an ongoing commitment to safeguarding your digital fortress. Regular security assessments, audits, and continuous monitoring are essential to ensure that your applications remain resilient in the face of evolving threats.

In summary, implementing application security controls is akin to fortifying a medieval castle, where every layer of defense plays a critical role in protecting valuable assets. By understanding the threat landscape, following secure coding practices, and employing a comprehensive security strategy, organizations can ensure that their applications stand strong against attackers. Much like the vigilant castle defenders of old, those responsible for application security must remain diligent and adaptable to maintain the safety and integrity of their digital domains.

Chapter 6: Network Segmentation and Microsegmentation

Let's embark on a journey to explore the fascinating realm of network segmentation—a strategy that not only enhances security but also improves network performance and management. Imagine your network as a vast city with different districts, each serving a unique purpose. Network segmentation is akin to dividing this city into distinct neighborhoods, each with its own set of rules and security measures.

At its core, network segmentation is about creating virtual barriers within your network to separate different types of devices, applications, or users. Think of it as erecting partitions within a building to allocate specific areas for various functions. By doing so, network administrators gain granular control over who can access what, thereby reducing the attack surface and limiting the potential impact of security incidents.

One of the key benefits of network segmentation is enhanced security. It's like placing locked doors and security guards at the entrances to different parts of your city. By segregating sensitive data and critical systems from the rest of the network, you can thwart lateral movement by attackers. Even if one neighborhood is breached, the intruder's access remains limited, preventing them from traversing the entire city.

Moreover, network segmentation simplifies network monitoring and management. Imagine having a sprawling garden where each section has its own irrigation system. Network administrators can focus their attention on specific segments, making it easier to detect and respond to anomalies or security threats. It's like tending to one section of the garden without worrying about the entire expanse.

Scalability is another advantage of network segmentation. Think of it as adding new wings to a building while keeping each section self-contained. As your organization grows, you can expand your network without compromising security. This flexibility is crucial in adapting to evolving business needs.

Network segmentation also improves network performance. It's akin to optimizing traffic flow in a bustling city by creating dedicated lanes for different types of vehicles. By isolating high-bandwidth applications from less critical ones, you ensure that important data receives priority, resulting in smoother network operations.

Now, let's explore the principles that underpin effective network segmentation:

Firstly, understanding your network's architecture is crucial. It's like having a detailed map of your city before dividing it into neighborhoods. You must know the layout, traffic patterns, and assets within your network to plan an effective segmentation strategy.

Identifying what needs protection is the second principle. Consider it as recognizing the city's valuable assets that require extra security. Critical systems, sensitive data, and privileged accounts should be isolated in their own segments.

Once you've identified what to protect, the third principle is to establish clear security policies. Think of it as defining the rules and regulations for each neighborhood in your city. Access controls, firewall rules, and security policies should be well-defined and consistently enforced.

The fourth principle is to implement segmentation gradually. It's like building new neighborhoods one at a time instead of completely overhauling the city. Start with critical areas, test your segmentation strategy, and gradually expand it to cover the entire network.

Fifth, monitoring and auditing are essential. Imagine having surveillance cameras and regular patrols in every neighborhood. Continuous monitoring helps detect security breaches or policy violations promptly.

Regularly reviewing and updating your segmentation strategy is the sixth principle. It's akin to renovating and modernizing different parts of your city to meet changing needs. As technology evolves and your network grows, your segmentation strategy should adapt accordingly.

Lastly, educate your network users about segmentation. Consider it as informing the city's inhabitants about the security measures in their neighborhood. Users should understand their roles in adhering to security policies and reporting any suspicious activity.

In summary, network segmentation offers numerous benefits, including enhanced security, simplified management, scalability, and improved performance. By following key principles, such as understanding your network, identifying assets to protect, setting clear security policies, and implementing segmentation gradually, organizations can create a robust and adaptable security strategy that protects their digital domains just like a well-segmented city guards its diverse neighborhoods.

Let's delve into the concept of microsegmentation—an advanced approach to network security that takes the principles of network segmentation to a whole new level. Microsegmentation is like creating individual homes within each neighborhood of our city, ensuring that even the smallest unit is protected and isolated.

In traditional network segmentation, we divided our network into a few broad segments, each with its unique security policies. Microsegmentation, on the other hand, takes this idea further by breaking down those segments into even smaller, highly granular segments. It's like having a separate fortress for each house in the neighborhood, where the security measures are tailored to the specific needs of the inhabitants.

The primary goal of microsegmentation is to enhance security by reducing the attack surface to the absolute minimum. In essence, it's the cybersecurity equivalent of adding multiple layers of security to each building in our city. Attackers find it exceedingly challenging to move laterally within the network because each microsegment has its unique set of access controls and security policies.

Let's explore why microsegmentation is becoming increasingly important in today's threat landscape. Imagine that our city has faced a surge in sophisticated burglaries, and standard security measures are no longer sufficient. In such a scenario, microsegmentation acts as a force multiplier for your network defenses.

One of the key benefits of microsegmentation is its ability to protect critical assets and sensitive data with precision. Think of it as placing an impenetrable vault in each house to safeguard valuables. With microsegmentation, you can allocate the highest level of protection to the most critical resources while ensuring that the rest of the network remains secure.

Moreover, microsegmentation enables fine-grained control over network traffic. Imagine having individual traffic signals for each house in the neighborhood. You can dictate which applications and services are allowed to communicate within a microsegment, minimizing the risk of lateral movement by malware or unauthorized users.

In terms of compliance, microsegmentation can simplify the process. Think of it as having separate compliance checks for each building in our city, tailored to its specific function and requirements. Compliance can be enforced at the microsegment level, ensuring that each segment adheres to its unique regulatory requirements.

Scalability is another advantage of microsegmentation. Imagine that our city keeps growing, and we need to add new structures. With microsegmentation, you can easily expand your security strategy without disrupting existing segments. It's like adding new houses to the neighborhood without compromising the security of the existing ones.

Now, let's explore the practical aspects of implementing microsegmentation:

Firstly, thorough planning is essential. It's like designing the blueprint for each house in our city before construction begins. Identify the specific assets and data that require protection, and determine the desired security policies for each microsegment.

Segmentation policies should be based on the principle of least privilege. Think of it as giving keys to different rooms within a house only to those who need access. Ensure that each microsegment has precisely the level of access required for its function and nothing more.

Next, implement microsegmentation gradually. It's like building additional layers of security for each house one at a time. Start with the most critical segments and progressively expand the strategy to cover the entire network.

Continuous monitoring and auditing are crucial. Imagine having surveillance cameras in each house to ensure security is maintained at all times. Regularly review and update the security policies for each microsegment to adapt to evolving threats and network changes.

Automation can play a significant role in managing microsegmentation. Think of it as having smart locks and security systems that can adapt to different situations.

Automation tools can help enforce policies, detect anomalies, and respond to security incidents swiftly.

Lastly, educate your network users about microsegmentation. Consider it as informing the residents of our city about the enhanced security measures in their homes. Users should understand how microsegmentation benefits them and their role in adhering to security policies.

In summary, microsegmentation takes network security to a new level by creating highly granular segments with tailored security policies. It offers precision protection, fine-grained traffic control, and scalability while simplifying compliance. By following best practices, organizations can implement microsegmentation effectively, making their networks as secure as a city with individually fortified homes.

Chapter 7: Zero Trust Architecture: A Paradigm Shift in Network Security

Let's embark on a journey into the realm of Zero Trust—a revolutionary approach to cybersecurity that challenges traditional network security paradigms. Imagine a world where trust is no longer based on location or network boundaries but on continuous verification and strict access controls.

At its core, Zero Trust is like having a vigilant guardian at the entrance of every building in our city, scrutinizing everyone who seeks entry, regardless of their origins. This approach assumes that threats can originate both from external sources and within the network, prompting a fundamental shift in how we approach security.

The guiding principle of Zero Trust is simple: "Never trust, always verify." In our city, this means that even long-time residents must provide valid identification before entering a building. Similarly, every user, device, or application attempting to access the network must prove their trustworthiness at all times.

One of the key tenets of Zero Trust is the concept of "least privilege." Think of it as providing access to specific parts of a building based on a person's role or need. In the Zero Trust model, users are granted the least amount of access required to perform their tasks, reducing the attack surface and limiting potential damage if a breach occurs.

Zero Trust also emphasizes continuous monitoring and assessment. It's akin to having surveillance cameras in every room of every building, with automated alarms that trigger when suspicious activity is detected. In the cybersecurity context, this means constant scrutiny of network traffic, user behavior, and access patterns to identify anomalies and potential threats.

Segmentation is a fundamental component of Zero Trust. Picture our city divided into countless secure zones, each with its own security checkpoints. In the same vein, the Zero Trust model segments the network into microsegments, where each segment has its access controls and security policies. This way, even if one segment is compromised, the rest remain secure.

Authentication and identity management are paramount in Zero Trust. Imagine our city residents carrying electronic IDs that are checked at every building entrance. Similarly, in the Zero Trust model, strong authentication methods, such as multi-factor authentication, are used to verify users' identities.

Zero Trust also advocates for encryption as a means of securing data in transit. It's like having armored vehicles transporting valuables within our city. In the digital world, encryption ensures that even if data is intercepted, it remains unreadable to unauthorized parties.

Now, let's delve into the practical aspects of implementing Zero Trust:

Firstly, identify and classify your assets and data. Think of it as cataloging the contents of every building in our city. Determine what is sensitive, valuable, or critical to your organization's operations.

Second, implement strong access controls and user authentication. Picture installing robust security checkpoints at every building entrance, ensuring that only authorized personnel gain entry.

Continuous monitoring is crucial in the Zero Trust model. Imagine having a security team in our city that watches over every building 24/7. Implement security information and event management (SIEM) systems and threat detection tools to monitor network traffic and user behavior for anomalies.

Segmentation plays a pivotal role. Consider it as dividing our city into secure zones with strict access controls. Implement microsegmentation within your network, isolating different parts to limit lateral movement by attackers.

Encryption should be used extensively to protect data in transit and at rest. Imagine securing valuable assets within our city's buildings with state-of-the-art safes. Implement encryption for communication channels and data storage to ensure data remains confidential.

Implement a robust identity and access management (IAM) system. It's like having a unified identification system for all residents of our city. Ensure that user identities are managed effectively, and access is granted on a need-to-know basis.

Lastly, educate your organization about the Zero Trust model. Consider it as informing our city's residents about the enhanced security measures in place. Users and employees should understand the importance of Zero Trust and their role in maintaining security.

In summary, Zero Trust is a paradigm shift in cybersecurity that challenges traditional notions of trust and access. It emphasizes continuous verification, least privilege, segmentation, encryption, and robust identity management. By implementing these principles and practices, organizations can establish a security posture that's as vigilant as a city with guards at every building entrance, ensuring that trust is never assumed but continually verified.

Imagine building a fortress around your digital kingdom, one where trust is no longer granted by default but earned at every step. This is the essence of implementing a Zero Trust network—a transformative approach to cybersecurity that challenges traditional notions of network security.

At the heart of Zero Trust is a fundamental shift in how we view trust in a networked world. It's like transforming a once-open city into a walled fortress, where every entry point is fortified, and every individual, regardless of their origin, must prove their identity and purpose.

The core principle of Zero Trust is simple yet profound: "Never trust, always verify." In this paradigm, trust is no longer based on the network perimeter but on continuous validation and authentication of users, devices, and applications.

Think of your network as a medieval castle surrounded by a moat. In the past, this moat represented the network perimeter, protecting everything inside. In a Zero Trust network, however, the moat is replaced by layers of security that exist not just at the perimeter but within the network itself. This means that even if an attacker breaches the outer defenses, they still have to contend with multiple layers of security within.

Implementing Zero Trust begins with the notion of "least privilege." It's akin to granting access to specific areas of your castle based on an individual's role and need. In the same vein, users, devices, and applications are given the least amount of access necessary to perform their tasks, minimizing the potential for harm if a breach occurs.

Continuous monitoring is a cornerstone of Zero Trust. Picture a vigilant watchtower atop your castle, scanning the surroundings for any sign of intrusion. Similarly, in a Zero Trust network, automated monitoring tools are in place to scrutinize network traffic, user behavior, and access patterns. Any suspicious activity triggers alarms and immediate investigation.

Segmentation is another critical component. Think of your castle as divided into distinct, well-fortified zones. In a Zero Trust network, segmentation creates microenvironments with their own security policies and access controls. Even if one segment is compromised, the rest remain protected.

Authentication and identity management are paramount in Zero Trust. Imagine if every person entering your castle had to undergo thorough identity checks. In the digital realm, this involves strong authentication methods, such as multi-factor authentication (MFA), to validate users' identities.

Encryption plays a vital role in securing data in transit and at rest. Consider it as safeguarding the treasure within your castle with impenetrable locks. Encryption ensures that even if data is intercepted, it remains unreadable to unauthorized eyes.

Now, let's explore the practical steps to implement a Zero Trust network:

Begin by conducting a thorough inventory of your digital assets. Think of this as cataloging the treasures within your castle. Identify what's sensitive, valuable, or critical to your organization.

Next, establish strong access controls and user authentication mechanisms. It's akin to fortifying the entrances to your castle and allowing only authorized personnel to enter.

Continuous monitoring is essential. Imagine having guards patrolling your castle's walls day and night. Implement security information and event management (SIEM) systems and threat detection tools to constantly watch over your network.

Segmentation creates secure zones within your network. It's like dividing your castle into separate fortresses with their own defenses. Implement microsegmentation to isolate different parts of your network.

Encryption should be used to protect data in transit and at rest. Picture your treasure chest sealed with an unbreakable lock. Ensure that all communication channels and data storage are encrypted.

Implement a robust identity and access management (IAM) system. It's like having a central registry of everyone allowed inside your castle. Manage user identities effectively and grant access based on a need-to-know basis.

Lastly, educate your organization about Zero Trust. Consider it as informing your castle's inhabitants about the enhanced security measures in place. Users and employees should understand the importance of Zero Trust and their role in maintaining security.

In summary, implementing a Zero Trust network is like fortifying your digital castle against modern-day threats. It revolves around the principles of continuous verification, least privilege, segmentation, encryption, and robust identity management. By embracing these principles and taking practical steps, you can create a network that's as secure and vigilant as a medieval fortress, ensuring that trust is never assumed but continually validated.

Chapter 8: Advanced Endpoint Protection and Response (EDR)

Picture your computer, smartphone, or tablet as the gates to your digital kingdom—a realm filled with personal data, sensitive information, and valuable assets. In the ever-evolving landscape of cybersecurity, protecting these endpoints has become more critical than ever before. Endpoint security technologies are your digital knights, tirelessly guarding against threats, securing your devices, and ensuring the safety of your digital world.

Antivirus software is your first line of defense, acting as the vigilant sentinels of your digital realm. These programs scan your device for malicious code, known as malware, and neutralize any threats they encounter. It's akin to having a team of knights protecting your castle from marauding invaders.

But the battle against malware extends beyond the traditional antivirus. Today's threats are dynamic and ever-changing, often disguising themselves to avoid detection. This is where next-generation antivirus (NGAV) steps in, using advanced techniques like machine learning and behavioral analysis to identify and stop emerging threats. It's like having not just knights but also wizards with magical insights into the enemy's tactics.

Firewalls are like impenetrable walls surrounding your digital fortress. They monitor incoming and outgoing network traffic, allowing or blocking data based on a set of predetermined security rules. Firewalls stand guard at the gates, deciding who enters and who is kept out, much like gatekeepers of a medieval city.

Endpoint Detection and Response (EDR) solutions are the vigilant watchmen of your digital castle. They continuously monitor endpoint activities, looking for signs of suspicious behavior or potential breaches. When they detect unusual activities, EDR tools spring into action, investigating the threat and, if necessary, quarantining the infected device. Think of them as digital sentinels patrolling the halls of your castle, always on high alert.

Patch management is akin to repairing the cracks in your castle walls. It involves keeping your software and operating systems up-to-date by applying patches and updates. Outdated software can have vulnerabilities that attackers exploit. Regular patching ensures your digital fortress remains resilient against known threats.

Data encryption is your trusted scribe, ensuring that your messages and information are written in a secret code. Encryption transforms your data into an unreadable format, which can only be deciphered by someone with the right key. It's like sending secret scrolls that can only be deciphered by those with the magic words.

Mobile device management (MDM) is your loyal steward, managing and securing your mobile devices. Whether it's your smartphone or tablet, MDM helps enforce security policies, remote wipe capabilities, and ensures that only authorized devices can access your digital kingdom.

Endpoint security platforms are the generals of your digital army, orchestrating the defense of all your endpoints. They bring together various security tools and technologies into a unified system, providing a holistic view of your endpoint security. It's like having a seasoned commander who can strategize and coordinate the efforts of your knights, wizards, and watchmen.

Behavioral analytics is your trusted counselor, studying the behavior of your digital subjects to detect anomalies. By establishing a baseline of normal behavior, it can spot deviations that might indicate a security breach. It's like having a wise advisor who can foresee potential threats and advise on defensive measures.

Zero Trust security principles are the new guard doctrine in the ever-evolving landscape of cybersecurity. Instead of assuming trust within your digital kingdom, Zero Trust operates under the principle of "never trust, always verify." Every request for access, regardless of its source, is treated as potentially hostile until proven otherwise. It's like turning every visitor to your castle into a potential intruder until they've provided the proper credentials.

Multi-factor authentication (MFA) is your reliable lock and key system. Instead of relying solely on a password, MFA requires users to provide two or more authentication factors, such as a password and a fingerprint or a one-time code sent to their mobile device. It's like having a multi-layered lock on the gates to your castle, making it significantly harder for unauthorized access.

Security awareness training is your method of educating your digital subjects. Just as a well-informed populace is crucial for the safety of a kingdom, educating your employees and users about cybersecurity best practices is essential. It's like providing your citizens with the knowledge and tools to recognize and report suspicious activity.

Cloud security is your expanding territory, protecting not just your castle but also your outlying estates in the cloud. With more businesses embracing cloud services, ensuring the security of data and applications stored in the cloud is paramount. Cloud security tools and practices extend your security umbrella to cover this vast digital landscape.

Now, imagine implementing these endpoint security technologies not as individual knights but as a cohesive army defending your digital kingdom. A well-integrated and layered security approach is the key to fortifying your endpoints effectively. Just as a medieval castle's defenses were stronger when knights, archers, and watchmen worked together, your endpoint security is most robust when these technologies complement and reinforce each other.

In summary, endpoint security technologies are your digital guardians, protecting your devices and data from a myriad of threats. From vigilant antivirus software to the advanced capabilities of next-generation antivirus and the watchful eyes of endpoint detection and response tools, these technologies form the bulwark of your digital defenses. By implementing a comprehensive and layered approach to endpoint security, you can ensure the safety and resilience of your digital kingdom in an ever-evolving cybersecurity landscape.

Imagine a bustling city, complete with its businesses, homes, and infrastructure, all functioning smoothly until an unforeseen disaster strikes. It could be a fire, an earthquake, or a flood. The key to minimizing the damage and getting the city back on its feet is a well-organized and efficient response. In the digital realm, your endpoints are like the buildings and streets of your city, and just as you need a disaster response plan for your city, you need one for your digital kingdom.

This is where Incident Response (IR) with Endpoint Detection and Response (EDR) solutions comes into play. Think of it as your digital disaster response team, ready to spring into action when threats and breaches occur in your digital city.

The first step in incident response is detection. Just as smoke detectors alert you to a fire, EDR solutions continuously monitor your endpoints for signs of trouble. These signs could be unusual patterns of behavior, unexpected file changes, or suspicious network traffic. When they detect something amiss, they raise the alarm, letting you know that there might be a digital fire to extinguish.

Once an alert is raised, the incident response team swings into action. This team consists of security professionals who are trained to investigate and mitigate security incidents. They assess the severity of the threat and gather information to understand what has happened. It's like sending firefighters to assess the situation and determine the best course of action.

If the threat is confirmed, containment is the next step. This involves isolating the affected endpoint to prevent the threat from spreading further. It's like creating a firebreak to stop a wildfire from consuming an entire neighborhood.

Once containment is achieved, eradication begins. This is where the incident response team works to remove the threat from the affected endpoint. It's like firefighters dousing the flames and ensuring that the fire is completely extinguished.

After eradication, recovery efforts kick in. This may involve restoring affected systems and data from backups. It's similar to rebuilding structures that were damaged in a disaster.

During this entire process, communication is key. Just as emergency services keep citizens informed during a crisis, your incident response team should maintain clear communication with stakeholders, including employees, customers, and the public. Transparency and timely updates are essential to maintain trust and ensure everyone is aware of the situation.

But the work doesn't end with recovery. Just as a city evaluates its disaster response after an incident to identify areas for improvement, your organization should conduct a post-incident review. This helps identify weaknesses in your security posture and allows you to refine your incident response plan for the future.

Incorporating EDR into your incident response plan is like having a team of highly trained specialists at your disposal, ready to investigate, contain, and mitigate security incidents in real-time. EDR tools provide visibility into endpoint activities, enabling rapid threat detection and response.

Automation plays a vital role in incident response. EDR solutions often come with automated response capabilities that can isolate compromised endpoints, terminate malicious processes, and even roll back changes made by attackers. This automation is like having an army of digital responders that can react within seconds, minimizing the impact of an incident.

One of the significant advantages of EDR solutions is their ability to conduct detailed forensic investigations. Just as detectives collect evidence at a crime scene, EDR tools record vast amounts of data about endpoint activities. This data can be invaluable for understanding the scope of an incident, identifying the root cause, and preventing future attacks.

To effectively incorporate EDR into your incident response plan, it's crucial to have well-defined processes and procedures in place. Your incident response team should be well-trained in using EDR tools and have a deep understanding of your network and endpoints.

Additionally, EDR solutions can provide threat intelligence, helping your organization stay informed about the latest threats and attack techniques. This intelligence is like having access to reports on criminal activities in your city, allowing you to anticipate and prepare for potential threats.

In summary, incident response with EDR solutions is your digital disaster response plan. It's a coordinated effort to detect, investigate, contain, and mitigate security incidents in your digital city. Just as in a real disaster, clear communication, automation, and thorough investigations are crucial components of an effective incident response strategy. By integrating EDR into your security arsenal and having a well-trained incident response team, you can ensure that your digital kingdom remains secure even in the face of unexpected threats.

Chapter 9: Cloud Security: Protecting Data and Applications in the Cloud

In the ever-evolving landscape of information technology, cloud computing has emerged as a transformative force. Imagine it as a vast, interconnected realm where data, applications, and services are hosted on remote servers, accessible from anywhere with an internet connection. It's like having the ability to access your digital resources from virtually anywhere in the world.

This shift to cloud computing has offered businesses and individuals unprecedented flexibility, scalability, and cost-efficiency. However, this digital paradise isn't without its challenges, especially when it comes to security.

One of the fundamental cloud security challenges is the shared responsibility model. In this model, cloud providers are responsible for securing the underlying infrastructure—the physical servers, networking components, and data centers. It's akin to a building's owner being responsible for the security of the entire property, including the walls, doors, and locks.

On the other hand, cloud users, or tenants, are responsible for securing what they put into the cloud—their data, applications, and configurations. This is like a tenant being responsible for locking their apartment door and protecting their belongings inside.

Navigating this shared responsibility can be tricky, as it requires a clear understanding of where the provider's responsibilities end and the tenant's responsibilities begin. It's akin to knowing when to call the building maintenance crew versus when to call a locksmith.

Cloud security also faces challenges related to data privacy and compliance. With data traversing the cloud, it may cross geographic boundaries, raising concerns about where the data is stored and who has access to it. This is similar to wondering who can enter and exit a borderless, virtual city.

To address these concerns, many cloud providers offer data residency options, allowing users to specify where their data is stored. Think of it as choosing a secure storage location within the virtual city limits.

Another cloud security challenge stems from the dynamic nature of cloud environments. Unlike traditional data centers with fixed configurations, cloud environments can scale up or down rapidly. This scalability is akin to a city's population expanding or contracting based on events or seasons.

However, this dynamic nature can lead to security blind spots. Misconfigurations, forgotten resources, and unpatched vulnerabilities can lurk in the shadows, waiting to be exploited. It's like having hidden alleyways and backdoors in a sprawling city that criminals can use to their advantage.

To combat this, organizations must implement robust cloud security measures, including continuous monitoring, automated compliance checks, and rapid incident response. This is akin to having a vigilant city watch that patrols the virtual streets, ensuring everything is in order.

Cloud security also faces challenges related to the identity and access management of users and applications. In a cloud environment, users and applications often access resources remotely, and verifying their identities becomes crucial. It's like having secure access checkpoints at every entry point to the virtual city.

Multi-factor authentication (MFA) and identity and access management (IAM) tools play a vital role in ensuring that only authorized individuals and services can enter the cloud. These security measures are akin to requiring both a key card and a biometric scan to access a secure facility.

Moreover, cloud security must address the threat landscape unique to the cloud. Attackers are continually devising new methods to exploit cloud vulnerabilities. Security teams must stay vigilant and adapt their defenses to the changing threat landscape. This is akin to having a dedicated team of security experts who study criminal behavior patterns and devise strategies to counter them.

Cloud providers themselves invest heavily in security, offering a range of tools and services to help users secure their cloud environments. These include firewalls, encryption, identity management, and threat detection. It's like having a city government that provides essential services such as law enforcement and public infrastructure.

Despite these challenges, the benefits of cloud computing are too compelling to ignore. The key to harnessing the power of the cloud while mitigating its security risks lies in a proactive and comprehensive approach to cloud security. It's like building a virtual city that not only offers the convenience and opportunities of the cloud but also ensures the safety and security of its digital denizens. In summary, cloud security is a critical aspect of modern IT, akin to building a safe and thriving virtual city in the digital landscape. While challenges exist, including the shared responsibility model, data privacy concerns, dynamic environments, and identity management, organizations can address these challenges through a combination of best practices, security tools, and vigilant monitoring. Just as a well-managed city can thrive and prosper, a well-secured cloud environment can unlock the full potential of cloud computing while keeping digital assets safe and sound. In the ever-evolving landscape of information technology, cloud computing has become a cornerstone of modern business operations and personal convenience. It's like having a virtual vault where you can store, access, and manage your data, applications, and services from anywhere in the world, unlocking unprecedented flexibility and scalability.

However, this digital utopia comes with its own set of challenges, particularly in the realm of security. Just as you would secure your physical assets in the real world, it's imperative to safeguard your digital assets in the cloud. Here, we'll delve into some best practices for ensuring the security of your cloud-based resources.

First and foremost, access control is paramount in cloud security. Think of it as the key to your virtual fortress. Only authorized individuals and systems should have access to your cloud resources. Implement strong authentication methods, like multi-factor authentication (MFA), to ensure that the right people are accessing your digital kingdom.

Next, encryption is your shield against data breaches. Encrypt data both at rest and in transit. This is like locking your valuables in a safe and ensuring they're transported securely when needed. With encryption, even if an intruder gains access to your data, it remains unintelligible without the decryption key.

Regularly monitoring your cloud environment is akin to having vigilant sentinels patrolling your virtual domain. Employ automated tools to detect any suspicious activities or unauthorized access. By identifying and addressing issues promptly, you can thwart potential threats before they escalate.

A robust backup and disaster recovery plan is your safety net in the digital world. Imagine it as a magical spell that can restore your kingdom after a catastrophe. Regularly back up your data and ensure that you can quickly recover from any unexpected incidents, such as data breaches or system failures. Security patches and updates are the equivalent of fortifying the walls of your castle. Keep your cloud resources up to date with the latest security patches and software updates. Hackers often exploit known vulnerabilities, so staying current is crucial in maintaining a strong defense.

Network segmentation is your strategy for dividing and conquering potential threats. Think of it as building separate strongholds within your kingdom. By isolating different parts of your cloud environment, you can contain any security breaches, preventing them from spreading to other areas.

Establishing clear security policies and procedures is like drafting the rules of your kingdom. Ensure that everyone in your organization understands and follows these guidelines. Regularly review and update these policies to adapt to the evolving threat landscape.

Security training and awareness programs are your way of arming your citizens with knowledge. Educate your team about the latest security threats and best practices. An informed workforce is your first line of defense against social engineering attacks like phishing.

Cloud providers often offer a range of security tools and services as part of their platforms. Utilize these resources to bolster your defenses. It's like having a dedicated security force that's ready to assist you in safeguarding your digital realm.

Regularly conduct security audits and assessments. Think of it as hiring an independent inspector to evaluate your castle's defenses. By identifying vulnerabilities and areas for improvement, you can continuously strengthen your security posture.

Lastly, establish an incident response plan. Imagine it as a battle strategy for when the walls are breached. Define roles and responsibilities, and outline the steps to take in the event of a security incident. A well-prepared response can minimize damage and hasten recovery.

In the dynamic landscape of cloud computing, security is an ongoing process. It's not a one-time endeavor but a continuous effort to protect your digital assets. Just as a vigilant ruler ensures the safety and prosperity of their kingdom, a vigilant approach to cloud security is essential to harness the full potential of cloud technology while safeguarding your valuable digital assets.

In summary, cloud security is a vital aspect of our modern digital world. By following best practices such as access control, encryption, monitoring, backup and recovery, patch management, network segmentation, policy development, security training, utilizing cloud provider tools, conducting audits, and having an incident response plan, individuals and organizations can fortify their defenses and enjoy the benefits of cloud computing with confidence. Like a well-protected kingdom, a well-secured cloud environment ensures that your digital assets remain safe and your operations run smoothly in the cloud.

Chapter 10: Red Team vs. Blue Team: Simulating Advanced Attacks and Defense

In the complex realm of cybersecurity, the concept of Red Team and Blue Team plays a pivotal role in safeguarding digital environments. Picture it as a strategic game where one team tries to outsmart the other, but the stakes are high, involving the protection of critical data and assets.

The Red Team is the group of individuals or cybersecurity experts tasked with acting as adversaries. They simulate cyberattacks and employ various techniques to exploit vulnerabilities in a system or network. This role is akin to that of cunning infiltrators or hackers probing the defenses of a castle. Their objective is to uncover weaknesses, gaps, and potential security breaches that could be exploited by real-world attackers.

The Red Team operates with the mindset of an attacker, constantly seeking ways to bypass security measures, infiltrate systems, and exfiltrate sensitive information. They use a variety of tools, tactics, and procedures, much like an adversary would in the wild. The goal is to expose vulnerabilities before malicious hackers can find and exploit them, ultimately strengthening the organization's defenses.

On the other side of this cybersecurity chessboard is the Blue Team, the defenders of the digital realm. They are the organization's internal security experts responsible for maintaining and enhancing cybersecurity measures. Their role is comparable to that of vigilant guardians protecting a kingdom from external threats.

The Blue Team's primary responsibility is to detect, respond to, and mitigate cyber threats and attacks. They constantly monitor the network and systems for any signs of suspicious or unauthorized activity. Much like guards patrolling the castle walls, they use security information and event management (SIEM) systems, intrusion detection systems (IDS), and other monitoring tools to keep a watchful eye on the organization's digital assets.

When the Red Team launches simulated attacks, the Blue Team's mission is to detect and respond to them effectively. This practice, often referred to as Red Team vs. Blue Team (RTBT) exercises, provides a controlled environment for both teams to refine their skills and improve the organization's overall cybersecurity posture. These exercises mimic real-world scenarios, helping the Blue Team develop incident response plans and fine-tune security controls.

The collaboration between the Red Team and Blue Team is essential for comprehensive cybersecurity. While the Red Team identifies vulnerabilities and weaknesses, the Blue Team learns from these findings and implements improvements to shore up defenses. This continuous cycle of testing, learning, and enhancing security measures is crucial in today's dynamic threat landscape.

Additionally, the Red Team and Blue Team roles extend beyond the boundaries of cybersecurity exercises. In many organizations, they work together to proactively assess and improve security measures. The Red Team may provide valuable insights to the Blue Team on emerging threats and attack techniques, enabling the organization to better defend against real-world cyberattacks.

Furthermore, the insights gained from Red Team exercises can inform the development of more robust security policies, procedures, and training programs. By understanding how adversaries operate, the organization can take proactive steps to prevent and mitigate potential threats effectively.

In summary, the Red Team and Blue Team are integral components of modern cybersecurity practices. They represent the constant battle between attackers and defenders in the digital realm. While the Red Team mimics adversaries to uncover vulnerabilities, the Blue Team stands ready to detect, respond to, and thwart potential threats. Their collaborative efforts are essential in fortifying an organization's cybersecurity defenses, ensuring that the kingdom of data remains protected from the ever-present dangers of the cyber world.

In the ever-evolving landscape of cybersecurity, organizations must adopt proactive measures to defend against an array of threats, vulnerabilities, and attacks. One of the most effective methods for testing and enhancing an organization's cybersecurity defenses is through the practice of Red Team and Blue Team exercises. These exercises are akin to war games in the digital realm, allowing organizations to simulate real-world cyberattacks and responses in a controlled environment.

The Red Team, as we've previously discussed, assumes the role of the adversary. Their mission is to emulate the tactics, techniques, and procedures (TTPs) of cybercriminals or nation-state actors seeking to breach an organization's defenses. This team of skilled cybersecurity professionals, often independent of the organization's internal security team, operates with the singular goal of uncovering vulnerabilities and weaknesses.

During Red Team exercises, the team uses a wide array of tools and techniques to mimic potential attackers. They may employ phishing emails to target employees, attempt to exploit vulnerabilities in the network infrastructure, or simulate advanced persistent threats (APTs) that persistently probe for weaknesses over an extended period. Their actions are designed to mirror the tactics used by real adversaries.

The primary objective of the Red Team is to identify vulnerabilities and security gaps that might go unnoticed in routine security assessments. By thinking like an attacker, they help organizations understand where they may be exposed to risk. This approach allows organizations to proactively address vulnerabilities and improve their overall cybersecurity posture.

On the other side of this digital battleground is the Blue Team, representing the organization's internal security personnel. Their mission during these exercises is to detect and respond to the simulated attacks launched by the Red Team. This involves continuous monitoring of network traffic, system logs, and security alerts.

The Blue Team leverages a range of cybersecurity tools, including intrusion detection systems (IDS), intrusion prevention systems (IPS), firewalls, security information and event management (SIEM) solutions, and endpoint protection platforms. These tools provide real-time visibility into the organization's digital environment, enabling the Blue Team to identify suspicious or malicious activity promptly. When the Red Team initiates an attack, the Blue Team's response is critical. They must work swiftly to assess the situation, identify the attack vector, and implement countermeasures to mitigate the threat. The response may involve isolating compromised systems, blocking malicious network traffic, and conducting forensic analysis to understand the extent of the breach.

The synergy between the Red Team and Blue Team is crucial during these exercises. It's not a matter of one team trying to outperform the other, but rather a collaborative effort to strengthen an organization's security posture. After each exercise, both teams come together to review the results, share insights, and identify areas for improvement.

These exercises also provide an opportunity to evaluate the organization's incident response procedures and communication protocols. It's essential that everyone involved, from IT and security teams to senior leadership, understands their roles and responsibilities during a cybersecurity incident. Red Team and Blue Team exercises help refine these processes and ensure a coordinated response.

Moreover, Red Team and Blue Team exercises go beyond technical assessments. They serve as valuable training opportunities for cybersecurity professionals. Members of the Red Team gain experience in crafting and executing sophisticated attacks, while those on the Blue Team enhance their skills in threat detection, incident response, and decision-making under pressure.

Incorporating these exercises into an organization's cybersecurity strategy is a proactive measure that can significantly enhance its defenses. By identifying vulnerabilities and weaknesses before real adversaries do, organizations can fortify their security measures and reduce the risk of successful cyberattacks.

Additionally, Red Team and Blue Team exercises contribute to a culture of continuous improvement within an organization. They foster a mindset of vigilance and preparedness, where cybersecurity is not viewed as a static challenge but as an ongoing effort to adapt to the ever-changing threat landscape.

In summary, Red Team and Blue Team exercises are integral components of modern cybersecurity practices. They provide a controlled environment for simulating cyberattacks and responses, helping organizations identify vulnerabilities, improve defenses, and enhance incident response capabilities. By working together, these teams play a vital role in fortifying an organization's digital fortress against the relentless tide of cyber threats.

BOOK 4
EXPERT-LEVEL NETWORK SECURITY
MASTERING PROTOCOLS, THREATS,
AND DEFENSES

ROB BOTWRIGHT

Chapter 1: Advanced Protocol Analysis and Exploitation

Protocol analysis, often referred to as packet analysis, is a fundamental practice in the world of networking and cybersecurity. It involves the detailed examination of network packets, the fundamental units of data that flow across computer networks. By delving into these packets, analysts can gain invaluable insights into network behavior, diagnose problems, and even uncover security vulnerabilities.

To understand protocol analysis, it's crucial to grasp the concept of network protocols. Network protocols are a set of rules and conventions that dictate how data should be formatted, transmitted, received, and processed in a network. They define the language that devices on a network use to communicate with each other. Common examples of network protocols include the Transmission Control Protocol (TCP), Internet Protocol (IP), and Hypertext Transfer Protocol (HTTP).

Protocol analysis involves capturing and inspecting network packets as they traverse the network. This process typically employs specialized tools known as packet analyzers or packet sniffers. These tools can capture packets from the network and display their contents for analysis.

One of the primary uses of protocol analysis is troubleshooting network issues. When a network problem arises, such as slow performance or connectivity problems, protocol analysis can help pinpoint the root cause. Analysts can examine packet captures to identify anomalies, errors, or bottlenecks in the network traffic. For example, they may discover excessive retransmissions of packets, which could indicate network congestion or packet loss issues.

Another essential aspect of protocol analysis is security. Cybersecurity professionals use packet analysis to detect and investigate potential security breaches. By examining network traffic, analysts can identify suspicious or malicious activity, such as unusual patterns of data transfers or unrecognized protocols. This insight can lead to the discovery of intrusion attempts or malware infections.

Protocol analysis tools provide various features for analyzing captured packets. Analysts can filter packets based on criteria such as source or destination IP addresses, port numbers, and packet content. They can also perform time-based analysis to understand the sequence of events in a network communication.

Beyond basic packet capture and analysis, protocol analysis techniques can become quite sophisticated. For instance, deep packet inspection (DPI) involves examining the payload of packets, not just their headers. DPI can reveal the content of web requests, emails, and other application-level data. This level of scrutiny is essential for identifying threats, but it also raises privacy concerns, as it can potentially expose sensitive information.

In addition to troubleshooting and security, protocol analysis plays a crucial role in network optimization and performance tuning. By studying the behavior of network traffic, organizations can make informed decisions about network capacity, optimize application performance, and improve overall network efficiency.

Protocol analysis is not limited to real-time monitoring. Analysts can save packet captures for later analysis, enabling them to review historical network activity. This is especially valuable for investigating security incidents or recurring network problems.

One of the challenges in protocol analysis is dealing with the sheer volume of network traffic. In large networks, capturing and analyzing every packet is often impractical due to the sheer volume of data generated. Analysts must carefully select which packets to capture and analyze, focusing on those that are most relevant to their objectives.

Moreover, as networks evolve and encryption becomes more prevalent, protocol analysis faces new challenges. Encrypted traffic is opaque to traditional packet analyzers, making it difficult to inspect the contents of packets. This shift towards encryption has prompted the development of techniques like SSL/TLS decryption, which allows analysts to inspect encrypted traffic for security purposes.

In summary, protocol analysis is a vital practice in the realms of networking and cybersecurity. It involves the examination of network packets to troubleshoot issues, enhance security, and optimize network performance. By dissecting these packets, analysts can gain deep insights into network behavior, helping organizations maintain robust and secure networks in an increasingly complex digital landscape.

Exploring the world of network security and cybersecurity, one often encounters the term "protocol vulnerabilities." These vulnerabilities are akin to hidden traps within the intricate framework of network communication protocols. To understand them better, we need to delve into the realm of protocols and how they can become the Achilles' heel of network security.

At its core, a protocol vulnerability is a flaw or weakness in a network protocol's design or implementation that can be exploited by malicious actors. Think of it as a flaw in the blueprint of a secure building, allowing a skilled intruder to find a way inside. These vulnerabilities exist in various forms, but they all share a common trait: they can be leveraged to compromise network integrity, confidentiality, or availability.

To appreciate the gravity of protocol vulnerabilities, let's first explore what network protocols are and why they matter. Network protocols are the rules and conventions that govern how data is exchanged between devices on a network. They serve as the language of the digital world, ensuring that different devices, often from different manufacturers, can communicate seamlessly.

Common network protocols include the Transmission Control Protocol (TCP) and Internet Protocol (IP), which form the foundation of the internet, and Hypertext Transfer Protocol (HTTP), which powers the World Wide Web. These protocols are essential for the internet to function, and countless others ensure the smooth operation of various applications and services.

Now, consider what happens when a vulnerability is discovered within one of these critical protocols. This vulnerability may allow an attacker to exploit a weakness in the protocol's design or implementation, potentially leading to a breach in network security. It's akin to finding a chink in the armor of a medieval knight - a small but critical vulnerability that can be exploited.

Protocol vulnerabilities can manifest in numerous ways. They might involve improper input validation, where a protocol fails to adequately verify the data it receives, allowing an attacker to inject malicious code or manipulate the system. Another common type is buffer overflow vulnerabilities, where attackers overwhelm a system by sending more data than it can handle, often leading to system crashes or unauthorized access.

These vulnerabilities often result from human error or oversight during the design or coding phase of a protocol. Sometimes, the vulnerabilities may remain hidden until discovered by security researchers or, more alarmingly, exploited by malicious hackers. When they are exposed, it becomes a race against time to patch or mitigate the vulnerability before widespread attacks occur.

One infamous example of a protocol vulnerability is the Heartbleed bug discovered in OpenSSL, a widely used cryptographic library. This vulnerability allowed attackers to steal sensitive data, such as usernames and passwords, from secure websites and services. It sent shockwaves through the internet community, highlighting the critical role that protocol security plays in our digital lives.

Mitigating protocol vulnerabilities requires a multi-faceted approach. It starts with proactive measures during protocol design and implementation, emphasizing rigorous security testing and code reviews. Security best practices, such as input validation and secure coding, should be integrated into the development process.

Furthermore, it's crucial to stay vigilant for emerging vulnerabilities and apply timely patches and updates. The Heartbleed incident serves as a stark reminder that even widely adopted and trusted protocols are not immune to flaws.

Security researchers and organizations play a vital role in identifying and reporting protocol vulnerabilities responsibly. Once a vulnerability is discovered, responsible disclosure ensures that the protocol's maintainers have a chance to fix the issue before it is widely exploited. This collaborative approach safeguards the integrity of critical network protocols.

To protect against protocol vulnerabilities, network administrators and cybersecurity professionals must continuously monitor their networks for signs of suspicious activity. Intrusion detection systems (IDS) and intrusion prevention systems (IPS) can help identify and mitigate attacks targeting protocol vulnerabilities.

Encryption can also serve as a powerful defense against protocol vulnerabilities. By encrypting data transmitted over a network, even if attackers intercept it, they cannot decipher the information without the encryption keys. This safeguards the confidentiality and integrity of sensitive data, even if protocol vulnerabilities exist.

In summary, protocol vulnerabilities are the hidden weak points in the complex web of network communication. They remind us that in the digital age, where our lives and businesses rely heavily on networked systems, securing the protocols that underpin our communication is paramount. By understanding these vulnerabilities and taking proactive steps to address them, we can build a more resilient and secure digital world.

Chapter 2: Deep Dive into Advanced Persistent Threats (APTs)

Advanced Persistent Threats, often referred to as APTs, are a class of cyber threats that stand out in the world of cybersecurity due to their unique characteristics and the level of sophistication they exhibit. To grasp the significance of APTs, we need to explore what sets them apart from run-of-the-mill cyberattacks and how they operate in the shadows of the digital landscape.

First and foremost, APTs are characterized by their persistence and long-term focus. Unlike many cyberattacks that are swift and noisy, APTs are patient and stealthy. They don't seek immediate results; instead, they aim to maintain a foothold in a victim's network for an extended period, often going undetected for months or even years. This persistence is one of the defining features of APTs and sets them apart from other, more opportunistic attacks.

To understand why APTs exhibit such patience, it's essential to recognize their objectives. APT actors are typically well-organized and have specific goals that go beyond a quick financial gain. These objectives may include corporate espionage, intellectual property theft, or gaining access to sensitive government information. APTs are often associated with nation-states, organized crime groups, or highly motivated and well-funded hackers.

Another characteristic of APTs is their adaptability. These threats are not bound by a single set of tools or tactics. Instead, APT actors continuously evolve their techniques to evade detection and maintain access to their targets. They are like chameleons in the cyber realm, changing their appearance and methods to blend into their surroundings.

APTs often begin their campaigns with a reconnaissance phase, during which they gather intelligence about their target. This can include studying the target's network architecture, identifying vulnerabilities, and profiling potential victims. The attackers are patient and meticulous, gathering information to tailor their attacks for maximum impact.

Once armed with this intelligence, APT actors craft sophisticated and customized malware to breach the target's defenses. These malware strains are often designed to evade traditional antivirus and intrusion detection systems. They use techniques like polymorphism, which changes the malware's code each time it infects a new system, making it challenging to detect.

To further enhance their stealth, APTs often employ zero-day vulnerabilities. These are previously unknown security flaws that attackers exploit before software vendors can develop patches. Zero-day vulnerabilities are incredibly valuable in the world of cyber espionage, as they provide APT actors with a window of opportunity to compromise their targets.

One of the key aspects of APTs is their use of command and control (C2) infrastructure. APT actors maintain communication channels with their malware-infected systems through C2 servers. These servers act as a bridge between the attacker and the compromised network, allowing the APT actor to exfiltrate data, issue commands, and maintain control over the target environment.

Intrusion detection and prevention systems often struggle to detect APTs because their activities mimic legitimate network traffic. APT actors use encryption and other evasion techniques to make their communications appear benign. This means that traditional network security measures are often ill-equipped to identify and stop APTs.

To combat APTs effectively, organizations must adopt a multi-layered security approach. This includes continuous monitoring of network traffic and endpoints, employing threat intelligence feeds to stay informed about emerging threats, and implementing robust access controls to limit lateral movement within the network.

User education is also a critical component of defending against APTs. Phishing attacks, which often serve as the initial infection vector for APTs, can be thwarted if users are trained to recognize and report suspicious emails and links.

In summary, understanding the characteristics of Advanced Persistent Threats is essential for modern cybersecurity professionals. APTs are not your run-of-the-mill cyber threats; they are patient, adaptable, and highly motivated. By staying vigilant, employing advanced security measures, and educating users, organizations can better defend themselves against these persistent and elusive adversaries.

Advanced Persistent Threats (APTs) are a formidable challenge in today's cybersecurity landscape, but there are effective detection and mitigation strategies that organizations can employ to safeguard their networks and data. To successfully defend against APTs, it's crucial to understand how these threats operate and the tools and techniques available for detection and mitigation.

One key aspect of APT detection is establishing a baseline of normal network behavior. This involves continuously monitoring network traffic and system activities to identify deviations that could indicate an APT presence. Tools like intrusion detection systems (IDS) and security information and event management (SIEM) solutions play a crucial role in establishing this baseline and detecting anomalies.

Behavioral analysis is another essential component of APT detection. Rather than relying solely on known signatures of malware or specific attack patterns, behavioral analysis looks for abnormal actions and behaviors within the network. This approach is effective against APTs because they often use custom malware and tactics that may not have known signatures.

Threat intelligence feeds provide valuable information for APT detection. These feeds offer insights into the latest APT campaigns, malware strains, and tactics. Security teams can use this intelligence to proactively update their detection tools and develop specific countermeasures against known APT threats.

Endpoint detection and response (EDR) solutions are increasingly critical in APT detection and mitigation. EDR solutions monitor endpoint devices, such as workstations and servers, for signs of suspicious activity. They can detect indicators of compromise (IoC) and behavioral anomalies that may indicate APT activity on a device.

Sandboxing technology is a powerful tool for APT detection. Sandboxes allow security teams to execute suspicious files or code in a controlled environment to observe their behavior without risking the network's security. This helps identify APT-related malware and vulnerabilities that traditional antivirus solutions may miss. Network segmentation is a strategy that limits lateral movement within the network, making it harder for APT actors to traverse the environment once they gain access. By segmenting the network into isolated zones with strict access controls, organizations can contain APTs and minimize their impact.

A robust incident response plan is essential for mitigating APTs effectively. This plan should outline the steps to take when an APT is detected, including isolating affected systems, identifying compromised data, and removing the threat from the network. An incident response team should be trained and ready to execute this plan swiftly.

Threat hunting is a proactive strategy for APT detection. Rather than waiting for automated tools to flag suspicious activity, threat hunters actively search for signs of APTs within the network. This can involve analyzing logs, reviewing network traffic, and investigating any anomalies or IoCs.

Deception technology is an innovative approach to APT detection. It involves deploying decoy assets within the network that appear enticing to APT actors. When attackers interact with these decoys, they trigger alerts, allowing security teams to detect and respond to APTs before they can access valuable assets.

Machine learning and artificial intelligence (AI) are increasingly utilized in APT detection. These technologies can analyze vast amounts of data and identify patterns that human analysts might miss. Machine learning models can be trained to recognize APT behavior based on historical data, improving the accuracy of detection.

Continuous monitoring is crucial for APT detection. APT actors may remain dormant within a network for extended periods, so ongoing monitoring is essential to identify their activities. Automated tools can help monitor network traffic, system logs, and endpoint behaviors 24/7.

Collaboration with external organizations and sharing threat intelligence can enhance APT detection efforts. By participating in information-sharing initiatives and industry-specific security groups, organizations can access a broader range of threat intelligence and stay informed about APT trends and tactics.

Employee training and awareness programs are vital in APT detection and mitigation. A well-informed workforce can recognize suspicious emails, links, or attachments, reducing the likelihood of successful APT-related phishing attacks.

In summary, APT detection and mitigation strategies encompass a range of techniques and technologies. These include behavioral analysis, threat intelligence feeds, EDR solutions, sandboxing, network segmentation, incident response plans, threat hunting, deception technology, machine learning, continuous monitoring, collaboration, and employee training. By implementing a holistic approach that incorporates these strategies, organizations can enhance their resilience against APTs and minimize the potential impact of these persistent and sophisticated threats.

Chapter 3: Insider Threats and Behavioral Analytics

Insider threats are a growing concern for organizations, and being able to recognize the indicators of such threats is crucial in mitigating risks. These indicators, often subtle, can help organizations detect and respond to insider threats effectively.

One common indicator of an insider threat is a sudden change in an employee's behavior or work patterns. For example, an employee who has always been punctual and dedicated suddenly becomes disengaged, misses work frequently, or shows signs of dissatisfaction. Such changes can be indicative of an insider contemplating malicious actions.

Excessive access privileges or permissions granted to an employee can also be a red flag. If an employee has more access to sensitive information or systems than their job role requires, it may indicate that they have the opportunity to misuse these privileges for personal gain or malicious purposes.

Unusual or unauthorized access to sensitive data or systems is a clear indicator of an insider threat. Monitoring access logs and being vigilant about unexpected access can help detect such incidents early. For instance, an employee accessing confidential files or systems outside of their normal duties may be a cause for concern.

Data exfiltration attempts are critical indicators of insider threats. Employees attempting to transfer sensitive data outside the organization's network, especially through unapproved channels or devices, should raise alarms. It's essential to have mechanisms in place to detect and prevent data exfiltration.

Changes in an employee's communication patterns can also be indicative of insider threats. For example, increased communication with external parties, especially competitors or unauthorized individuals, can signal an insider's involvement in unauthorized activities.

Financial irregularities can be another sign. Sudden changes in an employee's financial situation, such as unexplained wealth or financial distress, can be indicative of insider activities, especially if it aligns with the timing of data breaches or unauthorized access.

Employees who exhibit a lack of awareness or adherence to security policies and procedures may pose insider threats. Failure to follow password policies, neglecting to encrypt sensitive information, or bypassing security protocols can be indicators of an insider's intention to compromise security.

Social engineering attempts targeted at employees can also reveal insider threats. If an employee falls victim to phishing, spear-phishing, or other manipulation attempts, it could be a sign that they are susceptible to coercion or persuasion by malicious actors.

Disgruntled employees or those facing disciplinary actions may be at a higher risk of becoming insider threats. It's important for organizations to monitor and support employees who may be experiencing difficulties at work to prevent potential malicious actions.

Insiders with knowledge of security measures and the ability to bypass them can pose a significant threat. Suspicious activities, such as disabling security software, disabling alarms, or tampering with surveillance cameras, should be investigated promptly.

Behavioral anomalies in an employee's online activities can also be indicators of insider threats. Frequent visits to inappropriate websites, unusual downloads, or a sudden increase in communication with suspicious contacts can suggest malicious intent.

Employee loyalty and engagement can play a significant role in mitigating insider threats. Engaged employees are less likely to become insider threats, so organizations should focus on creating a positive work environment and fostering a sense of belonging.

In summary, recognizing insider threat indicators is vital for organizations seeking to protect their sensitive information and systems. By monitoring employee behavior, access privileges, data handling, communication patterns, financial activities, adherence to security policies, susceptibility to social engineering, and engagement levels, organizations can proactively detect and respond to insider threats before they result in significant damage. It's essential to strike a balance between trust and security, ensuring that employees feel valued while also safeguarding critical assets and data.

Behavioral analytics is a powerful tool in the realm of insider threat detection, offering a proactive approach to identifying potential threats within an organization.

By analyzing the behavior of employees and other users, organizations can gain valuable insights into their activities and detect anomalies that may indicate insider threats.

The concept behind behavioral analytics is simple: every individual within an organization has a unique pattern of behavior when it comes to accessing systems, data, and resources.

These behavior patterns are shaped by an individual's role, responsibilities, and typical activities. They include factors like the time of day an employee typically logs in, the systems they usually access, the files they commonly work with, and the frequency of their interactions with certain applications or databases.

In essence, behavioral analytics establishes a baseline of normal behavior for each user within an organization. Any deviations from this established baseline can be flagged as potential indicators of insider threats.

One of the key benefits of behavioral analytics is its ability to detect subtle and sophisticated threats that may go unnoticed by traditional security measures.

For example, consider an employee who has always logged in during regular business hours but suddenly begins accessing sensitive data late at night. This deviation from their established behavior pattern could indicate that something unusual is happening.

Behavioral analytics can also identify insider threats that involve gradual and subtle changes in behavior over time. For instance, an employee may slowly increase their access to certain confidential files or systems, which might not be apparent when looking at a single access event but becomes conspicuous when analyzed over an extended period.

Another valuable aspect of behavioral analytics is its ability to correlate data from various sources to build a comprehensive picture of user behavior.

By integrating data from sources like network logs, user activity logs, access control systems, and even physical access records, organizations can create a more accurate and detailed behavioral profile for each user.

This holistic view enables security teams to identify patterns that might otherwise remain hidden. For instance, if an employee's physical access records indicate multiple unauthorized entries into a secure area, it can be correlated with their digital behavior to provide a clearer understanding of their activities.

Behavioral analytics also plays a crucial role in addressing the challenge of false positives, which can overwhelm security teams and lead to alert fatigue. By focusing on behavioral anomalies that are truly significant, organizations can reduce false positives and ensure that security teams prioritize their efforts effectively.

One of the keys to effective behavioral analytics is machine learning and artificial intelligence. These technologies can process vast amounts of data quickly and accurately, identifying subtle patterns and anomalies that might be missed by manual analysis.

Machine learning models can be trained on historical data to recognize normal behavior patterns and then alert security teams when deviations occur. Over time, these models can become more refined and accurate in detecting insider threats.

For example, a machine learning model might notice that an employee typically accesses certain financial records only when they are working on a specific project. If the model detects access to those records outside of the usual project context, it can flag this behavior as suspicious.

Behavioral analytics can be used to detect a wide range of insider threats, including data exfiltration attempts, unauthorized access to sensitive information, and even malicious actions taken by employees with privileged access.

In some cases, behavioral analytics can identify signs of an insider who is being coerced or manipulated by external actors. For instance, if an employee suddenly begins accessing classified information or engaging in unusual online conversations, it could indicate that they are being pressured to provide sensitive data.

While behavioral analytics is a powerful tool, it's essential to implement it carefully and ethically. Privacy concerns must be addressed, and organizations should be transparent with employees about the data that is being collected and analyzed.

Additionally, behavioral analytics should be just one component of a broader insider threat detection strategy. It should complement other security measures, such as access controls, data loss prevention, and employee training.

In summary, behavioral analytics is a valuable approach to insider threat detection, leveraging the power of data analysis and machine learning to identify suspicious behavior patterns. By establishing a baseline of normal behavior for each user and flagging deviations from that baseline, organizations can proactively address insider threats before they result in significant damage. As technology continues to advance, the capabilities of behavioral analytics will only become more robust, helping organizations stay ahead of the ever-evolving landscape of insider threats.

Chapter 4: Advanced Network Forensics and Incident Response

Advanced forensic analysis tools have become essential instruments in the field of digital forensics, offering investigators powerful means to examine, recover, and analyze digital evidence.

These tools enable forensic experts to unravel complex digital mysteries, whether they involve cybercrime investigations, legal cases, or incident response activities.

One of the fundamental features of advanced forensic analysis tools is their versatility. These tools are designed to work across various operating systems, file systems, and device types, ensuring that investigators can analyze a wide range of digital evidence sources effectively.

Whether it's a Windows computer, a macOS device, a Linux server, or a mobile phone running Android or iOS, advanced forensic analysis tools can access and extract data from these platforms, making them invaluable in cross-platform investigations.

Moreover, these tools provide forensic experts with the capability to recover deleted or hidden data, a crucial function in many investigations. Whether data has been intentionally deleted to conceal evidence or accidentally lost, advanced forensic analysis tools employ sophisticated techniques to uncover and restore it.

File carving is one such technique, where these tools search for file signatures and structures in unallocated disk space, piecing together fragments of deleted files. This process can help investigators retrieve valuable evidence that would otherwise be lost.

Another essential aspect of advanced forensic analysis tools is their ability to acquire data in a forensically sound manner. This means ensuring that data remains unaltered during the acquisition process, maintaining its integrity and admissibility in legal proceedings.

These tools often use write-blocking mechanisms or other safeguards to prevent any changes to the original data source while creating a forensic copy for examination. This is a crucial step to ensure the chain of custody and preserve the evidentiary value of the data.

Advanced forensic analysis tools also excel in their capacity to analyze various types of digital evidence. From examining hard drives and solid-state drives to scrutinizing memory dumps and network traffic, these tools provide a comprehensive approach to digital forensics.

For example, when dealing with volatile memory analysis, these tools can capture the state of a running computer system, including active processes, open network connections, and data in RAM. This information can be invaluable for investigating live cyberattacks or uncovering malicious activity in real-time.

Furthermore, advanced forensic analysis tools are equipped to handle a wide array of file formats, including documents, images, videos, emails, and databases. This capability allows investigators to uncover hidden information within different file types, even if they have been encrypted or obfuscated.

Advanced forensic analysis tools also provide extensive support for timeline analysis. This involves reconstructing a chronological sequence of events related to digital evidence, helping investigators understand the sequence of actions taken by a suspect or attacker.

By examining timestamps, file metadata, and system logs, these tools can create a timeline that reveals when files were created, modified, or accessed. This information can be crucial in building a case, establishing an alibi, or tracing the origin of a cyberattack.

Moreover, these tools offer powerful search and keyword indexing capabilities. Investigators can search large volumes of data for specific keywords, phrases, or patterns, streamlining the process of identifying relevant evidence in complex investigations.

Another notable feature of advanced forensic analysis tools is their support for data visualization. They often provide graphical representations of relationships between files, user activities, and network connections, making it easier for investigators to identify patterns and anomalies.

Additionally, these tools incorporate advanced hashing and hashing analysis capabilities. Hashing allows investigators to verify the integrity of files and data by comparing their cryptographic hashes before and after acquisition or analysis. This ensures that no unauthorized changes have occurred.

Furthermore, hashing analysis can identify known files or data across multiple investigations, helping investigators link evidence to previous cases or threats.

Incorporating machine learning and artificial intelligence, advanced forensic analysis tools are becoming increasingly adept at automating parts of the analysis process. Machine learning algorithms can help identify suspicious patterns or anomalies in large datasets, reducing the time and effort required for manual analysis.

For example, these tools can automatically flag files or activities that exhibit behaviors consistent with malware or insider threats. They can also assist in the categorization and prioritization of evidence, enabling investigators to focus on the most relevant leads.

Moreover, advanced forensic analysis tools are designed to provide robust reporting capabilities. Investigators can generate comprehensive reports that document their findings, methodologies, and the chain of custody, ensuring that their work is transparent and admissible in legal proceedings.

These reports often include detailed information on the evidence analyzed, the results of examinations, and any conclusions drawn from the data.

Overall, advanced forensic analysis tools have become indispensable in modern digital forensics investigations. Their versatility, data acquisition capabilities, support for various evidence types, timeline analysis features, search and indexing capabilities, data visualization, hashing and hashing analysis, and integration of machine learning and artificial intelligence make them invaluable assets for forensic experts worldwide. With cyber threats continually evolving, these tools are at the forefront of efforts to uncover digital evidence, solve cybercrimes, and ensure justice is served.

In the dynamic and ever-evolving landscape of cybersecurity, advanced incident response strategies have become essential to effectively combat and mitigate the impact of sophisticated cyberattacks.

These strategies represent a proactive and strategic approach to dealing with security incidents, going beyond traditional reactive methods. They encompass a comprehensive set of processes, technologies, and practices designed to detect, respond to, and recover from security incidents efficiently and effectively.

One of the key elements of advanced incident response strategies is the emphasis on continuous monitoring and threat detection. Rather than waiting for a security incident to occur, organizations proactively monitor their networks and systems for signs of potential threats. This involves using advanced tools and technologies, such as intrusion detection systems (IDS), security information and event management (SIEM) solutions, and threat intelligence feeds.

Continuous monitoring allows security teams to identify unusual or suspicious activities, such as unauthorized access attempts, malware infections, or abnormal network traffic patterns, in real-time. Early detection is crucial in minimizing the impact of security incidents and preventing them from escalating into major breaches.

Another critical aspect of advanced incident response is the development of incident response playbooks and workflows. These documented procedures outline how different types of incidents should be handled, providing a structured and consistent approach to incident response.

Playbooks detail the roles and responsibilities of various team members, the steps to be taken during an incident, and the tools and resources to be used. By having predefined playbooks in place, organizations can respond rapidly and effectively to security incidents, reducing the risk of errors or delays in the heat of the moment.

Advanced incident response strategies also prioritize threat intelligence integration. Threat intelligence involves collecting, analyzing, and sharing information about emerging threats, attack techniques, and known threat actors. By incorporating threat intelligence feeds into their security operations, organizations can stay informed about the latest threats and adapt their defenses accordingly.

For example, if a threat intelligence feed reports a new malware variant being used in targeted attacks, security teams can proactively update their antivirus signatures and intrusion detection rules to detect and block that specific threat.

Furthermore, advanced incident response strategies emphasize the importance of threat hunting. Threat hunting is a proactive and iterative process of searching for signs of malicious activity or threats within an organization's network and systems. It involves skilled analysts using advanced tools and techniques to investigate anomalies and uncover hidden threats.

Threat hunting goes beyond automated detection and leverages human expertise to identify sophisticated threats that may evade traditional security measures. It allows organizations to take a proactive stance against potential threats and significantly reduces the dwell time of attackers within their networks.

In addition to proactive threat detection, advanced incident response strategies prioritize containment and eradication efforts. Containment involves isolating affected systems or segments of the network to prevent the spread of the incident. This step minimizes the attacker's ability to move laterally within the network and limits the damage caused.

Eradication, on the other hand, focuses on removing the root cause of the incident. This often involves conducting a thorough investigation to identify how the attacker gained access and ensuring that all compromised systems are clean and secure.

Advanced incident response also incorporates legal and regulatory considerations. Organizations must be prepared to comply with data breach notification requirements and other legal obligations in the event of a security incident. Advanced strategies include processes for coordinating with legal counsel, notifying affected parties, and meeting reporting obligations.

Moreover, advanced incident response strategies recognize the importance of post-incident analysis and lessons learned. After an incident is resolved, a detailed post-incident analysis is conducted to evaluate the effectiveness of the response, identify areas for improvement, and update incident response playbooks and procedures accordingly.

This iterative process ensures that organizations continually enhance their incident response capabilities and adapt to evolving threats.

Finally, advanced incident response strategies emphasize collaboration and coordination among different teams within an organization. This includes IT, security, legal, communications, and executive leadership. Effective communication and cooperation are essential for a swift and effective response to security incidents.

In summary, advanced incident response strategies are vital in today's cybersecurity landscape, where cyber threats are increasingly sophisticated and persistent. These strategies encompass continuous monitoring, incident response playbooks, threat intelligence integration, threat hunting, containment and eradication efforts, legal and regulatory considerations, post-incident analysis, and collaboration among different teams.

By adopting advanced incident response strategies, organizations can enhance their ability to detect, respond to, and recover from security incidents, ultimately strengthening their overall cybersecurity posture and resilience in the face of evolving threats.

Chapter 5: Threat Hunting: Proactive Detection and Response

In the realm of cybersecurity, threat hunting methodologies have emerged as a proactive and critical approach to identifying and mitigating security threats that may evade traditional security defenses. Threat hunting involves the systematic and continuous search for signs of malicious activity within an organization's network and systems. It goes beyond automated detection tools and relies on the skills and expertise of cybersecurity professionals to uncover hidden threats and vulnerabilities.

At the heart of threat hunting is the recognition that determined attackers often employ sophisticated tactics and techniques that can bypass traditional security measures. Rather than waiting for alerts from security tools, threat hunters take the initiative to actively seek out threats that may be lurking within an organization's infrastructure.

One of the fundamental methodologies in threat hunting is the development of hypotheses. Threat hunters start by formulating educated guesses or hypotheses about potential threats based on their understanding of the organization's environment and threat landscape. These hypotheses are informed by threat intelligence, known attack vectors, and an analysis of historical security incidents.

For example, a threat hunter may hypothesize that a particular group of threat actors known for targeting organizations in the financial sector could be operating within their network. This hypothesis is based on recent threat intelligence reports and indicators of compromise associated with that threat group.

Once hypotheses are formulated, threat hunters proceed with data collection and analysis. They gather data from various sources within the organization, such as logs from firewalls, intrusion detection systems, endpoint security solutions, and network traffic. They also collect external threat intelligence feeds and open-source intelligence to enrich their data.

The analysis phase involves meticulously examining the collected data to look for anomalies, patterns, or indicators of compromise that align with the formulated hypotheses. This process requires a deep understanding of the organization's normal network behavior and an ability to distinguish between benign and malicious activities.

During the analysis, threat hunters often use a combination of automated tools and manual investigation techniques. Automated tools can help sift through large volumes of data, while manual analysis allows for the identification of subtle, context-specific indicators that automated tools may overlook.

As part of their analysis, threat hunters may also perform network packet analysis to gain insights into network traffic and communication patterns. This level of granularity can uncover covert or encrypted communications used by attackers to maintain a foothold in the network.

Threat hunters also engage in endpoint analysis, examining the behavior of individual devices and systems. They look for signs of compromised endpoints, such as unusual process behavior, registry modifications, or suspicious network connections.

In addition to hypothesis-driven threat hunting, another methodology involves proactive threat hunting without predefined hypotheses. In this approach, threat hunters conduct open-ended investigations, searching for any signs of unusual or suspicious activity within the network. This method is particularly valuable for discovering previously unknown threats or vulnerabilities.

Threat hunting methodologies also place a strong emphasis on collaboration and knowledge sharing. Threat hunters often work closely with incident response teams, security analysts, and threat intelligence analysts to leverage their collective expertise. Collaborative efforts enhance the effectiveness of threat hunting by combining different perspectives and skill sets.

Furthermore, threat hunters document their findings and create reports that provide a clear picture of the identified threats, their potential impact, and recommended actions for mitigation. These reports are valuable for incident response teams and senior leadership, enabling informed decision-making and timely responses to security incidents.

In summary, threat hunting methodologies represent a proactive and dynamic approach to cybersecurity. They involve the formulation of hypotheses, data collection and analysis, the use of automated tools and manual investigation techniques, network and endpoint analysis, and collaborative efforts. Threat hunters play a critical role in identifying and mitigating security threats that may evade traditional defenses, ultimately strengthening an organization's overall cybersecurity posture.

Proactive threat hunting techniques represent a crucial aspect of modern cybersecurity strategies, focusing on actively seeking out potential threats and vulnerabilities before they can inflict harm on an organization. These techniques are grounded in the understanding that cyber threats continually evolve, becoming increasingly sophisticated and evasive. Rather than solely relying on reactive measures like intrusion detection systems or incident response, proactive threat hunting empowers cybersecurity professionals to take the initiative and be ahead of the curve.

The first key technique in proactive threat hunting is the development of a threat hunting hypothesis. This hypothesis serves as a starting point for the investigation, and it's crafted based on a combination of factors, including historical threat data, industry-specific threat intelligence, and an understanding of an organization's unique IT environment.

For instance, a threat hunting hypothesis might revolve around the notion that a certain type of malware has been targeting organizations in the same industry, and there's a possibility that it could be present within the organization's network.

Once the hypothesis is established, the threat hunting team embarks on a systematic data collection process. This involves gathering relevant data from various sources across the network, including logs from firewalls, antivirus solutions, DNS servers, and endpoint detection and response (EDR) systems. Additionally, external threat intelligence feeds and indicators of compromise (IoCs) are incorporated to enrich the dataset.

With a comprehensive dataset in hand, threat hunters proceed to the data analysis phase. This is where their expertise and intuition play a critical role. Threat hunters meticulously scrutinize the data, looking for anomalies, patterns, or suspicious activities that might align with the established hypothesis. They differentiate between normal network behavior and potentially malicious activities.

A combination of automated tools and manual analysis techniques is employed during this phase. Automated tools are useful for processing large volumes of data efficiently, while manual analysis allows for a nuanced understanding of the context and helps identify subtle indicators of compromise.

Network traffic analysis is another integral aspect of proactive threat hunting. By inspecting network packet data, threat hunters can unveil hidden communication channels or patterns that may have eluded traditional security measures. They pay close attention to unusual traffic patterns, encrypted communications, and other signs that might indicate malicious activity.

Endpoint analysis is equally crucial. Threat hunters examine the behavior of individual devices or endpoints to identify signs of compromise. This could include unusual processes running on a device, unauthorized changes to system configurations, or evidence of lateral movement across the network.

While hypothesis-driven threat hunting is a common approach, there's also room for open-ended, hypothesis-free hunting. In this mode, threat hunters explore the network without specific assumptions, relying on their expertise and experience to detect anomalies or potential threats that might not have been anticipated. This approach can be particularly effective in discovering novel threats or vulnerabilities.

Collaboration and knowledge sharing within the threat hunting team and across security departments are highly encouraged. Threat hunters often work closely with incident response teams, security analysts, and threat intelligence specialists. Combining their diverse skill sets and perspectives enhances the effectiveness of threat hunting efforts.

Documentation is a key part of proactive threat hunting. Threat hunters meticulously record their findings and observations, creating comprehensive reports. These reports provide a clear overview of identified threats, their potential impact, and recommended actions for mitigation. Such documentation not only assists incident response teams but also helps senior leadership understand the security landscape and make informed decisions.

In essence, proactive threat hunting techniques embody a forward-thinking approach to cybersecurity. They involve hypothesis development, systematic data collection, meticulous data analysis, network and endpoint inspection, and often hypothesis-free exploration. Collaboration and knowledge sharing are fundamental, and detailed documentation facilitates effective response and decision-making. By adopting these techniques, organizations can strengthen their security posture, stay one step ahead of evolving threats, and safeguard their digital assets.

Chapter 6: Network Access Control (NAC) and Posture Assessment

Implementing Network Access Control (NAC) is a pivotal step in securing an organization's network, serving as a gatekeeper that ensures only authorized devices gain entry. NAC is a multifaceted security strategy that encompasses various components, policies, and technologies, all working in tandem to enforce strict control over network access. In a rapidly evolving threat landscape, NAC plays a critical role in safeguarding sensitive data, mitigating risks, and maintaining the integrity of an organization's digital infrastructure.

At its core, NAC is all about verifying the identity and security posture of devices attempting to connect to the network. To implement NAC effectively, an organization must begin with a clear understanding of its network architecture, assets, and security requirements. This foundational knowledge is crucial for tailoring NAC policies and configurations to the organization's specific needs.

One of the primary components of NAC is endpoint assessment. Before granting network access, NAC systems evaluate devices seeking entry. This assessment includes checks for up-to-date antivirus software, the presence of required security patches, and adherence to security policies. Devices that meet these criteria are allowed onto the network, while non-compliant or suspicious devices are quarantined or provided with limited access until they meet the necessary security standards.

NAC solutions leverage various technologies to enforce access control. These may include 802.1X authentication, which requires users or devices to provide valid credentials, such as usernames and passwords or digital certificates, before accessing the network. This authentication process ensures that only authorized users or devices gain entry.

In addition to 802.1X, NAC can incorporate MAC address filtering, which permits or denies access based on the device's physical hardware address. While this method is less secure than 802.1X, it can still be useful in certain scenarios.

Network segmentation is another critical aspect of NAC. By dividing the network into distinct segments or VLANs, organizations can isolate different types of traffic and devices. This segmentation helps contain potential threats and limits lateral movement in case of a breach. NAC solutions often play a role in enforcing these segmentation policies.

Device profiling is yet another technique employed by NAC systems. When a device connects to the network, NAC solutions gather information about it, such as its operating system, installed applications, and hardware attributes. This data helps in classifying devices and ensuring that they adhere to the organization's security policies.

Posture assessment is a key step in NAC. This involves evaluating the security posture of a device based on predefined criteria. For example, the NAC system might check if the device's firewall is enabled, its antivirus definitions are up to date, or it has the latest security patches installed. Non-compliant devices can be quarantined or directed to remediation portals to update their security configurations.

One of the major benefits of NAC is its ability to automate responses to security incidents. If a device is found to be non-compliant or poses a threat, NAC can take actions such as isolating the device, alerting security personnel, or blocking network access entirely. This rapid response minimizes the risk of a security incident spreading throughout the network.

NAC solutions are highly adaptable and can integrate with other security systems. They often work alongside intrusion detection and prevention systems (IDS/IPS) to provide real-time threat detection and response. By analyzing network traffic patterns and endpoint behavior, NAC can help identify potential threats early and take immediate action.

NAC policies should align closely with an organization's security objectives and regulatory requirements. They should be periodically reviewed and updated to adapt to evolving threats and technology changes. Regular audits of NAC configurations and policies ensure that the system remains effective in maintaining network security.

User education and awareness are also vital components of successful NAC implementation. Users should be informed about the importance of compliance with security policies and the potential consequences of non-compliance. Training programs can help users understand their role in maintaining a secure network environment.

In summary, implementing Network Access Control (NAC) is a strategic imperative in today's cybersecurity landscape. NAC serves as a gatekeeper, verifying the identity and security posture of devices seeking network access. It encompasses various technologies, including authentication, segmentation, device profiling, and posture assessment. NAC systems automate responses to security incidents, enhance threat detection, and integrate seamlessly with other security solutions. Regular policy reviews, audits, and user education are essential to the ongoing success of NAC implementations, helping organizations protect their networks from evolving threats and vulnerabilities.

Posture assessment for endpoint security is a critical process that organizations employ to ensure that their devices meet specific security standards and are capable of defending against various threats in today's ever-evolving cybersecurity landscape. This assessment is a proactive approach to evaluating the security posture of endpoint devices, such as computers, mobile devices, and servers, to identify vulnerabilities, non-compliance with security policies, and potential risks. In a world where cyberattacks are becoming increasingly sophisticated, having a robust posture assessment strategy is essential to protect sensitive data, mitigate risks, and maintain the overall security of an organization's digital infrastructure.

At its core, posture assessment involves evaluating the security configuration, settings, and compliance of endpoint devices. This assessment checks various factors that can impact the security of a device, such as the presence of up-to-date antivirus software, the status of security patches and updates, the configuration of firewall settings, and adherence to security policies defined by the organization. It's important to note that posture assessment is not a one-time event but an ongoing process that helps maintain the security of devices throughout their lifecycle.

Posture assessment is typically carried out using specialized security software or tools that are designed to scan and analyze endpoint devices. These tools can perform a wide range of checks, including verifying the presence of antivirus software, checking for the latest operating system patches, and assessing the status of encryption protocols. The results of these assessments provide organizations with valuable insights into the security health of their endpoints.

One of the primary goals of posture assessment is to ensure that all endpoint devices meet a baseline of security requirements. This baseline is typically defined by the organization's security policies and industry best practices. For example, an organization may require that all endpoints have antivirus software installed, that they receive regular updates, and that they have firewall settings configured to block malicious traffic. By continuously monitoring and assessing endpoints against this baseline, organizations can identify and remediate security vulnerabilities in a timely manner.

Another important aspect of posture assessment is compliance monitoring. This involves ensuring that endpoint devices adhere to the organization's security policies and regulatory requirements. Compliance monitoring helps organizations demonstrate their commitment to security and ensures that they meet the necessary legal and regulatory obligations. Non-compliance can have severe consequences, including legal penalties and reputational damage.

Endpoint security posture assessment plays a crucial role in risk management. By identifying vulnerabilities and non-compliant devices, organizations can take proactive measures to reduce their attack surface and mitigate potential risks. For example, if a vulnerability is detected in an endpoint device, organizations can prioritize the deployment of patches or updates to address the issue before it can be exploited by attackers.

Additionally, posture assessment is instrumental in incident response. In the event of a security incident, having an up-to-date inventory of all endpoint devices and their security posture is invaluable. This information allows organizations to quickly identify compromised devices, isolate them from the network, and initiate the appropriate remediation steps. It enables a swift response to contain the incident and prevent it from spreading further.

Organizations should consider the following best practices when implementing posture assessment for endpoint security:

Define Clear Security Policies: Establish comprehensive security policies that outline the minimum security requirements for endpoint devices. These policies should align with industry standards and regulatory requirements.

Select Appropriate Tools: Choose the right security assessment tools or solutions that can effectively scan, analyze, and report on the security posture of endpoint devices.

Regular Scanning: Conduct regular scans of endpoint devices to ensure that they remain compliant with security policies. These scans can be scheduled at predetermined intervals or triggered based on specific events.

Automate Remediation: Implement automated remediation processes to address security vulnerabilities and non-compliance issues promptly. Automation helps reduce manual intervention and accelerates response times.

Prioritize Vulnerabilities: Use risk-based prioritization to address the most critical vulnerabilities first. Not all vulnerabilities are equal, and some may pose a higher risk to the organization.

Education and Training: Provide ongoing education and training to end users to raise awareness of the importance of security posture and compliance.

Integration: Integrate posture assessment into the organization's broader cybersecurity strategy, including incident response and threat detection.

Regular Reporting: Generate regular reports on the security posture of endpoint devices to provide visibility to stakeholders and track progress over time.

In summary, posture assessment for endpoint security is a fundamental practice in modern cybersecurity. It involves evaluating and monitoring the security configuration and compliance of endpoint devices to identify vulnerabilities and non-compliance with security policies. By implementing an effective posture assessment strategy, organizations can reduce risks, enhance incident response capabilities, and maintain the overall security of their digital assets. This proactive approach is essential in a constantly evolving threat landscape where cybersecurity is paramount.

Chapter 7: Secure Software Development and Code Review

Secure coding practices are the foundation of building resilient and secure software in today's digital age, where cyber threats and vulnerabilities are rampant. Writing secure code involves adopting a set of principles, techniques, and best practices to ensure that software applications are robust and capable of withstanding malicious attacks. This chapter delves into the world of secure coding, exploring why it's essential, what it entails, and how developers can implement these practices to create safer and more reliable software.

Imagine software as the intricate architecture of a building. Secure coding is akin to using sturdy materials, constructing strong foundations, and implementing safeguards to protect against potential threats like storms and intruders. In the digital realm, developers are the architects and builders, and their code forms the structure of software applications. Just as architects must adhere to building codes for safety, developers must follow secure coding practices to protect against cyber threats.

Secure coding is not an afterthought; it should be an integral part of the software development process from the very beginning. This approach, known as "security by design," emphasizes that security should be considered at every stage of development, rather than being tacked on at the end as a mere afterthought. By weaving security into the fabric of their code, developers can create software that is inherently resistant to attacks.

One of the cornerstones of secure coding is input validation. This practice involves scrutinizing and validating data that enters the application from external sources, such as user inputs or data received from network connections. Unvalidated input is a common entry point for attackers who attempt to inject malicious data or code into an application. By rigorously validating inputs, developers can thwart many common attacks, including SQL injection and cross-site scripting (XSS).

Another fundamental principle is the principle of least privilege. This concept asserts that every component of a software system, whether it's a user, a process, or a system, should be given the minimum level of access or permissions necessary to perform its function. Applying the principle of least privilege helps reduce the attack surface, limiting the potential damage that a compromised component can inflict.

Secure coding practices also encompass the use of secure APIs (Application Programming Interfaces). APIs are bridges that allow different software components to communicate with each other. Developers must ensure that APIs are designed securely and that they validate Inputs, authenticate users, and authorize access to sensitive resources correctly. Poorly designed APIs can introduce vulnerabilities that attackers may exploit.

Authentication and authorization are vital components of secure coding. Authentication involves verifying the identity of users or components attempting to access a system. Strong authentication mechanisms, such as multi-factor authentication (MFA), add an extra layer of security. Authorization, on the other hand, determines what actions or resources a user or component is allowed to access after authentication. Implementing fine-grained authorization controls is essential to prevent unauthorized access.

Secure coding practices extend to the handling of sensitive data. Developers must ensure that sensitive data, such as passwords, financial information, or personal data, is stored, transmitted, and processed securely. Encryption techniques, like SSL/TLS for data in transit and hashing for data at rest, are indispensable tools for protecting sensitive information.

Code reviews and testing play a pivotal role in secure coding. Regularly reviewing code for security flaws, such as buffer overflows or insecure dependencies, allows developers to catch vulnerabilities early in the development process. Additionally, conducting thorough security testing, including penetration testing and vulnerability scanning, helps identify and remediate issues before they can be exploited by attackers.

Secure coding practices extend to error handling as well. Developers must implement robust error-handling mechanisms that do not inadvertently reveal sensitive information to potential attackers. Error messages should be vague and non-specific to prevent attackers from gaining insights into the internal workings of the application.

One of the most prevalent security issues in web applications is Cross-Site Scripting (XSS). XSS attacks occur when malicious scripts are injected into web pages and executed in the browsers of unsuspecting users. Secure coding practices to prevent XSS include proper input validation, output encoding, and the use of security libraries that can automatically sanitize user inputs.

Similarly, Cross-Site Request Forgery (CSRF) attacks can compromise the integrity of web applications by tricking users into making unwanted requests. Developers can protect against CSRF attacks by implementing anti-CSRF tokens and ensuring that sensitive operations require explicit user consent.

In the realm of secure coding, it is crucial to keep abreast of emerging threats and vulnerabilities. Cyber threats are constantly evolving, and developers must stay informed about the latest attack techniques and security patches for the libraries and frameworks they use. Engaging in ongoing education and training is vital to maintain a high level of security awareness.

Secure coding practices are not limited to web applications. They apply to all types of software, including desktop applications, mobile apps, and embedded systems. Regardless of the platform, developers must adhere to secure coding principles to build resilient and trustworthy software.

Furthermore, secure coding practices are not solely the responsibility of developers. Organizations must foster a culture of security and provide developers with the necessary tools and resources to implement secure coding effectively. Security should be a shared responsibility, with input from development, operations, and security teams.

In summary, secure coding practices are essential for building software that can withstand the ever-evolving landscape of cyber threats. Developers play a crucial role in ensuring the security of their applications by following principles such as input validation, least privilege, secure APIs, strong authentication and authorization, data protection, code reviews, and security testing. By integrating security into the software development process from the outset, organizations can create applications that are robust, resilient, and capable of defending against modern cyber threats.

Code review for security is a critical practice in the realm of secure software development, serving as a fundamental line of defense against vulnerabilities and potential cyberattacks. It is like having a vigilant guardian who meticulously examines every nook and cranny of your software's source code to ensure its resilience against malicious actors.

Picture a code review as a thorough inspection of a new house before moving in. Just as you would want to identify and address any structural or safety issues, a security-focused code review aims to pinpoint vulnerabilities and weaknesses that could compromise the security of your software.

Security code reviews should ideally take place throughout the development process, not just as a final step. By incorporating security reviews into each phase, developers can identify and address issues early, saving both time and resources down the line.

The primary objective of a code review for security is to detect and rectify security flaws in the source code. These flaws can manifest in various forms, from poor input validation to improper authentication mechanisms. During a security-focused code review, a knowledgeable reviewer scrutinizes the code to uncover vulnerabilities that might be exploited by attackers.

Input validation is a common area of concern in code reviews. Ensuring that all input is properly validated is paramount because attackers frequently attempt to inject malicious data through user inputs. A security code reviewer meticulously examines how user inputs are handled and whether they are subjected to rigorous validation to prevent malicious input from causing harm.

Authentication and authorization mechanisms are also pivotal components of a security code review. Reviewers evaluate whether the code implements robust authentication techniques, such as multi-factor authentication (MFA), to protect user accounts from unauthorized access. Additionally, authorization checks must be thoroughly examined to ensure that users are granted only the privileges they legitimately need.

Secure coding practices should be apparent throughout the codebase. Security-conscious developers adhere to principles such as the principle of least privilege, which mandates that each component of the system receives the minimum level of access required for its function. Code reviewers assess whether these practices are consistently applied and whether over-privileged components are identified and rectified.

Another critical aspect of a code review for security is the examination of how sensitive data is handled. Protecting sensitive information, like passwords or financial data, is of paramount importance. A code reviewer checks whether data is securely stored, transmitted, and processed by evaluating encryption techniques used for data in transit and hashing for data at rest.

The usage of secure APIs (Application Programming Interfaces) is also scrutinized during a security code review. APIs serve as conduits for communication between different software components, and a poorly designed API can introduce vulnerabilities. Code reviewers evaluate whether APIs validate inputs, authenticate users, and authorize access to sensitive resources correctly.

Error handling is often overlooked but is nonetheless crucial in security code reviews. Proper error-handling mechanisms are necessary to prevent attackers from gaining insights into the internal workings of the application. Code reviewers ensure that error messages do not inadvertently reveal sensitive information and that they are vague and non-specific to thwart potential attackers.

Two common security vulnerabilities that reviewers look for are Cross-Site Scripting (XSS) and Cross-Site Request Forgery (CSRF). XSS attacks involve injecting malicious scripts into web pages, which are then executed in the browsers of unsuspecting users. Code reviewers assess whether proper input validation, output encoding, and security libraries are used to prevent XSS vulnerabilities.

CSRF attacks, on the other hand, exploit users' trust in a website. By tricking users into making unwanted requests without their knowledge, attackers can compromise the integrity of web applications. Code reviewers ensure that anti-CSRF tokens are implemented, and that sensitive operations require explicit user consent to protect against CSRF attacks.

While the primary focus of a security code review is on identifying vulnerabilities and weaknesses, it also plays a vital role in educating developers. Code reviewers provide feedback and guidance to developers, helping them understand why certain code practices are insecure and how to rectify them. This educational aspect fosters a culture of security within the development team, where secure coding becomes a shared responsibility.

Furthermore, security code reviews contribute to the continuous improvement of an organization's security posture. By identifying and addressing vulnerabilities early, code reviewers help prevent potential security incidents that could lead to data breaches or other catastrophic consequences. This proactive approach is far more cost-effective than addressing security issues after they have been exploited by attackers.

To summarize, code review for security is an essential practice in the software development process. It involves a meticulous examination of the source code to detect and rectify security flaws. During a security code review, input validation, authentication and authorization mechanisms, secure data handling, proper API usage, error handling, and protection against common vulnerabilities like XSS and CSRF are all thoroughly assessed. Beyond identifying vulnerabilities, security code reviews serve as an educational opportunity for developers and contribute to the overall security posture of an organization.

Chapter 8: Advanced Security Architectures and Design

Security by design principles represent a proactive approach to incorporating security considerations into every phase of a project, ensuring that security is an integral part of the development process. Think of it as designing a car with safety features from the ground up, rather than trying to add seatbelts and airbags as an afterthought. In the digital realm, security by design is a fundamental concept aimed at building secure systems from the very beginning.

One of the central tenets of security by design is the concept of "least privilege." This principle asserts that users, applications, and systems should only have access to the minimum level of permissions required to perform their intended tasks. It's akin to granting employees access to only the rooms in a building that they need to do their jobs, preventing them from entering restricted areas. Authentication and authorization mechanisms play a pivotal role in implementing the least privilege principle. Robust authentication ensures that only authorized users can access a system or application. Once authenticated, the authorization mechanism dictates what actions or resources a user can access. Security by design mandates that these mechanisms are thoughtfully implemented to align with the principle of least privilege.

Another essential principle is defense in depth, which can be likened to the layers of security in a bank vault. Rather than relying on a single security measure, defense in depth employs multiple layers of security controls to protect against various threats. This might include firewalls, intrusion detection systems, encryption, and access controls, all working in concert to safeguard a system.

Security by design extends beyond the technical aspects and encompasses secure software development practices. It involves threat modeling, where potential vulnerabilities and risks are identified early in the design phase. This proactive approach allows developers to address security issues before they become significant problems. It's akin to anticipating potential hazards on a hiking trail and taking precautions to avoid them.

Secure coding practices are a fundamental aspect of security by design. Developers are encouraged to follow coding standards and guidelines that minimize the risk of introducing vulnerabilities. Secure coding includes practices like input validation, output encoding, and avoiding common pitfalls such as buffer overflows or injection attacks. It's like building a house with solid construction practices to prevent structural weaknesses.

In the world of security by design, encryption is a critical tool. It's akin to using a secure envelope for a confidential letter. Encryption ensures that data remains confidential and tamper-proof, even if it falls into the wrong hands. It's an essential element of securing data in transit and data at rest.

Privacy by design is a principle closely related to security by design, emphasizing the importance of protecting individuals' privacy rights. It means that privacy considerations are embedded into the development process from the outset, ensuring that user data is handled with the utmost care and compliance with privacy regulations. Imagine designing a restaurant where customer privacy is a top priority, with discreet seating and strict data protection measures.

One of the overarching goals of security by design is to create a culture of security within an organization. This involves educating employees about security best practices and fostering a shared responsibility for security. It's similar to a neighborhood watch program where everyone looks out for each other's safety.

Security by design also recognizes the importance of secure configurations. Just as you would set up your home alarm system with the right settings, secure configurations involve optimizing the settings of systems, applications, and devices to minimize security risks. This includes disabling unnecessary services, using strong passwords, and applying security patches promptly.

Threat modeling is an essential practice within the security by design framework. It involves identifying potential threats and vulnerabilities in a system and assessing their impact. This process helps prioritize security measures and allocate resources effectively. It's like conducting a safety assessment before embarking on a long road trip, ensuring you have the right tools and plans in place to handle potential issues.

Security by design also embraces the principle of continuous improvement. It's not a one-time effort but an ongoing commitment to enhancing security measures as new threats emerge. This is akin to regularly maintaining and upgrading your home security system to stay ahead of evolving risks.

To sum it up, security by design principles are the cornerstone of building secure and resilient systems. These principles include least privilege, defense in depth, threat modeling, secure coding practices, encryption, privacy by design, and fostering a culture of security. By incorporating security considerations from the outset, organizations can create robust defenses against an ever-evolving threat landscape, much like building a fortress with multiple layers of protection.

Implementing advanced security architectures represents a crucial step forward in safeguarding digital assets and information. It's like upgrading your home security system to include smart locks, surveillance cameras, and motion detectors for enhanced protection. In the ever-evolving landscape of cybersecurity threats, traditional security measures may no longer be sufficient. Advanced security architectures offer a comprehensive and adaptable approach to tackling the sophisticated and multifaceted challenges posed by cyber threats.

At the core of advanced security architectures is the concept of network segmentation, which is akin to dividing your home into separate zones with different security measures. By dividing a network into segments or zones, organizations can limit the lateral movement of attackers and contain potential breaches. Each segment has its own security policies and access controls, ensuring that even if one segment is compromised, the entire network remains protected.

A key component of advanced security architectures is the use of next-generation firewalls (NGFWs). These firewalls go beyond traditional packet filtering and stateful inspection, incorporating advanced capabilities like deep packet inspection, intrusion detection and prevention, and application-layer filtering. NGFWs are like having a security team that not only checks IDs at the door but also analyzes everyone's behavior and flags suspicious activities.

Intrusion Detection Systems (IDS) and Intrusion Prevention Systems (IPS) are integral parts of advanced security architectures. IDS monitors network traffic for suspicious activities and alerts security teams to potential threats. IPS, on the other hand, not only detects but also takes proactive measures to block or mitigate threats automatically. It's like having security personnel who not only report suspicious behavior but also intervene to prevent any harm.

Secure access solutions are critical in advanced security architectures. This includes technologies like Zero Trust Network Access (ZTNA), which verifies the identity of users and devices before granting access. ZTNA is akin to having a stringent ID check and background screening for anyone entering your property. This ensures that only authorized users with clean credentials can access sensitive resources.

Advanced security architectures also emphasize the importance of endpoint security. Endpoint Detection and Response (EDR) solutions provide real-time monitoring and response capabilities on endpoints like computers and mobile devices. EDR solutions are like having security cameras and alarms in every room of your house, allowing you to detect and respond to threats at the endpoint level.

Cloud security is a significant consideration within advanced security architectures. With the growing adoption of cloud services, organizations need to extend their security measures to protect data and applications hosted in the cloud. Cloud Security Posture Management (CSPM) tools help organizations ensure that their cloud configurations align with best practices and security policies.

Advanced security architectures incorporate Security Information and Event Management (SIEM) systems for comprehensive threat detection and response. SIEM solutions collect and analyze data from various sources, allowing security teams to correlate events and identify potential security incidents. It's like having a central control room that monitors all security cameras and alarms in your home, providing a holistic view of security.

Machine Learning (ML) and Artificial Intelligence (AI) are becoming increasingly vital in advanced security architectures. These technologies can analyze large volumes of data to detect anomalies and patterns indicative of cyber threats. ML and AI are like having a security assistant who continuously learns and adapts to new threats, helping you stay one step ahead of attackers.

Identity and Access Management (IAM) solutions play a pivotal role in advanced security architectures by managing user identities and controlling access to resources. IAM solutions ensure that only authorized users can access specific applications and data. It's like having a personalized keycard system that grants access based on the user's identity and permissions.

As part of advanced security architectures, organizations need to adopt a proactive stance towards threat hunting. Threat hunting involves actively searching for signs of hidden threats within the network. It's like having a private investigator who looks for any unusual activities or footprints that might indicate an intruder's presence.

Advanced security architectures prioritize automation and orchestration. Security Orchestration, Automation, and Response (SOAR) platforms help streamline security operations by automating routine tasks and responses to security incidents. SOAR is akin to having a team of security experts who work tirelessly and efficiently to manage security events.

An essential aspect of implementing advanced security architectures is continuous monitoring and improvement. Security teams should regularly assess the effectiveness of security measures, identify weaknesses, and adapt their strategies to address emerging threats. It's like regularly inspecting your home security system and making upgrades to stay ahead of potential burglars.

Threat intelligence is another key element of advanced security architectures. Organizations should leverage threat intelligence feeds and services to stay informed about the latest threats and vulnerabilities. Threat intelligence is like having a network of informants who provide valuable information about potential threats in your neighborhood.

Security awareness and training for employees are crucial in advanced security architectures. Well-informed and vigilant employees can serve as an additional layer of defense against social engineering attacks and insider threats. Security training is akin to educating your family members about recognizing and responding to security risks.

Advanced security architectures also advocate for a robust incident response framework. This framework outlines the steps to take when a security incident occurs, ensuring a coordinated and effective response. It's like having an emergency response plan in place, complete with contact information and procedures to follow during a crisis.

In summary, implementing advanced security architectures is vital in today's complex and evolving threat landscape. These architectures incorporate network segmentation, next-generation firewalls, IDS/IPS, secure access solutions, endpoint security, cloud security measures, SIEM, ML/AI, IAM, threat hunting, automation, continuous monitoring, threat intelligence, security awareness, and incident response. By adopting these measures, organizations can create a robust defense against a wide range of cyber threats, similar to fortifying your home with advanced security systems to protect against modern-day burglars.

Chapter 9: Secure DevOps and Container Security

Integrating security into DevOps pipelines is like seamlessly weaving safety checks into the construction of a high-speed train—ensuring that it runs efficiently while keeping passengers secure throughout the journey. In today's fast-paced software development landscape, where agility and speed are paramount, DevOps practices have become the cornerstone of delivering applications rapidly and continuously. However, this breakneck speed can inadvertently introduce security vulnerabilities, making it crucial to incorporate security measures throughout the development process.

Think of your DevOps pipeline as a well-orchestrated assembly line in a manufacturing plant. It takes code from its inception and carries it through various stages, from development and testing to deployment and monitoring. The goal is to maintain a consistent and predictable process while ensuring the final product is of high quality and free from defects, much like ensuring each car that rolls off the assembly line is safe and reliable.

Now, let's delve into how security can be seamlessly integrated into each phase of the DevOps pipeline:

1. Planning: Just as architects carefully plan the design of a building before construction begins, security planning in DevOps involves defining security requirements and risk assessments at the project's outset. Teams should outline security objectives and incorporate threat modeling to identify potential risks. This stage is akin to developing a robust blueprint for a secure application.

2. Coding: Developers, like skilled craftsmen, write the code that forms the foundation of an application. Secure coding practices involve adhering to security guidelines and using tools to identify and rectify vulnerabilities. It's like ensuring that the materials used in a construction project meet safety standards, and any flaws are corrected during the manufacturing process.

3. Building: This phase involves compiling and assembling the code into executable software. Here, security scans can be integrated into the build process to catch issues early on, much like conducting quality checks during the construction of a vehicle to ensure it meets safety standards.

4. Testing: Rigorous testing, similar to quality control inspections in manufacturing, is essential in DevOps. Security testing, including static analysis, dynamic analysis, and penetration testing, should be part of the testing regimen to identify and rectify vulnerabilities. Think of this phase as conducting crash tests and inspections to ensure that a car performs safely under various conditions.

5. Deployment: Deployment in DevOps is like launching a spacecraft into orbit—it requires precision and care. Automation tools can help ensure consistent and secure deployments by validating configurations and ensuring that security measures are applied consistently across environments.

6. Monitoring: Continuous monitoring in DevOps is like having a team of engineers who keep an eye on a vehicle's performance throughout its lifespan. Security monitoring tools should be in place to detect anomalies and security breaches promptly. Teams should use metrics and logs to gain insights into system behavior, similar to analyzing

data from sensors in a vehicle to ensure optimal performance.

7. Feedback and Iteration: DevOps is all about continuous improvement. Teams should gather feedback from operations and security teams to identify areas for enhancement. Much like manufacturers receive feedback from customers and use it to improve their products, DevOps teams should use feedback to refine their security practices continually.

8. Collaboration: Collaboration between development, operations, and security teams is critical in DevOps, much like different departments in a manufacturing plant working together to ensure product quality and safety. Open communication and collaboration can help identify and address security issues efficiently.

9. Automation: Automation in DevOps is akin to implementing robotics in manufacturing processes. It reduces human error, enhances efficiency, and ensures that security checks and tests are consistently applied throughout the pipeline.

10. Container Security: When using containers, security measures must be in place. Just as cargo containers are inspected for safety, container security involves scanning container images, controlling access, and monitoring runtime behavior to prevent vulnerabilities.

11. Infrastructure as Code (IaC): Treating infrastructure as code is like having blueprints for a building. IaC allows for consistent and repeatable infrastructure deployment, with security controls embedded directly into the code.

12. Compliance and Governance: Regulatory compliance and governance in DevOps are akin to adhering to building codes and regulations in construction. Organizations

should ensure that their processes and practices align with industry standards and legal requirements.

13. Security as Code: Security as Code is like embedding security controls into the DNA of your application. It involves defining security policies and configurations as code, making it easier to automate security checks and enforce policies consistently. In summary, integrating security into DevOps pipelines is not just a best practice but a necessity in today's digital landscape. It's like ensuring that every step in building a complex structure, whether it's a vehicle, a building, or a software application, prioritizes safety and security. By seamlessly weaving security measures into the entire DevOps process, organizations can accelerate their development while mitigating risks, ultimately delivering secure and reliable software to their users. Container security is akin to safeguarding a vault full of valuable treasures, where each treasure represents a microservice or application component encapsulated in a container. As containers gain popularity in modern software development, ensuring their security becomes paramount. Think of containers as secure boxes that house your application's components, ensuring they don't interact with each other in harmful ways while also preventing unauthorized access from external threats. The beauty of containers lies in their ability to package an application and its dependencies into a single, lightweight unit, which can be easily deployed across different environments. However, this very convenience can pose security challenges if not managed properly. To protect your containerized applications, it's essential to adhere to container security best practices throughout their lifecycle.

1. Start with Secure Images: Just as you would want to ensure the materials used to construct a building are sturdy and free of defects, start with secure container images. Use trusted base images from reputable sources and regularly update them to patch vulnerabilities.

2. Container Scanning: Similar to employing X-ray machines at airports to scan baggage for prohibited items, use container scanning tools to analyze container images for vulnerabilities. These tools can identify and flag security issues within the image.

3. Isolation: Containers, like isolated rooms within a building, should run independently. Implement container isolation mechanisms, such as namespaces and cgroups, to ensure that each container operates in its own secure environment.

4. Least Privilege Principle: Just as you would restrict access to certain rooms or areas in a building to authorized personnel only, apply the principle of least privilege to containerized applications. Limit container permissions to only what is necessary for their operation.

5. Access Control: Implement access controls to restrict who can interact with your containers, much like using access cards to enter secure areas in a building. Employ Role-Based Access Control (RBAC) and container-specific access management tools to define and enforce access policies.

6. Network Segmentation: Network segmentation in container environments is akin to dividing a building into secure zones. Isolate container networks using technologies like Virtual LANs (VLANs) or overlay networks to prevent unauthorized communication between containers.

7. Orchestration Security: Container orchestration platforms like Kubernetes are the building managers of the container world. Secure them by applying security policies, using RBAC, and regularly updating to the latest version to benefit from security enhancements.

8. Monitoring and Logging: Just as surveillance cameras in a building help identify security threats, implement monitoring and logging for your containers. Collect logs and monitor container behavior to detect and respond to security incidents promptly.

9. Runtime Protection: Employ runtime security measures, such as runtime anomaly detection and container runtime security tools, to safeguard containers while they're running. This is like having security personnel continuously patrol a building.

10. Secrets Management: Safeguard sensitive information, such as passwords and API keys, using secret management tools specifically designed for containers. Treat secrets as valuable keys that unlock secure areas within your containerized application.

11. Patch Management: Regularly apply security patches and updates to your containerized applications, just as you would maintain and repair different parts of a building to prevent deterioration.

12. Image Signing and Verification: Use digital signatures to verify the authenticity of container images, much like verifying the identity of visitors before granting them access to a secure facility.

13. Runtime Policies: Implement runtime policies to enforce security controls, such as preventing containers from running as root or limiting the resources they can

consume. These policies act as rules governing behavior within the container environment.

14. Incident Response Planning: Prepare an incident response plan to address security breaches swiftly and effectively. This is similar to having fire evacuation plans and procedures in place within a building.

15. Backup and Recovery: Just as you would create backups of important data in a building, regularly back up your containerized applications and their configurations to ensure business continuity in case of an incident.

16. Security Training: Provide security training for development and operations teams to raise awareness about container security best practices. Educate team members about potential threats and how to respond to them.

17. Continuous Improvement: Regularly assess and improve your container security practices. Conduct security assessments and penetration tests to identify weaknesses and take corrective actions. In essence, container security best practices are all about safeguarding the valuable assets contained within your applications, ensuring they are protected from external threats and potential vulnerabilities. Just as you would take every measure to ensure the security of a valuable vault, organizations should adopt a holistic approach to container security that spans from image creation to runtime protection, and from access controls to incident response. By adhering to these best practices, you can enjoy the benefits of containers while keeping your applications and data secure.

Chapter 10: Future Trends in Network Security: AI, IoT, and Beyond

AI, in the context of network security, encompasses a range of technologies, including machine learning, deep learning, natural language processing, and more. These capabilities are harnessed to bolster various aspects of network security, from threat detection to incident response. Let's explore how AI contributes to each facet of network security.

1. Threat Detection: Imagine AI as a vigilant sentry that continuously scans your network's traffic, seeking patterns that deviate from the norm. Machine learning algorithms can detect anomalies, such as unusual data flows, unauthorized access attempts, or suspicious user behavior. These algorithms learn from historical data and adapt to evolving threats, making them highly effective in identifying new and sophisticated attacks.

2. Intrusion Detection and Prevention: AI-powered Intrusion Detection Systems (IDS) and Intrusion Prevention Systems (IPS) provide a formidable defense mechanism. They can identify known attack signatures and, more impressively, identify deviations from normal network behavior that might indicate novel attacks. Think of it as AI's ability to recognize not just familiar faces but also new ones in a crowd.

3. Behavioral Analysis: AI-based behavioral analysis goes a step further. It learns the usual behavior of users and devices in your network and detects deviations that might signify compromised accounts or devices. It's like an AI detective tracking down suspicious activities in a bustling city.

4. Threat Intelligence: AI can sift through vast volumes of threat intelligence data from various sources, including public databases, dark web forums, and historical attack data. It can connect the dots between seemingly unrelated pieces of information, providing security teams with valuable insights into potential threats.

5. Predictive Analysis: AI can forecast potential threats and vulnerabilities by analyzing historical data, attack trends, and emerging threats. It's akin to weather forecasting, but for network security. By anticipating potential risks, organizations can proactively implement security measures.

6. User and Entity Behavior Analytics (UEBA): UEBA leverages AI to scrutinize user and entity activities. It can identify insider threats, such as employees behaving unusually or accessing unauthorized resources. It's like having a trustworthy friend who knows your habits so well that they can spot when something is amiss.

7. Automated Response: AI can respond to threats in real-time, automatically isolating compromised devices or blocking malicious traffic. It can act swiftly and decisively, much faster than human intervention. Think of it as an AI-driven security guard capable of instant response.

8. Phishing Detection: AI-driven email security solutions excel at spotting phishing attempts. They analyze the content and context of emails to identify suspicious patterns and warn users about potential threats. It's like having a sharp-eyed assistant who scans your messages for hidden dangers.

9. Malware Detection: AI can identify known malware signatures and detect zero-day threats by analyzing file

behavior and attributes. It's like an AI microscope, magnifying file details to reveal hidden malicious code.

10. Network Traffic Analysis: AI can monitor network traffic and pinpoint unusual traffic patterns or malicious payloads. It's like having an AI traffic cop who detects reckless drivers and suspicious vehicles on the digital highway.

11. Security Analytics: AI-driven security analytics platforms can process large datasets to identify security trends, vulnerabilities, and areas that need attention. Think of it as an AI analyst who sifts through data to uncover valuable insights.

12. Threat Mitigation: AI can assist in devising and executing mitigation strategies, offering recommendations on how to address security incidents effectively. It's akin to an AI crisis manager who guides you through challenging situations.

13. Scalability: One of AI's remarkable attributes is scalability. It can handle vast amounts of data and adapt to the size and complexity of your network. It's like having an AI assistant who can effortlessly manage a bustling organization.

14. Reducing False Positives: AI can significantly reduce the number of false positives, allowing security teams to focus on genuine threats rather than wasting time on benign alerts. It's like having an AI filter that screens out noise, ensuring that you only pay attention to meaningful signals.

15. Adaptive Security: AI adapts to the evolving threat landscape. As new threats emerge, AI models can be retrained to recognize them, ensuring that your network's security remains up to date.

16. Threat Hunting: AI can assist security professionals in threat hunting activities. It can analyze vast datasets and identify subtle indicators of compromise that might elude human analysts.

17. User Education: AI-driven security solutions can provide real-time user education by alerting users to potential security risks and guiding them on safe practices. It's like having a digital mentor who imparts security knowledge.

In summary, AI is your network's digital ally in the battle against cyber threats. It complements human expertise by providing real-time threat detection, automated response, and proactive analysis. By leveraging AI's capabilities, organizations can enhance their security posture, reduce response times, and stay resilient in the face of ever-evolving cyber threats.

Securing the vast and expanding Internet of Things (IoT) landscape has become an imperative in the digital age, and in this chapter, we will delve into the intricacies of safeguarding IoT devices and networks. Picture a world where everyday objects, from thermostats to refrigerators, are interconnected, providing convenience and efficiency, but also creating new cybersecurity challenges. As we explore IoT security, we'll navigate the complexities, threats, and strategies to ensure your IoT ecosystem remains protected.

1. IoT Growth: The proliferation of IoT devices is astounding. Smart appliances, wearable technology, industrial sensors, and more are flooding the market. This growth creates a larger attack surface for cybercriminals.

2. Diverse Ecosystem: The IoT ecosystem is diverse, spanning various industries, including healthcare,

automotive, agriculture, and smart homes. Each sector brings unique security requirements and challenges.

3. Vulnerabilities: IoT devices often have limited processing power and memory, which can make them vulnerable to attacks. Many lack robust security features or receive infrequent firmware updates.

4. Entry Points: IoT devices can serve as entry points for cyberattacks. A compromised smart camera or thermostat can be used as a foothold to infiltrate a network.

5. Device Authentication: Ensuring the identity of IoT devices is critical. Robust device authentication mechanisms prevent unauthorized devices from connecting to the network.

6. Data Encryption: Data transmitted between IoT devices and the cloud should be encrypted to protect against eavesdropping. Strong encryption protocols should be employed.

7. Firmware Security: Manufacturers should prioritize secure firmware development and timely updates. Regular patches are essential to fix vulnerabilities.

8. Access Control: Implement strict access controls for IoT devices. Limit the privileges of each device and user, ensuring they can only perform necessary actions.

9. Network Segmentation: Isolate IoT devices from critical systems through network segmentation. This practice limits the potential damage a compromised IoT device can cause.

10. IoT Gateways: Use IoT gateways to act as intermediaries between IoT devices and the network. These gateways can apply security policies and inspect traffic.

11. Security Standards: Adherence to security standards is crucial. Organizations should select IoT devices that comply with recognized security guidelines.

12. Behavior Monitoring: Employ behavioral analysis to detect unusual patterns in IoT device behavior, which could indicate a compromise.

13. Over-The-Air Updates: IoT devices should support over-the-air updates, allowing manufacturers to deploy security patches efficiently.

14. Supply Chain Security: Ensure the security of the entire supply chain, from component manufacturers to the assembly line. Counterfeit components can introduce vulnerabilities.

15. User Awareness: Educate users about IoT security best practices. Simple measures like changing default passwords and updating device firmware can go a long way.

16. Vendor Relationships: Maintain a strong relationship with IoT device vendors. Promptly report and address security issues.

17. Incident Response: Develop an incident response plan specific to IoT security incidents. This plan should outline steps to isolate and remediate compromised devices.

18. Regulatory Compliance: Understand and adhere to relevant IoT security regulations and standards, such as the General Data Protection Regulation (GDPR) and IoT Cybersecurity Improvement Act.

19. IoT Security Solutions: Utilize specialized IoT security solutions that provide visibility, threat detection, and response capabilities for IoT devices.

20. Consumer IoT Security: For home users, consumer IoT devices like smart thermostats and voice assistants should be securely configured and regularly updated.

21. Industrial IoT (IIoT): In the industrial sector, IIoT security is paramount. Protecting critical infrastructure and industrial processes from IoT-related threats is essential.

22. Privacy Considerations: IoT devices often collect vast amounts of data. Respect user privacy and comply with privacy regulations when handling this data.

23. Continuous Monitoring: Continuously monitor IoT networks for anomalies and intrusions. Detection and response should be swift to mitigate threats.

24. Ethical Hacking: Consider employing ethical hackers to conduct penetration testing on IoT devices and networks. This can identify vulnerabilities before malicious actors exploit them.

25. Vendor Diversity: Avoid over-reliance on a single vendor or ecosystem for IoT devices. Diversity can reduce the impact of a single vendor's security issues.

In essence, securing IoT devices and networks involves a multifaceted approach that encompasses technical measures, user awareness, vendor collaboration, and compliance with security standards. It's a dynamic field that requires continuous adaptation and vigilance to stay ahead of emerging threats. By implementing these strategies and remaining proactive, organizations and individuals can navigate the IoT landscape with confidence, enjoying the benefits of connectivity while mitigating the associated risks.

Conclusion

In this comprehensive book bundle, "Network and Security Fundamentals for Ethical Hackers," we have embarked on a journey through the intricate and ever-evolving realm of network protocols, attacks, and defenses. Across the four books that make up this bundle, we have explored the diverse facets of network security, from the foundational concepts to the most advanced defense strategies.

In "Book 1 - Network Fundamentals for Ethical Hackers: A Beginner's Guide to Protocols and Security Basics," we laid the groundwork by delving into the essential building blocks of networking. We introduced you to the fundamental protocols, network architecture, and security principles that underpin the digital world. With this solid foundation, you gained a clear understanding of the elements that shape secure communication.

"Book 2 - Understanding Network Attacks: Intermediate Techniques and Countermeasures" took you a step further, providing insights into the intermediate techniques employed by cybercriminals to compromise networks. We examined the tactics, tools, and procedures used in real-world attacks, equipping you with the knowledge needed to recognize and thwart these threats. Armed with this intermediate-level expertise, you developed the skills to detect and respond to a wide range of network intrusions.

"Book 3 - Advanced Network Defense Strategies: Mitigating Sophisticated Attacks" elevated your security prowess to the next level. We explored advanced defense strategies to protect against increasingly sophisticated adversaries. From intrusion detection and prevention to threat intelligence and incident response, you gained the expertise required to safeguard networks against relentless and cunning attacks. By adopting a proactive stance and implementing these advanced defenses, you fortified your organization's security posture.

Finally, in "Book 4 - Expert-Level Network Security: Mastering Protocols, Threats, and Defenses," we delved into the intricacies of network security at the expert level. We dissected complex protocols, analyzed cutting-edge threats, and introduced you to state-of-the-art defense mechanisms. This book not only expanded your knowledge but also empowered you to become a true master of network security.

Throughout this bundle, we emphasized the importance of ethical hacking—a discipline aimed at using hacking techniques for the greater good. Ethical hackers, armed with their deep understanding of networks and security, play a pivotal role in identifying vulnerabilities and strengthening defenses. By applying the knowledge gained from these books responsibly and ethically, you are poised to make a significant impact in the field of cybersecurity.

As we conclude this journey, remember that network security is a dynamic field that continually evolves in response to emerging threats. It demands continuous learning, adaptability, and a commitment to staying ahead of adversaries. Whether you are a beginner taking your first steps into the world of network security or an expert seeking to hone your skills, the insights, techniques, and strategies presented in this bundle provide a valuable resource for your ongoing cybersecurity endeavors.

In closing, "Network and Security Fundamentals for Ethical Hackers" equips you with the knowledge, tools, and mindset required to navigate the complex landscape of network protocols, attacks, and defenses. We hope that you will continue to explore, innovate, and protect in the ever-expanding realm of network and security fundamentals.

About Rob Botwright

Rob Botwright is a seasoned IT professional with a passion for technology and a career spanning over two decades. His journey into the world of information technology began with an insatiable curiosity about computers and a desire to unravel their inner workings. With a relentless drive for knowledge, he has honed his skills and expertise, becoming a respected figure in the IT industry.

Rob's fascination with technology started at a young age when he disassembled his first computer to understand how it operated. This early curiosity led him to pursue a formal education in computer science, where he delved deep into the intricacies of software development, network architecture, and cybersecurity. Throughout his academic journey, Rob consistently demonstrated an exceptional aptitude for problem-solving and innovation.

After completing his formal education, Rob embarked on a professional career that would see him working with some of the most renowned tech companies in the world. He has held various roles in IT, from software engineer to network administrator, and has been instrumental in implementing cutting-edge solutions that have streamlined operations and enhanced security for businesses of all sizes.

Rob's contributions to the IT community extend beyond his work in the corporate sector. He is a prolific writer and has authored numerous articles, blogs, and whitepapers on emerging technologies, cybersecurity best practices, and the ever-evolving landscape of information technology. His ability to distill complex technical concepts into easily understandable insights has earned him a dedicated following of readers eager to stay at the forefront of IT trends.

In addition to his writing, Rob is a sought-after speaker at industry conferences and seminars, where he shares his expertise and experiences with fellow IT professionals. He is known for his engaging and informative presentations, which inspire others to embrace innovation and adapt to the rapidly changing IT landscape.

Beyond the world of technology, Rob is a dedicated mentor who is passionate about nurturing the next generation of IT talent. He believes in the power of education and actively participates in initiatives aimed at bridging the digital divide, ensuring that young minds have access to the tools and knowledge needed to thrive in the digital age.

When he's not immersed in the realm of IT, Rob enjoys exploring the great outdoors, where he finds inspiration and balance. Whether he's hiking through rugged terrain or embarking on a new adventure, he approaches life with the same inquisitiveness and determination that have driven his success in the world of technology.

Rob Botwright's journey through the ever-evolving landscape of information technology is a testament to his unwavering commitment to innovation, education, and the pursuit of excellence. His passion for technology and dedication to sharing his knowledge have made him a respected authority in the field and a source of inspiration for IT professionals around the world.

www.ingramcontent.com/pod-product-compliance
Lightning Source LLC
Chambersburg PA
CBHW071235050326
40690CB00011B/2129